# Fashion Advertising and Promotion

# Fashion Advertising and Promotion

**JAY DIAMOND**

**AND**

**ELLEN DIAMOND**

**Delmar Publishers**

I(T)P  An International Thomson Publishing Company

Albany • Bonn • Boston • Cincinnati • Detroit • London • Madrid • Melbourne
Mexico City • New York • Pacific Grove • Paris • San Francisco • Singapore
Tokyo • Toronto • Washington

## NOTICE TO THE READER

Cover Design: Marjolaine Arsenault

**Delmar Staff**

| | |
|---|---|
| Acquisitions Editor: | Christopher Anzalone |
| Developmental Editor: | Jeffrey Litton |
| Project Editor: | Eugenia L. Orlandi |
| Production Coordinator: | Jennifer Gaines |
| Art and Design Coordinator: | Douglas J. Hyldelund |

COPYRIGHT © 1996
By Delmar Publishers
a division of International Thomson Publishing Inc.
The ITP logo is a trademark under license.

Printed in the United States of America

For more information contact:

Delmar Publishers
3 Columbia Circle
Box 15015
Albany, New York 12203-5015

International Thomson Editores
Campos Eliseos 385, Piso 7
Col Polanco
11560 Mexico D F Mexico

International Thomson Publishing Europe
Berkshire House 168-173
High Holborn
London WC1V7AA
England

International Thomson Publishing GmbH
Königswinterer Strasse 418
53227 Bonn
Germany

Thomas Nelson Australia
102 Dodds Street
South Melbourne, 3205
Victoria, Australia

International Thomson Publishing Asia
221 Henderson Road
#05-10 Henderson Building
Singapore 0315

Nelson Canada
1120 Birchmount Road
Scarborough, Ontario
Canada M1K5G4

International Thomson Publishing - Japan
Hirakawacho Kyowa Building, 3F
2-2-1 Hirakawacho
Chiyoda-ku, Tokyo 102
Japan

1  2  3  4  5  6  7  8  9  10  XXX  01  00  99  98  97  96  95

**Library of Congress Cataloging-in-Publication Data**

Diamond, Jay.
    Fashion advertising and promotion / Jay Diamond and Ellen Diamond.
      p.  cm.
    Includes index.
    ISBN 0-8273-5626-9
    1. Advertising—Fashion.  2. Sales promotion.  I. Diamond, Ellen.
II. Title.
HF6161.C44D5  1996
659.1′9391—dc20

95-3904
CIP

# Contents

# Preface

The fashion industry, like any other, must make every effort to properly publicize itself if success is to be achieved. With all of the competition at every level of the field, a well-founded advertising and promotional program is essential to distinguish one participant from the others. While the merchandise is certainly of paramount importance, it often takes the creativity and genius of the advertising and promotion professionals to capture the attention of the potential purchasers.

*Fashion Advertising and Promotion* was written to examine every aspect of the field, drawing upon the principles and practices that have been used for many years, coupling them with latest, innovative concepts used today. It will provide an excellent basis of knowledge for those wishing to make advertising and promotion a career, and for those in any aspect of the fashion industry who wants a better understanding of how advertising interfaces with the other facts of the world of fashion.

The text is divided into five sections, each dealing with a specific aspect of advertising and promotion. Section 1, *The Spectrum of Advertising and Promotion,* focuses on the industry's background, the careers available to those wishing to become practitioners and the manner in which the various components of the industry use advertising and promotion for their specific needs.

Section 2, *Planning Advertising and Promotion,* examines the research that is undertaken before any advertising campaigns or promotional endeavors are undertaken, as well as the role played by the advertising agencies.

Section 3, *Advertising Media and the Fashion Segments They Serve,* explores the different media and the role each plays for the fashion industry's participants.

Section 4, *Creating Fashion Advertisements,* presents a technical look at how the copy and illustrations are developed and displayed in an appropriate layout, as well as the various techniques employed in translating the creator's ideas into the finished product.

Section 5, *Fashion Promotion Presentations and Techniques,* explores fashion shows and their production, special events such as the long-running Thanksgiving Day Parades, fashion videos, and how they are created, publicity and the way it serves the industry, and visual merchandising.

In addition to the sixteen chapters, a glossary of terms is provided to facilitate comprehension of the industry's language.

The text is significantly highlighted with specific advertising and promotional endeavors of many of the industry's leading companies, including designers, manufacturers, fashion retailers, advertising agencies, materials producers, and trade associations. Special campaigns from Marshalls and other advertisers are featured to show the magnitude of their efforts, as well as step-by-step procedures of how advertisements are created at the agency level and finally reproduced at the reproduction house. A wealth of photographs and line drawings are featured throughout the text to illustrate the various approaches used in the field.

Each chapter begins with learning objectives and concludes with discussion questions and exercises. An instructor's manual is available with solutions to each of the questions, as well as a test bank for each chapter.

The authors wish to acknowledge the many helpful suggestions made by the reviewers:

Deborah Fowler, East Tennessee State University, Johnson City, TN
Ruth Glock, Iowa State University, Ames, IA
Sharon Juergens, Bauder Fashion College, Grand Prairie, TX

# The Spectrum of Advertising and Promotion

SECTION 1

*An advertising*

*agency's creative*

*team developing*

*a concept*

# The Industry's Background and and Purpose

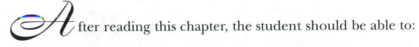

*A*fter reading this chapter, the student should be able to:

1. Describe the different advertising classifications that are used in the fashion industry.

2. Discuss the relationship among the participants in fashion advertising.

3. Explain the benefits of a campaign.

4. List the agencies involved and the methods used in advertising regulation.

5. Provide an overview of the various promotional tools used by the components of the fashion industry.

6. Discuss career opportunities in fashion advertising and promotion.

## Introduction

The world of fashion has a uniqueness all its own. It is constantly undergoing changes, trying to appeal to the fantasies as well as the practical needs of the consumer. The professionals in the field try to assess these needs and interpret styles that will satisfy them.

At every level of the industry, from the producers of the raw materials and the designers who turn them into usable products, to the retailers who develop merchandise collections, a host of other professionals design promotional activities to distinguish one participant's business and product line from the others.

Without considerable attention being paid to some form of promotional activity, be it advertising or a special event, customers might not be able to decide from which source they should make their purchases. Just as creativity must come from the hands of the couturier to make the fashion world sit up and take notice, so must creativity be employed by the promoters to achieve distinction for their companies.

As the pages of the fashion journals are turned, the windows of many stores are examined, or runway shows are attended, some come to the fore as being truly special. They collectively have certain qualities and characteristics that make indelible impressions in the minds of the observer. When such a level of achievement is reached, the company has the chance to rise above the others and make a mark in the industry.

The goal of fashion advertising and promotion, of course, is to bring prominence to a particular company, and to increase its chances for profit. To achieve this goal requires the participation of a wealth of professionals that include copywriters, artists, photographers, layout designers, visual merchandisers, fashion show directors, and managerial executives, as well as budgets that allow them to translate their thoughts into distinguished presentations.

In this chapter, as well as in the remainder of this text, every aspect of fashion advertising and promotion will be addressed, including: the planning that takes place before any direction may be taken; the media and how they interface with the various components of the fashion world; the creative aspects and production of advertising; and the numerous promotions and presentations utilized by the industry.

## Fashion Advertising

No matter how innovative a designer's new collection might be, how long or short the skirts for the new season will be positioned, or how spectacularly a new fabric is destined to become a winner, none will achieve its potential success without customer awareness. The power of advertising is such that it can quickly and succinctly deliver messages to specifically targeted groups anywhere in the world.

The delivery of the message not only serves the needs of the designers, retailers, or others in the game of fashion, but it also plays an important role for the recipients. In the case of the advertiser, the goals that may be achieved include increasing the awareness of a particular brand or collection and image enhancement—both of which provide the potential for increased sales. Consumers, on the other hand, benefit by learning about what is available to them, where purchases may be made, which companies offer the best prices, and, in general, how to become more informed shoppers.

**FIGURE 1-1**

*The first Neiman-Marcus*

*newspaper advertisement*

*(Courtesy of Neiman-Marcus)*

Although the use of advertising dates back to ancient Egypt, where merchants chiseled sales messages into stone tablets and placed them along public roads, it was not until the late 1800s that the fashion industry embraced it as a means of communicating with its customers. In 1880, John Wanamaker, the Philadelphia dry goods merchant, was the first major retailer to use the newspaper to deliver daily messages about his store and its merchandise to the people. The ads were fashioned in story form, with each day's installment concentrating on a different store activity or event. Neiman-Marcus followed the Wanamaker approach with ads that were similar in nature, following the "column" format, with drawings as enhancements.

Today, fashion advertisers regularly communicate with their audiences through a variety of means that run the gamut from the one-shot ad to total campaigns. The advertising programs range from the simplest to the most sophisticated, each hoping to increase customer awareness and sales volume.

## CLASSIFICATIONS OF FASHION ADVERTISING

The nature of fashion advertising is complex in that it attempts to reach different audiences and markets in different ways. The following text summarizes the focus of attention of each classification.

**BRAND ADVERTISING.** The lifeblood of any designer or manufacturer label is national recognition. The intent of this type of advertising is product or label recognition. Companies such as Ralph Lauren, DKNY, and Calvin Klein spend millions of dollars each year on national campaigns to get their names and images indelibly etched in the minds of the consuming public. They care not where the merchandise is purchased, only that it is their brand that is the one that is bought.

**RETAIL ADVERTISING.** Fashion retailers are primarily concerned with advertising that is locally oriented. Their intention is to get customers to either come to the store to buy or make purchases through mail or phone ordering. The effort is intended to increase sales, and necessarily to promote a particular line or product, unless, of course, it is one that is the store's own private label collection. Most fashion retailers participate in **cooperative advertising** programs with

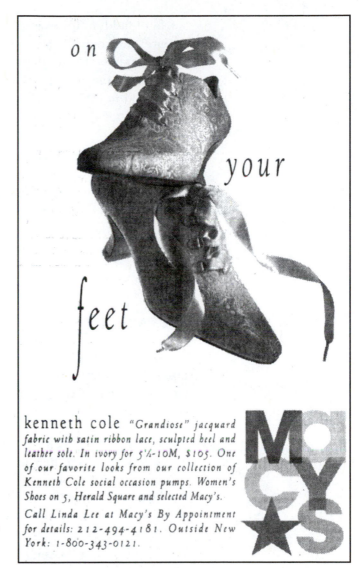

**FIGURE 1-2**

*A cooperative ad jointly*

*paid for by designer*

*Kenneth Cole and Macy's.*

*(Courtesy of Macy's)*

vendors. These arrangements provide for the cost of the ad to be jointly funded by the manufacturer or designer and the store. In this way, the retailer is able to stretch his or her advertising dollars.

**TRADE ADVERTISING.** Businesses "in the trade" are those that sell products or services to other businesses in the same industry. In the world of fashion, for example, the fiber producer's goal is to sell to the apparel designer, the shoe manufacturer to the retailer, and the trimmings supplier to the designer. Each business uses trade periodicals, papers, and magazines whose focus is on the fashion industry, such as *Women's Wear Daily,* to deliver their advertising messages.

**INSTITUTIONAL ADVERTISING.** Some companies spend a portion of their advertising budgets to promote their images rather than specific items. The message might focus upon a store's reputation for service, a company's dedication to quality control, or one that attempts to raise the consciousness for social issues. Companies like Benetton and Lands' End are two that regularly focus advertising on the institutional format.

## THE PARTICIPANTS

Getting the word out to the appropriate audience requires a collaborative effort that involves three key participants: the advertisers themselves; advertising agencies; and the media.

**THE ADVERTISERS.** In fashion, the following organizations use advertising to reach their markets:

- Materials Processors and Producers—They direct their advertising efforts to their primary customers, the apparel and accessories designers and manufacturers.
- Designers and Manufacturers—Advertising is earmarked for the retailers they serve and the consumers who purchase their products.
- Retailers—The consumer is the target.
- Retail Shopping Centers—They try to appeal to shoppers in their trading areas to come to visit the stores in their shopping arenas.
- Trade Associations—Their customers are the professionals in the field such as retailers, manufacturers, designers, and so on. Each attempts to promote their respective fashion organizations.
- Trade Expositions—These are events that are organized to sell merchandise to the various components of the fashion industry. Some

are directed toward apparel manufacturers, while others are primarily for retailers.

- Industry Sponsored Public Relations Groups—They serve the needs of a specific industry segment, with publicity attainment as their chief goal.

In Chapter 2, the Advertisers and Promoters of Fashion, an in-depth discussion will center upon the marketing focus of each advertiser and the advertising approaches they use to communicate with their markets.

**THE ADVERTISING AGENCIES.**   An advertising agency is a company that handles everything needed by the advertiser to create successful advertisements. Their involvement includes market analysis, strategy planning, creating the copy, artwork and ad layouts, production, and media placement. They come in all sizes, offer different specializations, and work on compensation arrangements that include commissions and fees.

In Chapter 4, Advertising Agencies and Promotional Services, the nature and role of these organizations are explored as well as how they interface with the advertiser and media.

**THE MEDIA.**   The third member of the team is the media. It includes the communication channels that the advertisers use in order to get their messages to the marketplace. The specific channels used depend upon the type of fashion operation and the locations of their customers. Retailers, for example, make use of newspapers in an attempt to interface with local audiences. Designers, on the other hand, generally opt for the fashion magazine in an attempt to reach fashion-minded readers throughout the world. While the broadcast media is of paramount importance to advertising, it is not as widely used by those in fashion. Other forms of media used include direct mail, outdoor, and transit.

As part of the team, a media representative has the responsibility not only to supply space and time costs for the advertisers, but to provide information to the advertisers regarding how their specific communication network will best serve their needs.

In Section III, Advertising Media and the Fashion Segments They Serve, five chapters are devoted to the forms of media employed by the industry.

**FIGURE 1-3**

*Newspapers, magazines,*

*and direct mail are some*

*of the media used by the*

*fashion industry.*

## THE ADVERTISING INITIATIVES:
## FROM CONCEPTION TO PRODUCTION

The beginning of any advertising initiative is based upon the company's goals and the strategy it will use to reach them. Fashion advertisers either use individual, one-time advertisements, or campaigns for major events and promotions. The **campaigns** are a series of related advertisements that are placed in one medium or a variety of media for a prescribed period of time.

**INDIVIDUAL ADVERTISEMENTS.**    When a fashion retailer is planning to run a one-day sale, it generally plans an individual advertisement in the newspaper or on television to notify consumers of the event. Similarly, a designer visit to a store might warrant a similar single advertisement. Sometimes these advertisements are placed at the last minute to take advantage of an unforeseen event. An impending snowstorm, for example, might motivate a shoe store to alert the public to its assortment of boots. Major advertisers have few problems with these eleventh-hour insertions because they generally contract for print space and air time for a specific period of time. Most individual advertisements are planned well in advance of their production, and fit the company's needs to achieve specific goals.

**CAMPAIGNS.**  The development of a campaign requires a great deal of company and product analysis before any strategy may be employed. The focus of attention may center upon the launching of a new product under a designer label, the opening of a branch store, the presentation of a special event, the promotion of a new designer name, the beginning of a holiday selling period, or anything that an organization wants to substantially promote.

**FIGURE 1-4**

*A multimedia campaign encompassing both the print and broadcast media (Courtesy of Macy's)*

**FIGURE 1-5**

*A representation of a newspaper campaign that features the theme of The Twelve Days of Christmas (Courtesy of the Asher Agency)*

In a single medium campaign, The Forum Shops at Caesar's, an upscale shopping facility in Las Vegas, Nevada, developed a newspaper campaign for the Christmas season with a theme based on "The Twelve Days of Christmas" and a variety of events to spark customer interest. Twelve different, but related, newspaper advertisements were run, one each day, until the last shopping days were reached. The continuity of the theme helped to implant the message in the shoppers' minds.

Campaigns often are of the multimedia type. That is, a variety of media are used to get the message across. It might involve a combination of newspaper and magazine advertisements, or perhaps, all of the media appropriate to the event.

**FIGURE 1-6A**

*Magazine*

*advertisement*

*(Courtesy of*

*Marshalls)*

## Radio/Copy

Hill, Holliday, Connors, Cosmopulos, Inc., Advertising

Client  Marshalls            Date  3/24/94B        Job Number
Description  Swimwear (sans tag)        Title  Competition        Time

MARSHALLS MUSIC IN

Woman:      Once again the winner of this year's swimsuit competition
            is... Marshalls. With the biggest swimsuit event in the
            country going on right now. Thousands and thousands of
            suits for only $16.99. That's 57% to 75% lower than the
            same suits at department stores. We've got a wide
            selection of styles, from one-piece to itsy-bitsy yellow
            polka dot bikinis, for just $16.99. Lots of sizes for lots
            of ages, just $16.99. At these prices, you can buy 2 or 3
            of our suits for the cost of one of theirs. And Marshalls
            has the brands you look for. [We can't tell you what they
            are but you'll know them when you see them.] So come in to
            Marshalls and judge for yourself. But hurry. At this price
            this swimsuit competition will be over before you know it.

SINGRS:     Never, never, never pay full price. Marshalls.

Anncr:      Come in now and register to win our Grand Prize, a 7-day
            Caribbean cruise for two aboard the SS Norway plus a $500
            Marshalls gift certificate. 84 second prize winners
            receive two tickets to anywhere American Airlines® flies
            in the continental US and Canada. Sweepstakes ends April
            20th, 1994. See official rules in store. No purchase
            required. Void where prohibited. For the store nearest you
            call 1-800-MARSHALLS.

1                    John Hancock Tower / 200 Clarendon Street / Boston, MA 02116   617-437-1600

**FIGURE 1-6B**

*Radio*

*advertisement*

*(Courtesy*

*of Marshalls)*

In order to maximize exposure to its vast consumer market for its "Dive/Competition" campaign, Marshalls chose the multimedia route utilizing newspaper, magazine, radio, and television. Each print and broadcast advertisement focused on swimsuit prices and how the consumer would benefit from the store's low prices. The visuals and copy in each of the media are interrelated. The major elements of the campaign are featured in the illustrations. Along with the finished pieces, the rough sketches that were used to develop the television spot are also shown.

A team effort is essential to the success of any campaign. It requires the participation of the advertiser, the advertising agency, and the media to carry the project to a fruitful conclusion.

Throughout the text, a wealth of individual advertisements and campaigns will be featured to show the way in which the fashion industry uses them, how they are created, and the production techniques that are employed for their insertions in print and on the air.

## INDUSTRY REGULATION

Before the beginning of the twentieth century, businesses dealt in a climate that revolved around *caveat emptor*, "let the buyer beware." It was the belief of industry that the consumer was sufficiently knowledgeable to make purchasing considerations and the advertising messages were simple to understand. The federal government, however, believed that unfair and inappropriate claims were being made by advertisers and the consumer was not really capable of knowing fact from fiction. In order to protect the citizenry, different agencies came into being, beginning with the Federal Trade Commission. Others on the federal and local governmental levels were also established along with industry groups that focused on self-regulation.

Those agencies that have some relationship with the fashion industry will be discussed.

### THE FEDERAL TRADE COMMISSION. Established in 1914, the Federal Trade Commission (FTC), a regulatory agency, with the powers generated by the Federal Trade Commission Act, became the major watchdog of the advertising industry. Initially developed as an agency to protect one business from another, it was not until 1938, and the pas-

sage of the Wheeler-Lea amendments that the FTC expanded its role to enable it to protect consumers from deceptive and misleading advertising. The commission not only holds the advertiser accountable for deception, but the advertising agency as well, since it is significantly involved in the creation of the advertising message.

Since deceptive advertising has not been clearly defined by Congress, the FTC rules on which advertisements are indeed deceptive. That is, they determine whether the consumer would take action based upon the advertisement's claims, or if they would not take action if the claims were not made.

The Commission is composed of five members appointed by the President, with confirmation by the Senate. The members serve for a seven-year term. Their investigations may come at the hands of their own initiative or the request of the President, Congress, governmental agencies, the Attorney General, referrals from the courts, or complaints from the public.

The approach that they take in the resolution of the problems may be any one of the following:

1. A case may be dropped if it is not in direct violation of the law.

2. Voluntary compliance may be suggested, and if adhered to, no further action will be taken. Retailers, for example, who have made claims concerning merchandise that was drastically reduced but unavailable when sought by customers and who convince the agency of its intention to stop the practice, will not be required to participate in other actions.

3. A Consent Order procedure may be initiated to avoid extensive hearings and negotiations. Under this arrangement, an agreement must be completed and submitted within thirty days to prevent further action.

4. Formal Cease and Desist proceedings may be used if no reply has been made to a complaint. If a reply is made, then a hearing is generally held before a trial examiner who hears both sides of the issue. A decision is made based upon the law and becomes the decision of the FTC, unless either side appeals it. In the case of an appeal, legal briefs are prepared, which result in either a dismissal of the case or in an order of cease and desist. This requires stoppage of the practice. Penalties of $10,000 per day are issued for noncompliance.

Some of the specific areas of concern for the Commission involve:

1. The use of substitute materials in demonstrations on television commercials to make them appear better. In some cases, if heat and light sensitivity affects the product, some substitutions may be made. The intent, however, may not be to enhance the product's appearance so that the viewer will see it as better than it actually is.

2. A product may not be advertised as "new" unless it actually is, or it has been changed from the original in some real way.

3. The area of testimonial endorsements is particularly difficult, especially when the endorser is a celebrity. In such cases, the endorsers must be considered to be users of the product. In cases where those giving testimony are actually engaging in deception, they, along with the advertiser, will be held liable.

4. False claims that are used to make a product seem superior are in violation of the act. "Puffery," a term used to describe the elevation of a product to a higher level, is not allowed. As an example, puffery is present when an advertisement states "mink of the highest quality" when it is actually an inferior grade. Misrepresentation goes one step further when the actual fur is muskrat that has been dyed to look like mink.

5. The word *free* must be used carefully. If the offer is for a free item, the conditions of the offer must be clearly stated. If, for example, the message says, "Buy one pair of shoes and get the second one free," that is appropriate. If the terms of the sale are not spelled out and only the word *free* is used, it is illegal.

A major role played by the FTC that affects advertisers is the enforcement of the Robinson-Patman Act established in 1936. The act prevents manufacturers from offering advertising allowances to one customer unless the same offer has been made to the competition on a "prescribed proportional" basis. That is, if giant retailers like Macy's and Bloomingdales are offered an arrangement where they would receive a 5 percent promotional allowance based on purchases, the smaller retailer must be provided with the same opportunity.

The advertising portion of the act actually eliminates price discrimination. Without such legislation, a manufacturer could claim that all of his accounts pay the same price for the same merchandise, but through the use of promotional incentives to major purchasers, they would, in reality, be receiving a rebate.

**THE FEDERAL COMMUNICATIONS COMMISSION.** The focus of this regulatory agency is the media. Unlike the FTC whose responsibility centers on the advertisers and the advertising agencies, the Federal Communications Commission (FCC) regulates the media. Its jurisdiction is solely with the broadcast media, radio, and television. While its control over advertising is somewhat limited, it does have the power to remove commercial messages from the air that are deceptive or in poor taste. Often, they work in conjunction with the FTC in the investigation of complaints.

One of the areas of the FCC's responsibility is the excessive amount of time and the number of commercials broadcast during a time period, as well as commercial content. The latter is often handled by other regulatory agencies such as the FTC, to whom the FCC directs the complaints.

There are other controls at the federal level that play an important role in advertising regulation such as the United States Postal Service. They have the right to stop the delivery of mail that seems to center on defrauding the public and could initiate force to close their businesses. They do a significant amount of watchdog coverage of the mail order business.

**LOCAL LEGISLATION.** While the FTC regulates advertising in **interstate commerce** where businesses have operations that cross over state lines, there are numerous states that have enacted advertising legislation of a local nature. Most of the local laws are based on the Printers' Ink Model Law of 1911. The law deals with fraudulent advertising and states, in essence:

> *Any person, firm, corporation, or association, who with intent to sell anything, directly or indirectly, to the public, makes, publishes, disseminates, circulates or places before the public, or cause to be placed before the public, an advertisement of any sort which contains any assertion, representation or statement of fact which is untrue, deceptive or misleading, shall be guilty of a misdemeanor.*

Originally written for the print media, most local laws now cover all of the media.

**SELF-REGULATION.** Although there is significant involvement by governmental agencies to oversee the advertising industry, it should not be construed as an industry that is wrought with fraud. Instead, the vast majority of participants in the advertising game, the advertisers themselves and the agencies, play by the rules. In an attempt to rid themselves of the blemishes caused by the unscrupulous, they have instituted programs of self-regulation.

At the national level, the most important advertising organizations responded to consumer outcry to form the National Advertising Review Council (NARC). They were the American Association of Advertising Agencies, the American Advertising Federation, and the Association of National Advertisers. They joined forces with the Council of Better Business Bureaus, Inc. (CBBB) to form the National Advertising Review Council (NARC). The major purpose of the group was to negotiate voluntary withdrawal of deceptive national advertising.

In order to meet the demands of the task, NARC established two individual units, the National Advertising Division (NAD) of the Council of Better Business Bureaus and the National Advertising Review Board (NARB). The former is a full-time agency comprised of advertising industry professionals. They are the first step in solving problems that are brought by consumers, industry, and advertising organizations. When advertisements of deception are called to their attention, they ask the advertiser to defend their claims, and if declared inappropriate, they are asked to change or withdraw them. If the situation cannot be resolved, the NARB takes over. The group is a fifty-member team that represents national advertisers and agencies. In handling the cases that come before them, a five-member panel consisting of three advertisers, an agency representative, and a public individual handles the review. The information from the hearing and the findings of the NAD are evaluated so that the situation may be resolved. If the process has been completed without any resolution, the case may be referred to the FTC. It should be understood, however, that the groups have no real power, and cannot do anything more than advise governmental intervention.

Understanding the impact of unfavorable publicity on their companies, the NAD/NARB has been extremely successful in correcting advertising deception.

At the local level, the individual Better Business Bureaus (BBB) have been successful in correcting misleading and deceptive advertising. Much like their national counterpart, they have no legal jurisdiction but assist businesses with understanding the legal aspects of advertising. They also keep files of advertising violations and assist governmental agencies in their investigations.

# Fashion Promotion

The bag of tricks used by promoters of fashion range from the simplest concepts, such as runway shows, to complex entries that might require the temporary physical transformation of a store into a special theme. While it is the merchandise that a company offers that determines whether or not there is customer interest, the methods of promotion are designed to enhance their salability.

As with advertising, some companies spend more on promotional activities than others, with some budgets soaring into the millions for a year's projects. Fashion retailers, for example, like Neiman-Marcus and Bloomingdale's are so promotionally oriented that not a week goes by without a special promotion or event. On most Sundays, Marshall Field's features a newspaper advertisement that spells out the different promotional happenings for the week.

The other segments of the industry, such as the materials producers and designers, also engage in a host of activities to create interest in

**FIGURE 1-7**

*A runway show*

*under the tents in*

*New York City's*

*Bryant Park*

their merchandise and to promote their images. The different classifications of promotion, and who the participants are in their development, follow.

## CLASSIFICATIONS OF FASHION PROMOTIONS

Reaching their markets through promotional endeavors generally takes the route of fashion shows, different types of special events, and a relatively new tool, the fashion video. The following is provided as an overview of some of the marketing tools, with detailed coverage throughout the chapters in Section V, Fashion Promotion Presentations and Techniques.

**FASHION SHOWS.**   Fashion shows range anywhere from informal modeling, where garments are worn by models and paraded throughout a store, to extravagant thematic shows that rival theatrical productions. The runway presentation, used by designers and manufacturers, is the one most generally used. It is simple to organize, can be featured in a manufacturer's showroom, a retailer's premises, a restaurant, or in just about any facility.

Detailed exploration of fashion shows, their production, and uses will be featured in Chapter 12.

**SPECIAL EVENTS.**   In-store visits by designers, "trunk shows," presentations of entire collections by a vendor in the store for use in special ordering by invited customers, institutional events that are used to enhance a company's image rather than specifically sell merchandise, such as the Thanksgiving Day parades, charity dinners, contests, celebrity appearances, salutes to foreign fashion centers, and anniversary sales are just some types of special events that are used. By their very nature, special events other than fashion shows are usually the work of retailers.

Many of the special events sponsored by the fashion industry will be examined in Chapter 13.

**FASHION VIDEOS.**   The pioneering of Norma Kamali and the later introduction of MTV has prompted the fashion video to be widely used as a promotional tool. Designers and manufacturers use them for a number of purposes. They sometimes have them continuously playing

**FIGURE 1-8**

*An Elvis impersonator*

*special event draws*

*a crowd to the mall.*

in the showrooms for the buyers to see while waiting for personal service, or send them directly to the buyers in the hope that they will be motivated to come and see the lines. Fashion retailers use them as mood-setting devices or to attract the attention of the passersby.

A full description of how they are produced and the manner in which they benefit their users is covered in Chapter 14, Fashion Videos.

## THE PARTICIPANTS

The development of a fashion promotion may be a simple matter, requiring only one participant, while others are complicated productions necessitating the involvement of scores of people.

Most fashion organizations, with business at the creative level, generally subscribe to outside resources for their promotional endeavors, except for an in-house publicist or special projects director who oversees such programs but uses specialized agencies to carry them out.

Fashion retailers often employ in-store teams to carry out their events, since promotion is a role played by the store each and every day.

**THE SPONSORING COMPANIES.**    Materials producers, retailers, retailing environments such as shopping centers, trade associations, trade expositions, and public relations groups are generally the companies that use promotional tools to increase potential customer awareness. Retailers such as Macy's, that subscribe to a wealth of these events, for example, have full staffs that produce everything from their world-famous parades and flower shows to less complicated formats. For the major events, outside teams are brought in to augment their own staffing. Manufacturers, on the other hand, wishing to mount a fashion show usually do so with the use of an independent agency. Since these shows are only given on occasion, the necessity for in-house staffing is unwarranted.

No matter which approach is taken, the sponsoring company must provide the outside professionals with the goals they expect to achieve from the event, as well as make certain that, at each step along the way, their needs are being met.

**OUTSIDE PROFESSIONALS.**    Throughout the fashion industry, a number of businesses have been established that solely develop promotional programs for clients. They might specialize in fashion show production, supplying everything from the commentary to the settings; publicity, where they have the knowledge necessary to get editorial coverage of their client's promotions in the media; arranging for celebrity personal appearances; developing media kits; and writing press releases. Some of the major promotion companies provide just about anything needed by their clients to bring attention to their businesses.

One such company, based in New York City, is Sophie Xuereb Associates. For clients, such as Guy Laroche, Joan and David Shoes, and Emilio Cavallini, her company has designed special promotions, directed advertising programs, achieved editorial coverage from the fashion press, and improved public relations.

Resident buying offices, generally thought of as businesses that advise on fashion and make purchases for their clients, also maintain promotional staffs that advise on activities that are appropriate for their retail members.

Chapter 2, The Advertisers and Promoters of Fashion, provides an in-depth overview of the participants and the roles they play.

# Careers in Advertising and Promotion

Few fields offer the excitement of advertising and promotion. Not only does the industry provide a variety of different opportunities, it does so throughout the United States and the rest of the world. Where other industries are often closely geographically centered, this one provides mobility for the pursuant.

While creative expression, account management, research, and production involvement might generate one's interest, it should be understood that the salaries, particularly those at the entry levels, are comparatively low. Job availability is often limited because of the large number of aspirants vying for positions.

As in any field, however, those with real interest should not be dissuaded from seeking opportunities. Opportunities are available. With the knowledge of who the employers are and the tasks performed by their companies, those with the essential credentials should find success.

Although careers in fashion advertising and promotion are generally interrelated, the specific jobs performed and often the necessary practical experience and educational backgrounds needed are different.

## ADVERTISING

Employment in the field is basically at three levels: the advertising agencies, the media, and the advertiser. Many of the jobs in each have the same basic requirements. In those cases, they will only be discussed one time.

While there are a great number of different types of positions in the field, only a representative sample of the most typical will be presented.

### ADVERTISING AGENCIES.   Located in every major country in the world, with more than 10,000 in operation, the agency is the most likely place to find employment. Of course, New York City, with three-quarters of the top fifty agencies, is an excellent place to begin.

The various positions are broken down into the creative, account management, media, research, production, and traffic areas.

*Creative Department.*    These jobs are essentially involved in writing the messages, preparing the artwork, developing the layouts, and, for television, producing the commercials.

- Copywriter–The headlines and the body copy are the responsibility of this person. Job acquisition is most often based upon evidence of a portfolio that contains samples of previously written pieces. Ideally, the successful candidate will have a degree in writing or communication to go along with a good portfolio. Salaries generally start at about $18,000 for an entry-level position and rise to $100,000 or more for senior writers.

- Art Director–The title alone indicates more than just a starting position. It is one that is achieved after many years at lower levels of work that include titles such as **bullpen artist**, a term used to describe an assistant who prepares "mechanicals" or does paste-ups; and **junior art director**, a person who specializes in the same preparatory work. They must also possess a portfolio of work showing their understanding and creativity used in print advertisements. Education should include graphics and design and a complete knowledge of the use of computer software used in developing advertisements. The salary levels of the art people are commensurate with those of the copywriters.

- Producer–For television commercials, the job of a producer is to make certain the commercial is made. He or she works with a copywriter and art director who develop the concept. The producer has the responsibility to decide whether or not their work will translate into a commercial. Other duties involve bidding the job, selecting the production company, overseeing the "shoot," and supervising every aspect of the commercial. Those interested usually begin as **production assistants**, for very little pay; and eventually may move up to **junior producer**, where responsibility involves testing concepts; and ultimately, **group head**, a position that has administrative as well as creative aspects. A successful candidate should have attended film school to gain an understanding of the technical aspects of production. The salaries are generally slightly less than those of the copywriters and art directors.

Of course, the most coveted position is that of **creative director**. He or she is the one who can make or break the agency by setting creativity standards, understanding the needs of the clients, and running the entire show. They come from the ranks of copywriters and art directors and earn anywhere from $75,000 at the smaller agencies to well over $350,000.

*Account Management.*   The people in account management primarily function as the managers of their clients' businesses within the agencies. They regularly interface with the clients in matters of marketing and communication.

- Assistant Account Executive–A beginning job, this position essentially involves carrying out all of the details necessary to satisfy the client's needs such as providing information on competitors, developing charts, following-up on artwork that should have been ready, keeping timetables for production, and so on. One in this line of work does everything asked for by his or her superior, the account executive. Salaries are low, with $15,000 to $20,000 being typical amounts. A liberal arts or business education is desirable.

- Account Executive–This job helps to improve the client's business. Such a person is responsible for the management of one brand or product inside the agency. Regular meetings with the creative teams, media, and research are commonplace to make certain that the advertising program is being carefully handled. Salaries range from $25,000 to $50,000.

- Account Supervisor–The work is much like that of the account executive, except that responsibility is usually for two to four products. With such a work load, the day-to-day activities are left to the individual account manager, with the supervisor primarily providing supervision. The job generally pays from $40,000 to $80,000, depending upon the size of the agency and the number of accounts overseen.

At the top of this division are **management directors** and an account director, with a salary potential of $65,000 to $200,000, depending upon the size of the agency. They are the chief managers of the clients' accounts.

*Media Planning and Buying.*   In this division, the participants develop media plans for the clients based upon what their goals are, who the competition is, and how to best reach the market. Once the plan is established, the buyers make the necessary print and broadcast purchases in which the advertisements will appear.

- Assistant Planner–This is an entry-level position requiring a lot of statistical analysis. It is very low paying, with about $14,000 to $16,000 being the typical range. A good marketing research or statistics background is essential.
- Junior Buyer–This is the counterpart beginning position to assistant planner. It requires a great deal of paperwork. Salaries are the same as those for the assistant planner.
- Media Planner–Responsibilities of this position include developing the media plan for the client and presenting alternative approaches. Salaries range from $20,000 to $50,000.
- Media Buyer–Media buyers make the media purchases, most often for the broadcast media. The salary range is the same as media planner.
- Media Director–As the department head, this individual coordinates all of the efforts of planning and purchasing and interfaces with management of the other divisions. Salaries start at about $60,000 and range to about $150,000.

*Research.*   The jobs in this area involve learning about consumer wants and needs and delivering them to the creative people to translate them into appropriate advertisements. A knowledge of numbers is essential to the job. This is probably the division that provides the least potential for employment, since only the largest companies in the industry have many people doing research.

The jobs begin at the level of **project director**, who amasses background information for the client. The pay ranges from $20,000 to $30,000. The next level is **research supervisor**, where the pay goes up to about $45,000. A **research director** is at the helm, with salaries that may be more than $100,000. A degree in research is imperative.

*Production.*   People involved in production are responsible for getting the efforts of the creative team reproduced in the print media. The work is highly technical and requires knowledge of the printing processes, color separations, four-color processing, and so forth. A knowledge of the computer is also essential since a great deal of manipulation of the creative work is done with advertising software.

- Production Assistant–This is the entry-level position. It pays somewhere in the range of $15,000. Paperwork, following-up details, and watching for deadlines are the most important parts of the job.
- Production Supervisor–This position is one that involves communicating with the printers and platemakers who produce the final project. The pay is anywhere from $20,000 to $30,000.

*Traffic Management.*   This area involves keeping on top of all of the pieces that are necessary to complete a project, making certain that deadlines are met, and moving the project along from one supervisor to the next.

- Traffic Assistant–This is another beginning job that primarily involves looking after details. The salary is commensurate with that of the production assistant. A high school diploma or a technical certificate is all that is necessary.
- Traffic Manager–They deal with the agency heads of the other departments and make certain that the pieces of the advertising puzzle fit and are moving along, from one to the next, in a timely fashion. The salary range is from $30,000 to $50,000.

**THE MEDIA**.   Those people who work for the print and broadcast media perform two major roles. One is involved in getting the work either directly from the advertiser or the advertising agency and placing it in the publication or on the air. The other functions in selling time or space. The former positions available parallel those already discussed under advertising agencies and will not be examined. Those with a sales orientation include:

- Sales Representative–They must have a knowledge of their company, the competition, the technical and creative aspects of advertising, and be able to communicate this information to prospective accounts. Salaries vary according to the size of the company, with commission being the most typical form of remuneration.

• Sales Manager–He or she has the responsibility for selling as well as managing the sales department. Often, there is a salary plus bonus arrangement for the position.

**THE ADVERTISERS.**    Some companies have their own in-house departments where the jobs are very much the same as those found in the agencies. That is, they employ copywriters, art directors, layout people, production people, traffic managers, researchers, and so on.

Retailers, in particular, often have these staffs since they do a great deal of direct-mail publication.

With the advent of **desktop publishing**, a term used to describe computers and software applications that produce copy ready for production, all sorts of direct-mail pieces can be produced in-house. Thus, most major retailers employ people with this sort of experience so they can turn out the necessary brochures, catalogs, and other mailers.

In addition to the traditional positions previously mentioned, there is a need for those trained in desktop publishing. These individuals are generally well-versed in advertising and have sufficient computer literacy to produce the aforementioned direct-mail pieces. The salaries generally start at $25,000 and upward for these specialists.

## PROMOTION

There are a number of different career opportunities available in the general area of promotion. They are available at the companies that use promotional activities to generate business, independent public relations organizations, market consulting firms, and promotional enterprises. The job titles may vary from company to company, but the following are generally the names by which they are known.

**PUBLIC RELATIONS DIRECTOR.**    This job is one that tries to get the media to provide editorial coverage for something that a company or its recognizable representatives do that is newsworthy. When, for example, a famous designer is going to make a personal appearance in a store, advertising might be the vehicle to announce the event. However, if the public relations director can convince the media that the appearance is worthy of a mention in a column or on the air, this will give it greater clout. Since it is not paid for, as is advertising, it is especially welcome. People in these positions must have the ability to write the "press releases," prepared statements that are used by the media, and develop "media kits," packets of materials that describe the promotion or event, for transmittal to the fashion editors. Their backgrounds should include a wealth of writing and communications courses. Salaries for these positions sometimes go as high as $100,000.

**SPECIAL EVENTS DIRECTOR.**   Most major retailers employ people to develop special events that bring attention to their stores. The events include personal appearances, fashion shows, charity dinners, contests, parades, marathons, demonstrations, and so forth. Creativity is at the core of this individual's expertise. The more original the event, the more likely it will attract attention. In addition, the individual must be totally organized and competent in management. There is no special training for such a position. Salaries are often very high, with some at the top of the field earning more than $100,000.

**FASHION SHOW SPECIALIST.**   One of the most important promotional tools in the industry is the fashion show. Most of the people who organize and produce the shows are **freelance** consultants. That is, they are in business for themselves. For a fee, they produce shows for designers, manufacturers, and retailers. They do everything including hiring the models, writing commentary, selecting music, arranging for runways and props, developing programs, preparing seating plans, and so forth. Generally, their formal education has included courses in fashion, communication, writing, and theater.

## REVIEW QUESTIONS

1. What are the goals of fashion advertising and promotion?
2. Who was the first major retailer to use advertising to get his message across to the public?
3. Define the term *brand advertising*.
4. How does retail advertising differ from brand advertising?

5. In what way does cooperative advertising benefit its users?

6. Why do stores use institutional advertising if it does not promote a specific item?

7. What is the role of the advertising agency?

8. List the three types of participants that must operate as a team in order for an advertising campaign to be successful.

9. What is the purpose of running an advertising campaign instead of individual advertisements?

10. Which major regulatory agency has the chief responsibility for advertising industry regulation? What role does it serve?

11. How does the advertising and promotion portion of the Robinson Patman Act benefit small merchants?

12. On what law are most local advertising laws based?

13. How much power does the Better Business Bureau have in regard to deceptive advertising?

14. What is a "trunk show"?

15. What purpose do in-store fashion videos serve?

16. Which segment of the advertising industry is the major employer?

17. What is the job of a television producer?

18. Describe the role of an account manager.

19. Why must staff personnel in a store's advertising department be knowledgeable about desktop publishing?

20. Discuss the role of the public relations director.

## EXERCISES

1. Collect a month's supply of newspapers for the purpose of locating a fashion advertising campaign. Generally, at a peak selling period, such as a holiday or the opening of a new season, retailers develop such programs.

   The pages in which the advertisements appear, along with the dates of publication, should be mounted on a large board, in order of their appearance in the campaign.

A short oral or written presentation should be prepared indicating the nature of the campaign and the features in each advertisement that tie the campaign together.

2. Contact an advertising agency for the purpose of interviewing someone whose job title interests you. Make an appointment to discuss the duties and responsibilities of that individual, how they got the job, the opportunities for advancement, and anything that would be of interest to those seeking such a position.

*A runway show*

*launches the new*

*collection of*

*Hubert Franco.*

# The Advertisers and Promoters of Fashion

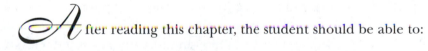

After reading this chapter, the student should be able to:

1. List the various business groups that advertise and promote fashion merchandise.

2. Explain the reasons why it is necessary for each business segment to participate in advertising and promotional campaigns.

3. Discuss the markets that each of the fashion industry segments focuses on through advertising and promotion.

4. Distinguish each level of fashion advertising and promotion from the others in the field.

## Introduction

Each and every day in the exciting world of fashion, companies are busy trying to capture their share of the market that will make their ventures profitable. It might be a grand-scale fashion show replete with internationally famous runway stars to launch a new designer collection, a store-sponsored charitable luncheon that brings attention to the retailer as well as serving the charity with donations, an advertising campaign that hopefully will fill the store with eager shoppers, or a host of other endeavors that will separate the participant's company from the competition.

The methodology used to generate sales for the individual companies range from the traditional or conventional to the unusual or unexpected. Each company, through its own in-house staff, outside agencies, or freelance specialists, must design and tailor programs that fit their specific needs. Whereas some of the techniques employed are utilized by every level of the fashion industry, other methods are generally reserved for one specific segment of the fashion industry. Retailers, for example, are the sole users of window displays as a promotional tool, while the fashion show has its place for materials producers, apparel designers, trade associations, and others.

Those who advertise and promote fashion are the materials processors and producers, designers, manufacturers of apparel and accessories, retailers, shopping centers, trade associations, trade fairs and expositions, and industry-sponsored public relations organizations.

In this chapter, emphasis will be placed upon a discussion of each segment of the fashion industry, the focus of their advertising and promotion attention, and some of the practices they employ to promote business and foster beneficial publicity for their companies.

## Materials Processors and Producers

The first stage of any fashion cycle begins with those businesses that are responsible for the processing or production of raw materials. Textile companies, leather tanners, fur processors, diamond miners, and others, through advertising and promotional campaigns, try to assure that their products will find a place in the market.

## THE MARKETING FOCUS

Those who are involved in this early phase of the fashion industry must get their messages across not only to the designers and manufacturers to whom they sell their goods, but to the consumers as well.

The manufacturers and designers are the ones who take materials such as textiles, furs, leather, precious metals, and stones, and turn them into wearable fashion items. They are the direct customers of the materials processors and producers.

While the ultimate consumer does not figure into the direct purchase of these unfinished goods, it is they who make the buying decisions of the fashion merchandise that utilize the materials. Recognizing the fact that an informed consumer is a better customer, the materials processors and producers understand that by making them aware of specific materials, they might chose one product over another. DuPont, for example, reaped a great deal of recognition and consumer attention from its "Bill Demby" promotion. Through an extensive television blitz, the world quickly learned that DuPont changed the life of a Vietnam veteran who lost both legs to a Vietcong rocket. With the use of a DuPont plastic, Demby was fitted with lifelike artificial limbs. The commercial not only depicted him as a citizen who could easily walk but dramatically showed how he was able to play basketball. No, this was not a fashion fiber that potential wearers could find in apparel and accessories, but it got Americans to remember the DuPont logo and label that was the same used on fashion products.

## ADVERTISING APPROACHES

Advertising is approached in a two-fold manner. One concentrates on the trade to whom it is going to sell its wares, and the other concentrates on the consumer. When manufacturers and designers are the targeted customers, a combination of print advertising in the trade journals and direct mail is often the choice. If the household consumer is the target, the media employed are usually magazines and television.

In the world of fashion, there are specific trade papers and magazines that are faithfully read by those in the industry. Women's wear designers faithfully read *Women's Wear Daily* or perhaps the *California Apparel News* if their business is more regional. Children's wear manufacturers regularly read the pages of *Earnshaw's*, and men's apparel and accessories producers are regulars in the pages of *DNR*, the *Daily News Record.* These, and hosts of other trade periodicals that specialize in other fashion markets, regularly feature the advertisements of the producers and processors of materials. An advertisement featuring DuPont's Micromatique, a microdenier fiber, might capture the attention of the designer who wishes to create a line that combines a luxurious "hand" with versatility and color clarity, benefits of the fiber. Similarly, the trimmings producer would advertise in the "trades" to alert the potential users to a new material enhancer.

Direct marketing is also a vital advertising approach. Through means of press kits and press releases, companies may quickly learn about some new and unique material that could peak their interests.

**FIGURE 2-1**

*Trade periodicals*

*regularly feature the*

*materials producers'*

*advertisements.*

Others choose the brochure route and develop a wealth of advertising pieces that are designed to bring customer inquiries. These might be simple black-and-white, two-page pieces, or masterfully produced, extravagant, full-color presentations. Some companies even publish magazines that are earmarked for industrial purchasers that rival the consumer periodicals in terms of size and quality. DuPont, for example, publishes *Lycra Magazine*, which features the creations of fashion designers and their Lycra-inspired fashions.

The consumer is part of a secondary market. That is, while they ultimately purchase products that feature specific materials, they are not the purchasers of these materials. With television, the focus of a large segment of the consumer market's attention, the materials producers use that medium to draw attention to their company and products. Magazines also play a significant advertising role in the dissemination of materials information. Fashion magazines (that are generally read to learn about new trends in terms of style, color, and silhouette) and apparel and accessories manufacturers and designers feature some materials advertisements. As the consumer "shops" the pages of the magazines to familiarize themselves with the season's hottest offerings, they come across the advertisements of the fiber giants that might motivate them to seek specific fibers and materials in their next purchases.

## PROMOTIONAL TECHNIQUES

In addition to their extensive advertising campaigns, materials producers and processors, especially those in the fibers and fabrics industry, utilize major promotional productions to publicize their companies.

First and foremost are the fashion show extravaganzas that rival the offerings of the professional theater. Monsanto, for example, has regularly mounted annual spectaculars that utilize original scripts, music, scenery, and imaginative lighting to alert the fashion world of designers about fibers and fabrics that will make future collections profitable ventures.

Runway shows, less formal in nature, are also used by the materials segment to underscore the value of their company's offerings. Garments specifically made for these occasions are paraded before an audience of designers and manufacturers who will hopefully be motivated to use the featured fibers and fabrics in future collections.

Breakfast seminar promotions are mainstays of some materials producers. Instead of the "live" fashion show, these meetings often feature video productions that parade models wearing the fabrics produced by the company. The advantage to this format is that it enables the video to be shown over and over again, without incurring the expense of numerous, in-person fashion productions.

Sometimes, the mills present workshops to prospective apparel manufacturer purchasers to present the latest in fiber innovation. Slide and video presentations are generally used, followed by a question-and-answer session to give the presentation a more personalized focus.

# Designers and Manufacturers

A visit to any major wholesale fashion market will immediately reveal the wealth of manufacturers and designers competing for the retailer's business. While creativity of design distinguishes one from the other and makes some more prominent than their competitors, it is advertising and promotion that is necessary to get the message to would-be purchasers. Each and every apparel and accessories company understands that even if their label is internationally recognized, a lapse in promotion would almost certainly result in diminished sales. It is the constant reminder, by way of innovative advertisements and creative promotions, that keeps the company's name and image in the forefront.

## THE MARKET FOCUS

The designers and manufacturers must naturally appeal to their prospective customers, the retailers, to sell their goods. They are the purchasers of the lines and the ones who may make or break a season. By being alerted to what their buyers will see during "market week," a period when new lines and collections are first shown, they might be motivated to review those products before any others.

This group, however, is not the only one on whom attention is focused. In the apparel and accessories industry, resident buying offices and other market consultants often play an important role for the manufacturer by alerting potential retail customers to what is hot in the market. They are the organizations that often cement a manufacturer's relationship with a retailer. They must be familiar with the fashion companies' new and innovative merchandise lines so they could communicate the information to their retail clients.

If the consumer is made aware of a specific designer's collection, he or she might be tempted to visit the retailer to examine the merchandise and hopefully purchase something. Through appropriate advertising and promotional use, whetted consumer appetites might help to presell the merchandise.

Finally, attention must be addressed to the media. They have the power to publicize a producer's collection to their readers and viewers without charging the manufacturer for the publicity. An "endorsement" by a renowned fashion editor or a segment on television shows like Adam Smith's *Money World*, which helped popularize Benetton, is worth untold sums to the fashion manufacturer.

## ADVERTISING APPROACHES

The creators of fashion merchandise use a host of advertising techniques and media to gain attention for their company names and collections. Included in these endeavors are both print advertisements and broadcast commercials in magazines, trade papers, television, and a wealth of press kits.

Magazine advertising is of paramount importance. Since the consumer publications *Elle, Harper's Bazaar, Vogue*, and *Glamour* are read by fashion shoppers, store buyers, merchandisers, and industry professionals, such as resident buyers, market consultants, and fashion journalists, they provide an excellent source of exposure. When Calvin Klein used a forty-page advertising insert in *Vogue* magazine, it underscored how important the medium is to getting the message out.

The readership of the trade papers is made up of the field's career participants. Knowing that store buyers spend at least a few minutes of each day scanning these journals, what medium is better to present a sample of a company's merchandise. One interesting item might sufficiently peak the retailer's interest to pay a visit to the showroom to review the entire line.

The press kit is a major player in the advertising programs of many designers and manufacturers. At the couture end of the spectrum, Karl Lagerfeld, Christian LaCroix, Yves Saint Laurent, and Bill Blass subscribe to this format, while "bridge" lines such as Jones New York and DKNY follow suit. Aimed at the retail buyers, merchandisers, and fashion reporters who hopefully will provide free publicity in their fashion columns if the "kit" offers something unique, it is a vehicle that can be produced relatively inexpensively.

# Calvin Klein

Calvin Klein was born in November, 1942, in the Bronx where he spent all of his childhood. As a boy he taught himself how to sketch and sew. "Since the age of five," he explains, "I've known I wanted to design clothes and have my own business." Klein attended the High School of Art and Design and the Fashion Institute of Technology. Five years as an apprentice in a coat and suit house on Seventh Avenue followed. During this period, Klein spent his nights and weekends working on his own designs.

In 1968 Calvin Klein joined with his close friend Barry Schwartz to create a coat business which would combine Klein's talent for designing and Schwartz's business acumen. Strangely enough, their first order was an accident; a buyer from Bonwit Teller stepped off the elevator at the wrong floor of the York Hotel and chanced upon Klein's workroom. Impressed by what he saw, he placed an order for $50,000, a considerable amount in 1968.

His coats a success, Klein took the advice of the members of the fashion pr...... executives who urged him to expand his business to include sportswear. Twenty-five years later Calvin Klein Collection for women, Calvin Klein Collection for men, cK Cal for men, cK Jeans, men's underwear, women's intimate apparel, footw socks, furs and swimwear.

Calvin Klein's fragrances, Obsession, Obsession for Men, Eternity, Eterni unprecedented success in America and have been introduced in Europ this fall.

For his work, Klein has won the prestigious Coty Award three times in c the youngest designer ever to win this distinction. In 1982, 1983 an Designers of America Award. He is a member of the Board of Directc and Parsons School of Design.

Calvin Klein defines his fashion as "modern clothes for the moder shapes, his designs are geared to the lifestyle of the modern woman for a busy, varied schedule. "Everything begins with the cut", he determine the function and beauty of any design. Klein also insis fibers: silk, cotton, wool and cashmere, leather and suede. The rich palette of muted colors to complete the effect of Klein's silhouettes. a distinctively American sense of style.

Klein has opened free-standing stores in Dallas, Chestnut Hill, Cl- unique stores house all Calvin Kloin clothes and accessories in a planned for major cities throughout the world. Klein also has lice Taiwan and Australia, as well as distributorships in Scandinavia

**FIGURE 2-2A AND B**

*The press kit enables prospective*

*buyers and fashion reporters to*

*learn about a designer.*

*(Courtesy of Calvin Klein)*

Television is significantly used by the fragrance and cosmetics industry. When a new fragrance is being launched, a television blitz is generally a major event. A look at the imaginative commercials that introduced Calvin Klein's Eternity and Obsession lines, and the millions of dollars spent to produce them and put them on the air, quickly reveals the power of the medium.

Newspaper advertising is not the forte of the manufacturer or designer, except as participants in cooperative arrangements with retailers. In these joint ventures, the product developers provide sums of money, sometimes as much as half of the cost of the advertisement, if the retailer features their merchandise. In this way, they get exposure to the consumer for a relatively modest expense.

## PROMOTIONAL TECHNIQUES

The major designers and manufacturers take part in a host of promotional formats, which give their companies and product lines meaningful exposure. The vast majority of those who subscribe to promotion have in-house public relations teams, or outside agencies, that create and develop the promotions. Among those most frequently used are runway shows, trunk shows, videos, personal appearances, charity events, demonstrations, and sampling.

When one reads the *Fashion Calendar,* an industry timetable of collection openings and noteworthy fashion events, the runway show appears as a dominant promotion. Television viewers who watch Elsa Klentch's *Style* program are also made aware of the importance of the runway format to introduce designer collections. The shows present manufacturers of men's, women's, and children's apparel, and hats, jewelry, and other accessories. They are presented to the press for potential exposure in newspapers, magazines, and television, and to store buyers who are responsible for merchandise purchasing. Couture and "bridge" collections are usually the mainstays of these programs.

The trunk show is a format that takes the line to the consumer. A designer, or company representative, moves the merchandise, "packed in a trunk," from store to store to show it to the consumer. Retailers run advertisements in the newspapers announcing these shows, or communicate with their steady customers by way of direct mail, inviting them to meet a company representative who will show and discuss the line. Since retailers are not always able to feature an entire collection, the trunk show provides the potential purchaser with everything available.

**FIGURE 2-3**

*Singer Melba Moore*

*helps promote the*

*DKNY collection with*

*an appearance at a*

*charity benefit.*

The trunk show format also helps the store's sales associates learn, first-hand, the features of the line, and what its salient points are. Department stores, specialty stores, and boutiques are regular stops on the trunk circuit.

One of the most exciting and productive approaches to fashion promotion is the video. Companies such as DKNY, Anne Klein, Liz Claiborne, and others produce fashion stories that feature their merchandise. A walk through any department store will reveal television screens mounted throughout the store to capture the customer's attention with the presentations. Initially the brain child of Norma Kamali, the fashion videos display apparel and accessories at every level.

Some people are motivated to visit a store when it is announced that a famous designer or a celebrity associated with a line will make a personal appearance. The more famous the personality, the more likely crowds will come. When the White Diamonds fragrance was first introduced, the company arranged for Elizabeth Taylor, its well-known spokesperson, to meet the customers. Designers such as Liz Claiborne and Karl Lagerfeld have attracted large crowds when they made their store appearances. Sometimes, even the use of a company representative will be enthusiastically greeted if the lines they are representing are well established. Generally, these appearances generate enough business to warrant the undertaking.

Fashion clinics are yet another promotional device that often result in consumer enthusiasm. Some companies send emissaries to the stores that carry their lines to teach eager shoppers how to best use their merchandise. It might be a suit manufacturer who focuses on appropriate business dress, an accessories consultant who can show how to easily transform a work outfit into one that may be appropriately worn after five o'clock by simply changing jewelry, or a cosmetics specialist who teaches the proper ways in which to apply the new season's colors and products.

Sometimes a fashion designer will enter into a cooperative venture with a retailer that benefits a charitable organization. In one successful event, Cancer Care benefitted through the joint efforts of designer

**FIGURE 2-4**

*Elizabeth Arden*

*representative offers*

*samples to shoppers.*

*(Courtesy of*

*Bloomingdale's)*

Donna Karan's DKNY line, which was featured in a runway show at Macy's New York, and highlighted by the appearance of singer Melba Moore. Since charity events often inspire many consumers to make contributions, they are generally regarded as a positive means for the presentation of a manufacturer's line of merchandise.

One can hardly pass through the aisles that house the numerous cosmetics counters in department stores without noticing the makeup demonstrations in progress. An experienced artist is generally working on the transformation of an average shopper into one who, with the proper makeup applications, is quickly changed into a "beauty." It is the individual cosmetic companies who send these demonstrators to the store to promote the line through this event. The ringing cash registers that often follow these types of performances prove that such promotions generate business.

By providing no-cost or low-cost samples of their products, the fragrance and cosmetics segment of the fashion world also reaps many benefits. In this industry, the plan was devised by Estee Lauder and ultimately followed by others. Given away, often with a small purchase, are samples of items that the companies are eager to have the customers try. If satisfied, future business will be generated.

## Retailers

From the giant department stores and chain organizations to the smallest sole proprietorships, retailers engage in a variety of advertising and promotional techniques. The vast amounts spent on these endeavors are to differentiate themselves from the competition, and to make the public aware of their presence in the marketplace.

It is the creativity of in-house staffs or outside agencies that often motivates customers to buy from specific stores. Given the similarity of merchandise offerings in retailing, it is necessary to mount programs that will give the retailer a fair share of the market.

### THE MARKET FOCUS

Unlike other segments of the fashion industry, which focus on more than one client group, retailers strictly promote their wares to the consumers.

Today's shopper presents an even greater challenge than those of yesteryear. As recently as the mid 1980s, retailer advertisements and promotions concentrated on female customers who, according to many studies, accounted for approximately 75 percent of retail purchases, with an even larger percentage for fashion merchandise. Typically, the woman of the household was someone who worked at home raising a family and made frequent store visits for their needs. At this point in time, the majority of women are employed outside of the home, and traditional in-store purchasing is often problematical.

With family incomes at levels higher than ever before, but with less time to leisurely shop the aisles, retailers have come to appeal to would-be customers in other ways. Since 1985, catalog shopping has become a way of life for many households. The 1990s has seen enormous growth in home shopping via cable television.

## ADVERTISING APPROACHES

The retailer's advertising forte is the newspaper. Inspection of such papers as the *Miami Herald, Los Angeles Times, Chicago Tribune,* and the *New York Times* reveals how important a medium it is. Particularly evident are those that feature fashion merchandise. Advertisements ranging from those targeted at the sophisticated customer to introduce the latest in designer creativity to the promotional variety that underscore clearance prices, are in every day's newspapers. These advertisements afford the giants like Macy's, Bloomingdale's, Marshall Field's, and Burdine's to quickly reach their audiences with timely fashion messages.

Although magazine advertising is also available to retailers, they use it more sparingly than the newspaper. Not only does the cost involved make its use less attractive, the audience that it reaches is often too broad to be effective. That is, while a striking fashion magazine advertisement might capture the attention of a reader, the individual might be too far away from the store to make the trip practical. Thus, such advertising is generally restricted to those major retailers with a significant number of branches that are easily accessible to shoppers in many trading areas. Stores like Lord & Taylor, Saks Fifth Avenue, Neiman-Marcus, Bloomingdale's, and Macy's, with stores from coast to coast, are users of the magazine format.

Most major retailers have utilized direct mail as a means of appealing to customers in their homes. Until the mid 1980s, the mailings were

**FIGURE 2-5**

*The newspaper is*

*the major medium*

*used by retailers to*

*communicate special*

*events. (Courtesy*

*of Dayton's)*

primarily part of the customer's monthly charge account statements with some seasonal catalogs. All of that has changed! The direct-mail catalog has become one of the most important means of communicating with regular and potential customers. With the use of toll-free numbers and twenty-four-hour service, the shoppers effortlessly order merchandise at their convenience.

The use of television is reserved for the largest of the fashion retailers. Its cost of production and air time are prohibitive for all but the industry's giants. When a particular campaign is being waged that necessitates reaching a vast audience, television is often the medium used. J.C. Penney, for example, in trying to establish itself with a new fashion image in the early 1990s, spent heavily on television advertising. With stores located from coast to coast, it was considered the most appropriate manner in which to reach their vast customer base.

Outdoor advertising on billboards has also become part of the retail scene. Placed at locations such as train terminals and bus stops, where potential customers wait for public transportation, stores like The Gap are spending significant sums. Without the competition imposed upon by numerous advertisements, such as in newspapers, this medium captures the viewer's undivided attention.

## PROMOTIONAL TECHNIQUES

In addition to their advertising commitments, retailers use a variety of promotional techniques to attract customers to their stores. The range is significant, as are the expenses involved in these undertakings. It might be as simple as running a special one-day sale to the extravagance of Thanksgiving Day parades.

The fashion show is typical of such promotions. They are presented as informal modeling, where the apparel and accessories are simply featured by participants who walk through the aisles of the store, structured runway shows that are held within the store's sponsoring department or community room, or collaborative efforts with specific designers.

Personal appearances also have proven to be successful with many retailers. It might involve a well-known fashion designer, who makes the rounds to stores that sell his or her collections, or celebrities who are spokespersons for particular manufacturers.

In-store video has become something of a promotional endeavor that has captured the attention of many major retailers. While some of the presentations are made available from product resources, some stores produce their own programs. Macy's, New York, for example, uses a video of their annual Flower Show in the store to show customers how the event was developed.

Fashion clinics are also extensively used. They might be directed at the traveler who is made aware of the proper way to select merchandise for that faraway trip, or potential interviewees who are uncertain about appropriate dress for their career interviews.

Stores such as Bloomingdale's and Neiman-Marcus have subscribed to special events on a very grand scale. The former's "salute" to a particular country and its merchandise, and the latter's promotion, also of a country, in the "Fortnight" celebrations, have brought crowds and profits to their respective companies.

College Boards, made up of students from various institutions of higher learning providing wardrobe advisement to new students, Teen Boards, representative bodies from the store's trading area schools assisting in the selection of apparel and accessories for students, seminars that feature a wide range of topics, and charitable luncheons are just a few others that retailers subscribe to in order to generate store traffic.

One of the more effective methods of promoting merchandise is through window and interior merchandise display. The major department stores have in-house teams to create and install their presentation, while the chain organizations use either staffs that move from unit to unit performing their duties, or display teams that create and photograph installations for their stories to be duplicated. Small

**FIGURE 2-6**

*The window display*

*attracts customer*

*attention and*

*hopefully motivates*

*them to enter the store.*

stores generally utilize freelancers for their installations or create the displays themselves.

Whatever format is subscribed to, the concept of display is to visually merchandise apparel and accessories in such a way that will motivate shoppers to seek out specific items. The stores use both window and interior displays for such purposes. The windows are often called the "silent salespersons" in that they are used to motivate shoppers to buy. Attractive window presentations that encompass a vast array of themes are used to tempt the shopper to enter the store. The interior formats are used to continue the enticement once the potential customer has entered the store. If the display efforts are successful, the merchandise will be purchased.

# Retail Shopping Centers

Although each retailer expends promotional dollars to inspire shopping in his or her particular organization, the arenas in which they are located often devise community efforts to bring attention to the environments in which a number of stores are clustered.

Some malls have central stages to use for promotional purposes. The regional malls at Owings Mills, Maryland, and Jacksonville, Florida, have a regular schedule of events that attracts customers to these environments. Once the presentations, such as fashion shows or musical performances, have been completed, it is the hope that the attendees will find their way into the stores. At that point, it is up to the individual retailers to motivate the shoppers to buy.

Many retail centers use advertising campaigns to focus the customer's attention on shopping there. The mall-sponsored advertising and promotional events are paid for by monies collected from the retailers who occupy space. Some shopping environments charge an annual fee for these joint promotional efforts, while others assess participants for each event.

## THE MARKET FOCUS

Retail centers serve only one customer market, the household consumer. With competition often so keen for their attention, retail centers must continuously remind those in the trading area of their existence. In Paramus, New Jersey, for example, there is a significant number of competing regional malls that vie for customers to patronize their stores.

Each geographical market is generally made up of subsegments. That is, in one general trading area, there might be different groups based upon such factors as income, age, ethnicity, and family size. Each must be carefully assessed to determine which group is the retail center's target customer. Often, these retail environments seem so similar in nature, that steady advertising and promotion is the only means of giving each its own identification. If shoppers are shown how one environment might better suit their individual needs, then that location will become more important to satisfy their needs.

## ADVERTISING APPROACHES

To attract substantial numbers of an appropriate market segment to a shopping center requires the use of advertising. The media primarily used to achieve this goal are newspapers, radio, and television.

At specific times, such as the beginning of the back-to-school shopping season or the period between Thanksgiving and Christmas, retailers are anxious to get the crowds to their environments. Mall marketing managers often develop newspaper advertisements that tell their potential customers that their center is better able to serve their needs than any other. The advertising campaigns might feature a list of tenants, services offered by the facility, or anything else that would tempt a visit. The newspaper is generally the medium of choice because of its ability to focus on a specific trading area, its relatively inexpensive cost, and its appeal to all potential family purchasers.

With the number of commuters who travel to their jobs by automobile, the radio has a captive audience. For a modest expense, when compared to the cost of television, the center can reach a wide range of customers. When Gurnee Mills, the giant retail shopping outlet in Gurnee, Illinois, developed its advertising campaign to alert consumers to its arrival, the radio was chosen as a major player.

Television has a lifelike appeal unachievable by any of the other media. Although it is costly to produce segments and present them at meaningful time slots, some retail developers use it. When the Mall of America, the largest shopping environment to open in the United States, opened its doors to the citizens of Bloomington, Minnesota, and its surrounding areas, television was a major medium that was used. The story of the ambience of the mall that includes entertainment attractions as well as stores was best told through the magic of the television camera.

## PROMOTIONAL TECHNIQUES

While advertising plays a major role in bringing the shopper to the mall, it is its promotions that often motivate the crowds to come. A wealth of techniques are carefully scheduled, throughout the year, that have both broad-based and specific customer appeal. The calendar of events include a host of different events.

One that is very popular throughout the United States involves the appearance of "soap opera" stars. The fanfare generated by the mere appearances of these personalities generally brings the largest crowds.

**FIGURE 2-7**

*The Easter Bunny in the Avenues Mall, Jacksonville, Florida, gets ready for a photo session.*

**FIGURE 2-8**

*Shoppers sample foods in*

*Town Center Mall with*

*a portion of the proceeds*

*earmarked for the*

*American Cancer Society.*

Of course, taking pictures with Santa or the Easter Bunny is another crowd pleaser. The lines are often long for these photo sessions that bring entire families to the malls. What better way is there to generate traffic for the retailers at holiday time?

Art fairs, antiques events, and automobile and boat shows are other attractions that bring the people. While these events usually provide business for the participants, it is the retailers who also benefit from the crowds who enter their stores after viewing the presentations.

Food fairs have become major attractions at malls. These are not to be confused with the food courts that regularly cater to the appetites of shoppers. In these special events, restauranteurs and chefs are invited to partake in presenting samples of their foods in the middle of the shopping aisles. In Boca Raton, Florida, the fashionable Town Center sponsored a three-day event that featured the gourmet fare of the local eating emporiums. To motivate the public to attend, shoppers were notified that a portion of the proceeds of the festival would go to a designated charity.

In special retail arenas, entertainment has become a key promotional ingredient to swell attendance. In Fort Lauderdale, Florida, the nation's second largest flea market, The Swap Shop features a broad range of fashion merchandise and regularly uses performers to attract the crowds of shoppers. In addition to a professional circus that offers performances throughout the day, world-renowned entertainers, such as Willie Nelson, perform their acts. All of this is free to the shopper. A look at the size of the crowds when these events are scheduled indicates the success of the promotion.

Needless to say, fashion shows that feature merchandise samplings of retail tenants, demonstrations, book signings, and other promotions are typical of many shopping arenas.

# Trade Associations

Most segments of the fashion industry have organizations that have designers and manufacturers as their members. The purposes of these associations vary. Some assess market conditions, determine the state of the industry, develop and promote functions of interest to members, and plan conferences.

Some of the high-profile trade associations include the National Retail Federation (NRF), the largest of the groups that represent retailers from all over the country; Footwear Industry of America; The Fragrance Foundation, and the Chambre Syndicale de la Couture Parisienne in France.

## THE MARKET FOCUS

Those to whom these groups have significant importance are the designers, manufacturers, and retailers in their membership and the different markets they serve. For example, The Fashion Footwear Association of New York (FFANY) represents shoe manufacturers and must communicate industry news to them. In addition, however, they also must interface with the retailers of shoes and the buyers who purchase the merchandise from their members.

They, and others who represent different product classifications, spread the word of the importance of their industries through a variety of advertising and promotional practices.

## ADVERTISING APPROACHES

The media most frequently used by these professional organizations to alert interested parties to their wealth of information are trade periodicals and direct mail.

When conference information is to be disseminated to participants of the group, brochures that feature the highlights of the upcoming meeting are sent. In order to attract new members, advertisements are run in national and regional trade papers. If a California-based apparel association wants to expand its membership, it might choose *Women's Wear Daily,* the nation's leading trade periodical for broad distribution, and the *California Apparel News* for a more focused approach.

Some organizations use professionally prepared publications to alert their colleagues to anything that is newsworthy. FFANY, for example, publishes high-quality, four-color magazines four times a year that feature articles on the state of the industry, organizational endeavors, promotions, and advertisements of those in the field.

Sometimes press kits and releases are used to announce special promotions of interest. These are sent to the membership and to the fashion press who might use the information in their periodicals and broadcasts giving free publicity to the group.

## PROMOTIONAL TECHNIQUES

Awards presentations and fashion shows are the two major promotions that are regularly sponsored by trade associations. The events range from those that are informal, to some that rival professional theatrical productions.

In the latter classification, FFANY, in conjunction with *SELF* magazine, presented a theatrical footwear presentation for spring 1993, in the Grand Ballroom of New York City's Hotel Pierre. It featured the latest in footwear cleverly shown with the benefit of an imaginative script, music, and dance. Through such events, the designers' and manufacturers' offerings are magically brought to the attention of prospective retailers.

# Trade Expositions

Throughout the fashion industry, trade fairs and expositions are regularly held for producers to exhibit their wares to prospective retail accounts. Each industry has one or more of these exhibits that are held during "market weeks," the times in which store buyers are shown the season's newest merchandise collections.

Some of these groups concentrate on one specific geographical locale, while others set up shop in various parts of the world's wholesale markets. In order to alert those who might have interest in such shows, various advertising practices are utilized.

## THE MARKET FOCUS

A trade fair, in which professional buyers and sellers are brought together under one roof, can only be successful if there is a sufficient amount of participation. Organizers of such events must constantly appeal to both groups to maintain steady attendance.

Before any retailer can be persuaded to travel to these fairs, they must be assured that the expense involved will be worthwhile. Thus, the sponsoring organization must first focus their attention on the manufacturers and designers whose presence will motivate buyer attendance. Only when a substantial number of merchandise producers join in these expositions, will the buyers attend.

Once the first group has been solidified, prospective retail customers must be convinced that their attendance will be beneficial to their companies. Trade shows sponsored by National Association of Display Industries (NADI), National Association of Mens Sportswear Buyers (NAMSB), International Trade Exhibitions in France (ITEF), and the International Boutique Show are major entries that account for a vast amount of merchandise to move from the producer to the retailer.

## ADVERTISING APPROACHES

In order to assure attendance, the groups use a combination of trade periodical advertising and direct mail.

Most of the marketing managers of these events choose publications such as *Daily News Record (DNR)*, a Fairchild publication, for menswear events such as the Designer Collective, or *Womens Wear Daily (WWD)* when the fair features women's apparel and accessories.

Some use trade magazines for their exhibition announcements. NADI generally features a full-page advertisement in *Visual Merchandising and Store Design*, since it is considered to be the most important publication for the display industry.

As is the case with trade associations, a wealth of brochures, press kits, and other direct-mail pieces are used to announce the date of the next trade promotion. Regular attendees receive these packets, along with others whose names might have been secured from marketing research firms who develop lists of prospective, interested parties.

## PROMOTIONAL TECHNIQUES

Aside from the typical line presentation and selling at the individual booths, the trade fair organizers use a variety of techniques to promote business.

Some of the fairs organize a host of different types of seminars that focus on specific topics that would be of interest to fair participants and attendees. At NADI, for example, there is generally a segment that focuses on "job openings." Some, such as Pitti Immagine Bimbo, a European children's exposition, feature a runway fashion show that gives buyers an overview of the market. Others, such as NAMSB, offer individual, informal fashion modeling at manufacturer's booths.

Many of the fairs present entertainment events that bring the buyers and sellers together in an arena that is away from where business is usually transacted. Such events often help interested parties get to know one another, which could later help solidify a sale.

# Industry-Sponsored Public Relations Group

Some segments of the fashion industry are represented, for publicity and promotional purposes, by public relations firms. The emphasis for each of these groups is to bring positive attention to their specialized fields. The Men's Fashion Association, better known as the MFA, and the International Linen Association are two such groups. Through a variety of promotional tools, they make certain that the industrial professionals are kept abreast of activities that are newsworthy.

## THE MARKET FOCUS

Each of these organizations focuses their attention on designers, manufacturers, retailers, the press, and sometimes consumers.

The press, in particular, is romanced by these public relations experts. If they are sufficiently fortunate to convince both the print and electronic media that their group has something that is fashion newsworthy, then they will be guaranteed coverage without cost in magazines, newspapers, radio, or television.

The producers, designers, and retailers benefit from the workings of these companies in that they are alerted to the current merchandise offerings in the field, news of innovation in technology, the climate of the consumer markets, and anything that will help them achieve greater profitability for their companies.

## ADVERTISING APPROACHES

The primary manner in which businesses interface with their members and the media is through the use of press kits. These packages are designed to bring attention to current state of the industry. They announce upcoming events, photographs of products that are typical of the season, and anything that would provide interest to the reader.

Some publish newsletters on a regular basis. The MFA version called *Currents* alerts members and the press to happenings in different wholesale markets, collection previews that are worth watching for, network programming that features specific menswear collections, and so forth.

Print advertising is placed in both trade periodicals and consumer publications. The former serves as a means of assuring trade representatives of season openings, fashion shows, and trade festivities such as awards receptions. The latter is used to promote the industry to the consumer. Through institutional advertising, for example, The Linen International Promotion Commission runs magazine advertisements in periodicals like *Glamour* and *Vogue* that tell the household purchaser of the benefits of their raw material.

## PROMOTIONAL TECHNIQUES

One way in which these groups gain significant attention is through annual awards nights. The MFA does its share in this category with a variety of these presentations such as the American Image Awards, which honor celebrated men of style and distinction; the Woolmark Awards, which salute fashion creativity and leadership; and the Aldo Awards, which recognize outstanding fashion journalism.

Fashion shows are also on the regular agendas of the public relations components of the fashion industry. The Leather Apparel

Association, for example, presents runway shows that feature the latest in innovative leather apparel design. The Council of Fashion Designers in America (CFDA) captures the design world's attention with its annual awards dinner and fashion show at New York City's Lincoln Center.

Along with these grand-scale promotions, other ways in which promotion is accomplished are through seminars, benefit luncheons, personal appearances of fashion forecasters and market consultants, and salutes to renowned industry leaders.

**FIGURE 2-9**

*Institutional advertisements help promote the linen industry and its products. (Courtesy of the International Linen Promotion Commission)*

If your shoes
are canvas,
does
that make
you an
artist?

Liz claiborne
sport shoes

## REVIEW QUESTIONS

1. Who is responsible for the development of the advertising and promotional endeavors of fashion-oriented companies?

2. Which segment of the fashion industry spends a considerable sum on display?

3. List the various types of organizations that are the users of advertising and promotion.

4. To whom do materials processors focus their marketing attention?

5. Which television campaign helped DuPont gain national recognition for its company?

6. In addition to the typical use of brochures, press kits, and press releases, what other quality direct-mail advertisements does DuPont use to gain attention for a particular fiber?

7. Which fashion industry segment is responsible for the fashion show extravaganzas that rival the offerings of professional theater?

8. In what way do fashion designers and manufacturers primarily make use of newspaper advertising?

9. Who was the initiator in the use of in-store video as a promotional device?

10. Discuss sampling as it is used as a promotional technique in the fragrance and cosmetics industry.

11. Why do a large number of retailers not subscribe to advertising in fashion magazines?

12. Define the term *college board*, and describe how it is used by fashion retailers to increase sales.

13. Describe some of the promotions that shopping malls use to generate traffic.

14. Explain why radio is used, in lieu of television, by some fashion retailers.

15. Which media are most frequently used by trade associations to reach their markets?

16. What is meant by the term *trade exposition*?

17. Describe some of the activities that industry-sponsored public relations firms such as MFA use to promote their segment of the fashion world.

**EXERCISES**

1. Select one company within a segment of the fashion industry and prepare a portfolio of advertisements and promotions it uses to generate business.

   The information and samples of their promotional endeavors might be obtained by writing to the organization, examining print and broadcast media, or through interviews with public relations managers.

2. Choose a print advertisement for each of the following:
   - designer
   - manufacturer
   - retailer
   - materials producer or processor

   Affix each on a foamboard for use in an oral presentation. Describe to the class the important points of each advertisement and the market for which it is intended.

3. Contact the mall manager of a major shopping center in your area to learn about special upcoming promotions. Visit the mall during this promotional period and photograph the activities of the event. Prepare a written report describing your observation.

# Planning Advertising and Promotion

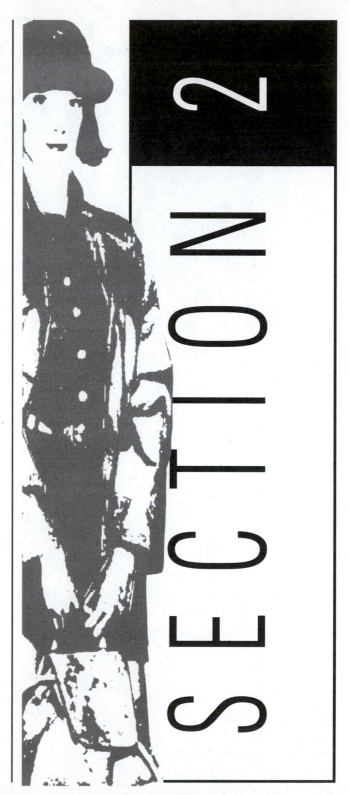

SECTION 2

*A researcher in*

*a mall gathers*

*information for*

*a study.*

# Research: Planning and Evaluation

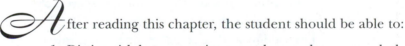

*A*fter reading this chapter, the student should be able to:

1. Distinguish between primary and secondary research that advertisers use in planning their campaigns.

2. List and describe the various sources of information that advertisers and promotion teams investigate prior to the actual development of an advertising or promotional campaign.

3. Discuss several methods used to gather the information necessary to make sound advertising and promotion decisions.

4. Explain the need to evaluate the actual advertisements before the final decision is made to use them in print or on the air.

5. Cite several methods used in the evaluation of an advertisement's effectiveness.

# Introduction

When the fashion model parades down the runway, the outburst of tumultuous applause is certainly indicative of the audience's reaction to the costume. On the other hand, little applause, or none at all, immediately reveals that the designer has failed to spark the viewing audience with his or her creation. It is at that time that the success or failure of the collection will be revealed. In the case of advertising, the applause is realized if the targeted consumer heads for the stores to purchase the advertised product. If he or she does not, the campaign will be considered a failure.

While it costs the fashion producers dearly to produce their lines, the expense generally pales when compared to the dollars expended for an advertising or promotional campaign. The multimillion dollar investments by Calvin Klein for the television advertising launch of a new fragrance and the enormous budget expended by Ralph Lauren in the fashion magazines at the beginning of each season are far more costly than the development of the products they are preparing for introduction to the world.

In order to assure the acceptance of a manufacturer's product, or motivate the consumer to choose a particular outlet for his or her fashion purchases, a great deal of advertising planning and evaluation must be undertaken. Although many successful campaigns have been on target because of the creativity of the promotional team, few ever get off the ground without some research effort. The corporate executives might have an enormous collective wealth of professional knowledge and a track record for positive results, but proceeding without the necessary research is considered to be risky business.

It should be understood that even after the most intensive study of the product and its targeted market, there are no guarantees in the field of advertising. The research might have been flawed, and even if it was not, the advertising team might have chosen to ignore some of its messages. Sometimes, an unorthodox approach might be considered, instead of one that the studies find appropriate.

In the early 1990s, Benetton ran the risk of departing from its traditional advertising posture that featured colorful apparel modeled by people of different ethnicities. Instead, they chose to use a radical print campaign that featured in one advertisement a priest kissing a nun, and in another, a patient dying from AIDS. Both sent shock waves around the world. Many professionals wondered out loud about the company's intentions. In 1994, they again went to an extreme position by featuring

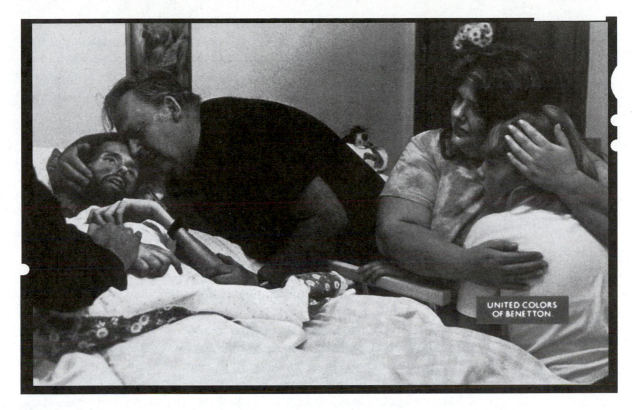

**FIGURE 3-1**

*A radical print advertisement campaign focused on unusual subjects. (Courtesy of O. Toscani for Benetton)*

the blood-stained uniform of a dead Bosnian soldier. Again the outrage was heard. Did Benetton guess right both times, getting enormous editorial coverage from the media, or did it turn the shopper away from its doors? The approach was certainly one of risk!

When one examines the sensuality of some of today's fashion advertisements with the more conventional approaches of the past, it appears that the public is often ready for another door to open. The world of advertising and promotion must be ready to go in the direction that best serves its users. A good way to learn about what the market is ready for is with research.

# The Research Process

The fashion companies that advertise and the agencies they employ to carry out the task generally follow a carefully planned procedure that has a two-pronged approach. The first determines the depth, scope, and focus of the advertisement's direct and promotional events the company is considering for use. The second is evaluative in nature, examining the effectiveness of the endeavor that has appeared in the media. While the expertise of the individuals involved plays a significant role in the ultimate advertising and promotional endeavors, research helps to guide the decision-makers in both the planning and evaluative stages.

Any aspect of research, not advertising alone, generally adheres to a specific procedure. For the planning and development of an advertising or promotional program, it begins with identifying the project and concludes with recommendations of the research team. Along the way, attention is focused on **secondary research**, which provides information that has already been published, and **primary research**, information that is gathered from original or firsthand sources. The information from each is scrutinized and evaluated and ultimately directs the advertiser towards an advertising or promotional direction.

The evaluative aspect of research involves assessing the campaign's effectiveness in terms of increased sales, customer awareness, or anything the company hoped to achieve through its promotional efforts.

Both of these research efforts may be carried out in one of two ways. The larger companies often have in-house advertising and promotional departments or divisions that perform every aspect of making their companies and products known, beginning with the research and concluding with the actual technical production of a campaign. Smaller businesses rely upon outside advertising agencies for the development of their programs. In the case of special campaigns, even the largest fashion organizations with their own staffs utilize the services of an agency to work with them.

Examination of the advertiser's research effort will first focus on the planning function and later on the evaluative aspect.

## DEVELOPMENT OF THE CAMPAIGN OR PROGRAM

Every fashion organization, no matter how large or small, must try any means necessary to make potential customers aware of its company's existence and product line. Without this recognition, it is unlikely that, in such a highly competitive field, success will be achieved. While it is without question that a strong organization and product line are

**FIGURE 3-2**

*Creative team in action at an*

*advertising brainstorming*

*session (Courtesy of Johnson's*

*Publishing Company)*

musts to achieve this success, getting the message out to the market is equally important.

Whether it is the development of a single advertisement, a full campaign, or a special promotional event, there must be a starting point that directs the endeavor and a point of conclusion that makes recommendations for the actual promotional route to take.

**IDENTIFICATION OF THE PROJECT.**   Each segment of the fashion industry has any number of projects that it wishes to bring to the attention of prospective customers. The retailer might wish to promote a new private label or announce the opening of a new unit. The fiber producer might want to alert its customers, the fashion designers, or the consumers to the benefits of a particular yarn. An apparel manufacturer's association might wish to call attention to its semiannual trade exposition in a particular city. The fragrance producer might want to launch a new product line.

The list of advertising needs seems to be endless. The initial step for any company wishing to embark upon a specific promotional effort is to specifically identify the project and its goals. A clear definition of the endeavor is a must. It is not sufficient to talk about "getting the message out" about a new exclusive arrangement between a store and a designer, but which consumer market is the best to target to ensure success for the collection.

The project's identification and how to proceed is often done through informal brainstorming by the advertiser's top management. At the designer level, it might be the designer, merchandising staff, and sales manager who might just sit around and throw out ideas that come from their own experiences with the line, its retail clients, and the public who might best be motivated to ultimately make the purchases. In the case of the department store wishing to advertise the opening of a new "spinoff operation," a specialty chain that it is about to begin, it might use several sessions attended by its buyers, product developers, merchandising managers, special events staff, and visual team to give birth to an advertising plan that would reach the potential market for the new chain.

Whatever the project, it must be carefully examined, with its goals defined, before any further action may be taken.

**MAKING THE STUDY.**   Once the decision-making team determines there is a need for the project and a budget has been established for it, the next planning phase is initiated. Initially, secondary research is conducted. If necessary, primary investigation is then undertaken.

## SECONDARY RESEARCH AND ITS SOURCES

Before an advertiser embarks upon original research, it chooses from a variety of sources that have information that has been published. The principle reasons for beginning with secondary research are cost and promptness of information collection.

Original research, as we will explore later in the chapter, involves any number of approaches to gathering information including the use of questionnaires, personal interviews, and focus groups. Each of these may be quite costly and sometimes out of the question for certain projects.

# CURRENTS

The Newsletter of The Fashion Association        Vol. V  No. 6        July 1993

## SATELLITING FATHER'S DAY FASHIONS

The question of what to get Dad for Father's Day was answered throughout the country on Wednesday, June 16. Tom Julian and television production company Piccoli & Piccoli hosted a satellite media tour throughout 20 local and national markets. This effort reached nearly 4.1 million people across the U.S.

Rather than models, real fathers and sons told the Father's Day story with a full range of gift ideas. Using a New York City studio as the backdrop, sets were designed to visualize a golf green, a brownstone and a backyard barbeque. Participating companies included: **The Polyester Council/Cotler, Johnston & Murphy, Code West, Dockers Footwear, Baume & Mercier, Champagne Diamonds** and **JCPenney.** (See Airwaves for placement.)

Looking ahead to the fall season, we are conceptualizing ideas and will keep you informed. ■

## CELEBRATING 25 YEARS OF STONEWASHING

A highlight evening during the Fall Press Preview included the 25th Anniversary Celebration of Stonewashing with Marithe and Francois Girbaud. On Thursday, June 3, industry and press gathered at Manhattan's Industria Superstudio. This hip photo studio was transformed into an indoor carnival — with aerial trapeze performers, dancers including The Pilobolus Dance Troupe, skateboarders and the Harlem Boys Choir. Blue margaritas were served along with "mood food" creating exotic crudite for picking off of waiters' vests. The music, clothing displays and trendy guests completed the surreal evening. Our photo montage highlights the party...

*Francois Girbaud talks "acrobatics" in French with Joni Fiore.*

*Continued on page 2*

## EXECUTIVE DIRECTIONS

It was a Press Preview — plus, plus!

The June 2 - 5 Press Preview attracted 135 national fashion journalists and over 175 industry representatives to the Sheraton New York headquarters and the Equitable Center Theatre for a program that created news from start to finish.

It also marked the official changing of our corporate identification. This was a natural evolution that began with a one-of-a-kind press program in 1955 as the American Institute of Men's and Boy's Wear (AIMBW). In 1968 we became the Men's Fashion Association, with a purpose to communicate fashion news.

As members of MFA moved into womenswear... and as more people questioned why there wasn't an MFA for womenswear...and, finally, as editorial travel budgets tightened up, it became clear that MFA had to broaden its scope to offer more information about every aspect of fashion. Hence, the change to The Fashion Association (TFA) was made. It may take a little getting used to — like changing the year you write on checks every January — but TFA has arrived and will be as good, dependable and professional as ever.

The Fashion Association has set January 12 - 15, 1994 as the dates for its Spring Press Preview at the Los Angeles Biltmore with the partnership of CaliforniaMart. Details are being worked out. Be there! It'll be another good one!

Norman Karr

**THE FASHION ASSOCIATION**

*tentative new logo for TFA*

## THANKS!

MFA/TFA offers its thanks to key people for the success of the Fall Press Preview. For helping to launch TFA's first women's wear program, we are grateful to Bernard Chaus, Jones New York, M.M. Krizia, and Theo Miles.

We give special thanks to Susie Watson of Timex for chairing the marketing committee and her team of Mary Ellen Barone of Anne Taylor Davis Communications, David Stamper of CaliforniaMart and Carol Edwards of JCPenney.

The interview sessions were "sweetened" by "2 Calorie Quest," which supplied cooling soft drinks. We appreciate Jerry Kean's photography and Michael Beckman & Associates' video taping. And, last but certainly not least, thanks to Chip Tolbert for all his production support. ■

## DID YOU KNOW???

Anniversaries are in the air, especially in the publishing world this fall. *The New Times Magazine* celebrates its 50th Anniversary in the second half of 1993. "50 Years Of Passion For Fashion" is the promotion's theme. Key issue dates are August 22, September 26 and October 24 which will feature fashion retrospectives. *Playboy* turns 40 in January and exciting plans include stories from notable authors Buck Henry and William F. Buckley. A special portfolio of legendary women who have appeared in the magazine will be featured. Congrats to both!

Now this famous face is wearing pants...he's a baseball Hall of Famer, holds many records for the Baltimore Orioles and looks great in underwear. Can you guess who? It's Jim Palmer, and he has teamed up with **Sansabelt** as their spokesperson. He will appear in advertising, wearing new slack styles which will appeal to contemporary males.

New product launches include...shirts from **Bass,** contemporary footwear from **J. Murphy,** watches from **Nautica by Timex,** train conductor watches from **Hypnotic Hats** and tailored clothing from **Garrick Anderson.** News from **Ron Chereskin** this season comes from two areas — outerwear and activewear. **Geoffrey Beene,** designer of classic men's shirts, is launching his first men's sweater collection. The look will be natural, in terms of both fiber content and coloration.

**Gold Toe** introduces a new promotion for the holidays. For every three pair pack of socks purchased, one dollar will be donated to children's charities. The program includes men's, women's and boy's lines.

Celebrity watching...Singer Jon Lucien dressed in tailored brights from **Everett Hall** on his recent CD cover, while Charles Barkley of the Phoenix Suns opted for Hall's black and white linen suit on the "Arsenio" show. Clint Eastwood dresses in Secret Service garb from **Nino Cerruti** in "In The Line Of Fire." The movie's costumer, Erica Phillips, uses Rue Royale suits in textured blue and grey.

Kurt Salmon Associates reports in the 1992 "Perspective"... **Genesco,** a footwear and tailored clothing manufacturer, increased profits 20-fold on a sales gain of 14%. Out of the top ten apparel companies leading in sales and earnings, five included menswear: **Levi Strauss, VF Corp., Liz Claiborne, Hartmarx** and **Phillips-Van Heusen.**

**The American Image Awards** is scheduled for Wednesday, November 10 at the Sheraton New York Hotel and Towers.

Colorful menswear will take to the runway on September 12 at the **Color Marketing Group's** annual convention in San Diego. Member companies are invited to participate free of charge and Tom Julian will present menswear news to 500 color specialists. Contact us for details. ■

---

**FIGURE 3-3**

Currents, *a trade association newsletter, is a secondary research source for the fashion industry.*

*(Courtesy of MFA)*

In terms of information acquisition, the secondary sources provide a wealth of data that is often quickly and simply obtained. In addition to already being available in some published formats, secondary sources might provide studies that could easily serve the advertiser as well as the original investigation.

Among the more frequented sources of secondary information utilized by fashion advertisers follow.

**TRADE ASSOCIATIONS.**    Every segment of the fashion industry has one or more trade associations that it can call upon to gather information on a variety of topics, including advertising and promotion. Fashion retailers, for example, as members of the National Retail Federation (NRF) are privy to a host of studies that the organization conducts. Using teams of industrial experts, the NRF examines and prepares a wide variety of reportS that range anywhere from point-of-purchase software availability to advertising trends. By examining the lists of studies that center on any aspect of promotion, the researcher might gain some meaningful insights into the promotional project he or she is exploring for the upcoming campaign.

Through the efforts of The Fashion Association, an organization that reports and advises on the menswear industry, designers and manufacturers of men's apparel might uncover information on media and the markets they serve. The February 1994 edition of their newsletter, *Currents*, for example, ran a feature that provided important information on the markets served by specific media and the names of contacts who might provide valuable suggestions on the targeting of market segments. Offered in the column was an overview of *Next Magazine*, a publication that focuses on the gay male population; *Action Sports Retailer*, one that concentrates on active-oriented merchandise; and *Columbia Magazine*, a periodical that features information on fashion trends. Advertisers interested in the gay market segment of the population would have easily found a way to do some further investigation by contacting the aforementioned *Next Magazine*.

Others that could supply specific advertising research for the fashion industry components include The Fragrance Foundation; The Fashion Footwear Association of New York; Leather Apparel Association, Inc.; New England Tanners Club; American Fur Industry; Cotton Incorporated; The Wool Bureau; American Textile Manufacturers Institute; and the American Gemological Society.

In cases in which specific agencies are unknown to the researcher or there is an insufficiency in terms of the available reports of those groups, there are associations that also provide studies of an advertising nature that might be appropriate. The American Association of Advertising Agencies, for example, offers numerous reports on every aspect of advertising from current media conditions to future trends in the field.

**GOVERNMENTAL AGENCIES.**  The various levels of the government provide a wide range of published information that is of value to the advertiser. For fashion operations with a narrow, local, potential clientele, approaching municipal agencies might serve their needs. For example, cities often gather statistics and prepare reports for their regions that include demographics such as age, occupations, and so forth. For more complete studies that focus on all important characteristics for decision-making, the federal government is the preferred choice. The Department of Commerce, for example, through its Census Bureau, provides data on housing, business, population, and so forth, all of which may impact potential advertising and promotion. In addition, the federal government publishes *The Monthly Catalogue of U.S. Governmental Publications*, which lists a host of reports that might feature information that is relevant to the advertiser's needs in terms of decision-making. The Federal Trade Commission (FTC) is a regulatory agency that, among other things, oversees advertising to make certain it does not foster any deception. Examining some of their decisions might guide the advertiser and prevent them from making costly mistakes.

Since there is little expense in obtaining government statistics, this is an excellent source for the researcher.

**PRIVATE SERVICES.**  Numerous companies, sometimes referred to as secondary research suppliers, are in business to gather information that would be of interest to marketers. Of particular importance to advertisers are companies such as A.C. Nielsen, who, among other things, reports on broadcast media audience measurement. Advertisers planning to use radio and television would certainly benefit from such findings of Nielsen. Another important secondary private source is Off-the-Shelf Publications, Inc., which supplies a host of papers on a variety of topics that would interest advertising planners.

**LIBRARIES.**    A starting point for many fashion advertisers and promoters is the library. At public branches throughout the United States and those housed in colleges and universities, a wealth of pertinent information is available. For the fashion world, the libraries at the institutions of higher learning that specialize in fashion advertising feature bookshelves full of periodicals that could help planners with their campaigns. Periodicals such as *Visual Merchandising and Store Design, Stores Magazine,* and *Advertising Age* are just a few of the titles that are regularly stored.

Many governmental publications and reports are also there, either in hard copies or on microfiche, which is often a quicker way of obtaining them rather than going directly to the government.

Invaluable sources of information available at the library are the publications of *Standard Rate & Data Service (SRDS),* which feature all of the rate-card information on the advertising media. While the major advertisers subscribe to *SRDS,* infrequent advertisers might find the copies at the library sufficient for their needs.

In every library, there is a professional who will guide the requester to the appropriate research materials, be they of an advertising nature or any other topic.

## PRIMARY RESEARCH AND ITS SOURCES

When all of the secondary research appropriate for the project has been explored and there is still a need for further investigation, the use of primary research is the next step to take. The advertiser's company may proceed with the original research if it has a staff capable of handling such a project or an outside marketing organization or advertising agency competent in terms of questionnaire preparation, interviewing procedures, observation techniques, and so forth, would be employed to handle it. Whether it is the in-house staff or a contracted specialist who directs the effort, the primary research methodology used is the same. If the choice is an outside firm, the *International Directory of Marketing Research Companies and Services,* produced by the American Marketing Association, might be examined to find the organization specializing in the needs of the advertiser.

**FOCUS GROUPS.**    More and more advertisers are choosing **focus groups**, panels of approximately a dozen individuals, to study the com-

**FIGURE 3-4**

*Focus groups are*

*important*

*primary sources*

*of information*

*for advertisers.*

pany and elicit information that will be helpful in the planning of an advertising campaign or a direction the company might take for its advertising and promotional programs.

The groups are selected for one session that lasts about two hours, or for several sessions. If the promotion is one that will have a national orientation, then the researcher might opt for several groups, one in each of its targeted markets. If the advertiser is a retailer with stores in a radius of 100 miles, the single group would be satisfactory. A company with international clienteles such as Ralph Lauren or Donna Karan might utilize a host of groups around the world in the research.

The format involves people seated around a table discussing any area of the advertiser's concern, with a trained moderator leading the group and noting their responses and reactions to specific questions and concepts. In cases in which the advertisement's sponsor wishes to learn firsthand about the participant's reactions, he or she is often an observer through a one-way mirror.

The advantages of this type of primary research are relatively inexpensive costs and immediacy of response. While the format continues to serve many advertiser's needs, most agree it cannot be relied upon for all decisions by itself. It is better used as an adjunct to the other types of primary research tools.

**QUESTIONNAIRES.**   If a fashion business is trying to assess a specific market, it might want to survey a **sample**, or representation, of the people in that group. One of the surest methods of culling information from prospective customers is through the use of a questionnaire. The format for information gathering might be on the telephone, through the mail, or in a face-to-face interview.

Each of these techniques hase their advantages as well as limitations. The telephone, for example, reaches the respondent faster than any of the other means, is relatively inexpensive, and may be carried out from a central point. However, more and more people are frowning upon the "nuisance" calls during inopportune times and are often reluctant to answer questions from people they are unable to see. Use of the mail allows respondents more time to study the questions, eliminates interviewer bias, and costs relatively little since a full staff is not needed. On the negative side, the rate of return is generally small, a deficiency that some researchers are trying to change by offering cash or prize incentives to respondents; costs are eventually high because of the small return rate; and the potential is great for misunderstanding the questions without the benefit of someone to clarify them. The asking of questions face-to-face, as is the case in personal interviewing, often gets more people to respond. Trained interviewers, additional probing of open-ended questions, and the recording of observations are the advantages offered by this technique. As in the case of the others, it too has disadvantages. Interviewer bias might color the answers, trained questioners are costly, and questions of age or income might be misrepresented because of the interviewee's potential to alter the truth.

If the questionnaire is the researcher's choice for investigation, its effectiveness will be enhanced if care is given to its design. The forms must be prepared first by considering the market to be examined and developing them with the use of language that is easily understood. In the case of a trade organization that wishes to study its market, the use of technical words in the questions is appropriate. Such terms as private label, confinement, pret-a-porter, and so forth, are sufficiently familiar to the field's professionals, and if used in questions will be entirely understood. The use of these exact terms when the surveyed audience is consumer oriented will undoubtedly be unclear. Thus, the choice of language is imperative when creating a questionnaire form.

Attention should also be paid to the avoidance of generalities in the questions, such as the words *usually* and *occasionally*, while arranging the questions in a sequential order so that one leads smoothly to the next. Its organization should be such that data tabulation will be simple to compile. It is also important that the questionnaire be limited in size. Forms that are too lengthy, more than two pages, are often quickly discarded, causing the rate of return to be affected.

**OBSERVATIONS.** In certain studies, observing people would provide better information than either the focus group or questionnaire methodology. A fashion retailer, for example, about to open a store in a mall and now ready to plan an advertising campaign to promote its arrival, might want to observe the mall's typical shoppers before a decision is made in terms of advertising format. Through the use of a form to record shopper appearance, general age classifications, and so forth, the advertiser might get a feeling about the best approach to use.

Another example of the fashion retailer's use of the observation technique might be in terms of selecting the best newspaper for the company's advertisements. Stationing observers at trainstations in the store's trading area and recording which publications are being read might signal where the advertisements should be placed.

It is the professional researcher who chooses one or more of the research tools to help a campaign or promotional program.

**EXPERIMENTAL RESEARCH.** Often, variations of the same advertisement are produced, with one ultimately being selected for showing. Where the advertiser or agency is uncertain as to which one has the potential for better results, an experiment might be conducted before the final decision is made.

In situations like these, an audience comprised of potential users of the product is invited to a screening of the commercials. The group is then divided into two equal parts, with each seeing just one of the productions. After the screenings, the two groups are questioned by a professional moderator in terms of what they liked, their comprehension of the message, and so forth. After studying the reactions of both groups, a decision is made as to which commercial will be aired.

**SAMPLE SELECTION.**    Once the methodology has been selected for the project, it is necessary to make a determination of the numbers of individuals or companies that need to be researched in order for the study to be credible. While the numbers in focus groups are generally small, as discussed earlier in the chapter, sometimes there is a need for expansion. When questionnaires or observations are used, there is a need to determine how many responses will be needed to make an accurate measurement. It should be understood that the investigation of an entire "market population" is not necessary for a realistic study. Marketers, through a number of means, choose a sample, or segment of the group to be studied. There are different types of samples used. They include a **probability sample**, in which everyone in the market has a potential for inclusion, and a **random sample**, which, with mathematical regularity, chooses names from a list.

The size of the sample and the type used is determined by professional researchers.

**DATA COLLECTION.**    After the forms have been designed, as in the case of questionnaires and observations, or the individuals have been assembled, as in the case of the focus group technique, it is necessary to gather the data.

If those involved in this data collection are not sufficiently trained, the results might not have the credibility needed to proceed with the project. Advertising agencies and marketing research organizations employ trained individuals who understand the appropriate techniques to use to gather information. If a telephone questionnaire is used, the professional understands the need for clearly reading the questions and not prejudicing answers by emphasizing certain words. In the use of an observation, the recorder knows to record as many people as possible and not to include or exclude any whom they might not consider good candidates for the research.

Sometimes, when costs need to be curtailed, the use of college students might be justified. Many colleges and universities offer majors in marketing research and train students to conduct interviews and use questionnaires. As long as the individuals are made aware of the purpose of the survey and understand the language of the industry, in this case fashion, the methodology would be appropriate.

**ANALYSIS OF THE DATA.**   Once the data has been collected, it must be analyzed so that a recommendation may be made to the advertiser. The data must be processed and arranged in a manner that makes analysis achievable. In the case of the focus group, there is no formal mechanism for data collection but merely a recording of the comments made by the participants. The moderator must sift through all of the responses, categorize them, and draw conclusions that would help determine the path the advertiser and promoter should take.

When questionnaires and observations are used, data processing and ultimate analysis may be more easily accomplished if the forms used to collect the data are properly **precoded**, that is, the assignment of a specific number next to each response in a category. Without the precoding, the responses must first be coded to fit the different responses.

The computer and its infinite variety of sophisticated programs enables the data to be quickly compiled and made ready for analysis and the ultimate recommendations of the researchers.

The final step involves the preparation of a report that includes the methodology for the collection of the data, its analysis, and the recommendations of the team responsible for carrying out the project.

## EVALUATIVE RESEARCH: THE FINAL DECISION

With the enormous expense involved in mounting a campaign, advertisers are often uncertain right up to the time of the publication or airing as to the final composition of the advertisement. With stakes so high, especially in the case of a national program that uses a multimedia mix, **evaluative research**, tests to measure advertising effectiveness, are often utilized before a full-scale, major campaign is mounted or after a lesser one has been published or aired.

There are numerous experts in the field who engage in this aspect of the research program. Some specialize in one medium, while others run the gamut that includes all of the media. If television is the medium to be used, then it is advantageous to employ the services of the specialist who deals exclusively with that medium. In addition to medium specialties, the methodology for testing varies from company to company. One may engage exclusively in recall testing, while others concentrate on recognition research.

Some of the better known companies whose forte is evaluative research are Burke Marketing Research, Gallup and Robinson, and Starch INRA Hooper. Before choosing any one agency to perform this task, it is best to make certain of their familiarity with the merchandise classifications being advertised.

Some of the more useful evaluative testing of fashion advertising follows.

**RECALL TESTS.**    In order to ascertain the degree to which a broadcast or print advertisement captured or held the reader's, listener's, or viewer's attention, a recall test is a sound approach. In cases in which the campaign will run for an extended period of time, the test often takes place immediately after its introduction.

The day after a television commercial is aired researchers use telephone interviews to contact those who have seen the advertisement. If the advertisement had national exposure, several hundred people who saw the advertisement are sought in a few different cities to test their recall. Of course, in order to reach the desired number of respondents, thousands would have to be called to get the number needed.

Typically, for television recall testing of a fashion product, the following questions will be asked: "Did you remember seeing a jeans commercial on television?" For negative responses, the follow-up question would be, "Do you remember a Calvin Klein jeans commercial?" This question attempts to aid the memory. If the respondent answers yes to the first or second question, additional questions such as, "Did you recognize the celebrity in the commercial?", "What was the commercial's setting?", and perhaps, "Which style did it feature?" The responses are carefully noted by the interviewers for later use in determining the advertisement's ability to capture attention of the viewer.

In cases in which there is uncertainty about the selection of a particular commercial in terms of its ability to motivate a market, some companies use recall testing in a research setting. In these cases, guests are selected at random to come to a theater to participate in an advertising test program. In the theater, they are shown a variety of commercials and are tested in much the same manner as described when the test takes place after a commercial is presented on the air.

Prior to the testing, guidelines are established to determine the percentage of recall necessary to go ahead with the project or to choose the better commercial from those featured.

Similar formats are used for print advertisement recall tests. Since there is no live action, pictures are used in place of video for the testing.

Professionals in the field use this form of measurement because it is relatively reliable and the costs are minimal. For television commercial testing of this nature, Burke Marketing Research, Cincinnati, Ohio, has been the most significant testing company.

**RECOGNITION TESTS.** The recognition test, a format used extensively for print advertising, is used extensively. *Starch Reports* are considered the hallmark technique for recognition, especially for magazine advertisements.

This form of research involves questioning people to first determine if they remember seeing a company's advertisements. Once the viewing has been confirmed, the interviewees are shown the publication in which the advertisements were featured and are asked a series of questions concerning the advertisement's components, such as the headline, illustration, use of a logo, and copy. The responses are then recorded and later assessed to determine which of the advertisements were remembered better. If two different versions of the advertisements were run in the same magazine, the one with the greater recognition is usually chosen for repeat insertions.

**PERSUASION TESTS.** Sometimes, advertisers wishing to test their television commercials use the theater format as described in the recall test category. In the former research, the participants are told they are going to examine a variety of television commercials to determine the commercial's effectiveness. With the persuasion methodology, the theatrical arena is again used, except the invited viewers are told their involvement is to help evaluate a **television pilot**, a show that is about to go on the air. In addition to showing the new program, the guests are also shown the commercials in their entirety.

In most of these persuasion tests, the members are asked about the products they prefer to use in the classification of those that will be featured in the commercials. After the conclusion of the presentation, they are asked to answer questions about the broadcast and then about product preferences. The reactions might assist the advertisers to make changes in the commercials.

**INQUIRY TESTS.** Some companies use inquiries or direct counts to research the effectiveness of their campaigns. As part of their advertisements, there is a coupon or 800 number that invites the observer to inquire about additional information or perhaps, a catalog of the company's wares.

Lands' End, the Wisconsin-based catalog operation, uses this type of approach in its print advertisements. Readers are invited to clip the provided coupon and return it to the company or call the toll-free 800 number for a catalog. To keep track of the worthiness of the advertisement in terms of direct response, each coupon is coded with two letters that indicate from which advertisement the coupon was taken, and thus, which of their advertisements were more effective.

**COMMUNICATION TESTS.** If you have ever walked through a mall, chances are that people with clipboards have been seen approaching shoppers to ask them certain questions. In order to motivate participation, they are often offered monetary rewards for their involvement. Those who wish to participate are then led to an interviewing area and are asked questions that aid in the assessment of advertisements.

After the advertisements are shown, be they television or print, questions pertaining to their thoughts as they examined the advertisements are asked, as well as their responses to specifics such as copy language, illustrations, and so forth.

The responses are recorded by the interviewer and later coded into categories that best describe their responses. Caution must be exercised in this type of research not to misjudge the category in which the responses are placed. If bias or misjudgment enters into the code assignments, the effectiveness of the research will be affected.

**IMPACT MEASUREMENTS.** Some fashion advertisers measure the advertisement's effectiveness by the results it brings. Fashion retailers, in particular, find this a good way to test their newspaper advertisements. It answers the questions, for example, "Did the Donna Karan

**FIGURE 3-5**

*The coupon in the*

*advertisement is used to*

*determine the*

*advertisement's*

*effectiveness and is coded*

*with the letters JV for ease*

*in evaluation.*

*(Courtesy of Lands' End)*

outfit sell better because of advertising?", or "Did the special sales promotion get the turnout it did because of the advertisement that was run?" By watching the sales before and after the advertising was utilized it could be determined whether or not it was the advertisement that impacted on sales.

Of course, for the retailer, other factors could have clouded the effectiveness of the advertisement such as inclement weather; a late spring snowstorm on the day the lightweight, linen suit was shown in the newspapers; a sudden series of disasters such as the earthquakes in Los Angeles in 1994; or crippling market conditions, such as an unexpected downturn in the stock market the day the advertisement appeared. Even with these unforeseen happenings, many retailers use this type of research testing.

**MISCELLANEOUS TESTS.**  Other measurement techniques are used in evaluative research, some of which were discussed in relation to the development of advertising campaigns and programs earlier in the chapter. The focus group, for example, is used for both the stages of planning as well as for evaluation purposes.

Some advertisers use **physiological testing**, a technique that measures emotional reactions to advertisements, and **frame-by-frame tests**, where each frame of a television commercial is examined separately, either in place of the aforementioned methods or in conjunction with them. In the fashion industry, those testing methods already discussed in detail are more typically used.

## Research: An Absolute Predictor or a Guide?

With all of the bustling excitement that surrounds advertising and promotional research, and the scientific focus it emphasizes, it should be understood that it merely serves as a guide for a company to use. The creative minds of advertising professionals play an important role in what direction a campaign should take.

In the stages of planning and developing, while sound research methodology guides a program, it does not absolutely enable the experts to deliver a sound approach. Creativity and "feeling" should be considered as well.

In the evaluative process, whether it is just prior to the running of what is considered to be the final version of a commercial or print advertisement or after some advertisements have been run, research is beneficial to assess the ability of the creative team to produce the right campaigns.

Research cannot be considered an absolute predictor because with all of its sophisticated tools those ventures that seem "safe," sometimes fail.

## REVIEW QUESTIONS

1. Is an advertising campaign guaranteed success if its research was carefully executed?

2. Briefly explain the meaning of the two-pronged approach to advertising and promotion research.

3. What first step must be taken by the research team in studying the development of the campaign?

4. Why is secondary research conducted before any original investigation takes place?

5. What are some of the sources of secondary research?

6. Does the fashion trade association play any role in advertising and promotion research?

7. If one wants to determine which publications are produced by the federal government for use in research studies, how should it be accomplished?

8. What is meant be the term *secondary research*?

9. May libraries play a significant role in advertising research?

10. Define the term *primary research.*

11. Discuss the operation of a focus group and how it aids researchers in their investigations.

12. What is meant by the term *sample*, as it relates to an advertising study?

13. Which method of questionnaire usage reaches the respondent the fastest?

14. Why is face-to-face interviewing often considered more advantageous than the use of mail questionnaires?

15. Briefly describe the methodology used in the observation techniques of research.

16. What is meant by evaluative research? When is it used?

17. Describe the recall test in advertising research.

18. What is considered to be the hallmark of recognition testing? For which medium is it used most extensively?

19. How does a researcher use the persuasion test?

20. Describe the mechanics of the inquiry test.

## EXERCISES

1. Pretend that your class has been approached by a local fashion retailer to conduct a research study to determine which medium is the one that is most motivating in enticing them to make purchases from the store.

   The class should plan a project that will eventually provide the necessary information to that retailer. In carrying out the project, a preliminary plan should be developed along the lines of the one featured in the chapter, including the design of the instrument that will be used to conduct the research.

2. Using the instruments that have been developed in Exercise 1, the class should then proceed to gather the information needed from the various groups identified as important to the store. Once the data have been collected it should be analyzed and put in report format for use by the store.

   Note: The size of the sample used in the research should be determined with the help of a marketing research professor in your school or a statistician who has experience with sample sizes.

*Creative director at the Christopher Thomas Advertising Agency designing layout for an advertisement*

# Advertising Agencies and Promotional Services

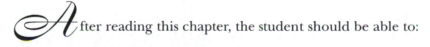fter reading this chapter, the student should be able to:

1. List and discuss the various functions and services that advertising agencies provide for their clients.

2. Research the marketplace and learn about the various agencies and their areas of specialization.

3. Prepare a set of guidelines to be used in the selection of an agency.

4. Discuss the methods of remuneration for agency representation.

5. Address the ways a client may maximize an agency's effectiveness.

## Introduction

The wealth of potential advertising possibilities available to the fashion industry requires expertise and knowledge that is generally far beyond the capacities of those who manage their companies. The abilities to create an applause-getting style or to merchandise a high-fashion retail emporium are different than those needed to make the potential customers aware of the company's existence. While many fashion industry practitioners may have a concept they would like to employ, in terms of advertising, they rarely have either the technical orientation or the skills needed to carry out their thoughts.

Advertising agencies provide the services needed by manufacturers, designers, retailers, and other industry components to make their individual companies stand out from the rest. Not only do they provide the creative services that go into the making of a print advertisement, broadcast commercial, outdoor poster, or direct-mail piece, but they offer managerial assistance, marketing direction, research, and anything necessary to make their client's promotional endeavors more achievable.

Just as there are different apparel designers and retailers that suit different needs there are agencies of every size, personality, and style to fit different client needs. They are located all over the world, ready to serve the demands of businesses regardless of their size.

With the enormous expense allocated for advertising by many fashion businesses, it is imperative that care be exercised before any final decision is made as to which agency shall represent them. Selection of the right agency is the first step toward assuring that the monies will be well spent.

## Scope of the Industry

With more than 10,000 advertising agencies in this country alone and many others located in all parts of the world, the fashion industry, which is also geographically dispersed around the globe, need not look very far to make a choice. The *Standard Directory of Advertising Agencies,* most often referred to as the *Agency Red Book,* provides an overview that includes a ranking of the world's top fifty advertising organizations, the top ten billing agencies for each of the media, and an alphabetized listing of the individual agencies and their specializations.

Although names like Saatchi & Saatchi Co., Young & Rubicam, Grey Advertising, BBDO, and Foote, Cone & Belding Communications are instantly recognizable in the world of advertising, there are literally thousands of smaller agencies from New York to Los Angeles and abroad that serve the needs of clients. In terms of geographic distribution, however, thirty-seven of the top fifty agencies are headquartered in New York. Chicago is a distant second, with three organizations.

While the major agencies represent businesses of most any type, there are some more moderately sized organizations that specialize in a particular industry. Some agencies specialize in fashion. Weiss, Whitten, Carroll, Stagliano Inc. represents Giorgio Armani, New York, A/X Armani Exchange, and Armani Couture, NY. Favara, Skahan, Raffle Advertising has as its clients American Legend Mink Co. and Blackglama Mink. Eisenman & Enock Inc. represents Susan Bennis/Warren Edwards, New York, retailers of high-fashion shoes.

# Types of Advertising Agencies

Today's fashion advertiser may choose from a variety of agency types to handle specific needs. The choices include the full-service agencies that handle all of their client's advertising tasks and the boutiques that primarily emphasize the creative services required by their users. Others include network, Rolodex, and media-buying services, and in-house agencies.

## FULL-SERVICE AGENCIES

In addition to planning and creating advertisements of every classification and placing them in the most appropriate media, the full-service agencies also provide a host of other functions such as the total management of the client's account, traffic control and production, marketing, and account management. Some of the larger agencies have added additional services of a promotional nature such as developing special events, designing shopping bags, and preparing publicity tools such as press kits. The full complement of services offered by advertising agencies will be examined later in the chapter.

## AGENCY NETWORKS

WPP Group, London
- Ogilvy & Mather
- Cole & Weber
- J. Walter Thompson

Interpublic Group of Companies, New York
- Lintas, Dailey & Associates

Omnicom Group, New York
- BBDO
- Gurian & Mazzel
- Lowe Group

Saatchi & Saatchi Co., New York
- Conill Advertising
- Klemter Advertising

Young & Rubicam, New York
- Chapman Direct
- Munsell, Fultz & Zirbel

Euro RSCG, Neuilly, France
- Robert A. Becker, Inc.
- Cohn & Wells

Grey Advertising, New York
- Beaumont-Bennet Group
- Font & Vaamonde

Foote, Cone & Belding Communications, Chicago
- Krupp Taylor
- IMPACT

Publicis-FCB Communications, Paris
- Publicis Inc.

D'Arcy Masius Benton & Bowles, New York
- Clarion Marketing

Note: The companies indicated directly below each group comprise their networks.

**FIGURE 4-1**

*The major advertising agency networks*

## NETWORKS

A number of giant organizations have been formed through the joining of independent agencies into networks. The result has been the mega-agency, which not only offers a full range of services to clients, but also shifts portions of accounts from one agency in the network to another. If, for example, one group is better able to handle the requirements of newspaper advertising and another group specializes in outdoor and transit, the client will benefit from the expertise of each. Some of these agency giants include the WPP Group, London, the largest in the world; Interpublic Group of Companies, New York; Omnicom Group, New York; and Saatchi & Saatchi Co., London.

## BOUTIQUES

Instead of the usual host of services, these smaller companies specialize in just one aspect of advertising. Most often it is the creative aspect. They provide the written and illustrative portions of the advertisements and layouts and assist in their placement in the appropriate media. Generally, they are paid on a fee basis for each of the assignments they handle.

## ROLODEX AGENCIES

Instead of having a regular staff handle all of their management and creative functions, these agencies hire specialists for each of their projects as they need them. Thus, if a creative writer is needed to write the script for a radio commercial, he or she is hired only for that project. If marketing attention is necessary, an expert in that area will be employed for that task.

## MEDIA-BUYING SERVICES

Today, the media is more complex than ever before and requires thorough analysis and study before decisions on appropriate use of advertising are made by advertisers. The major role played by these organizations is negotiating the best possible deal for the client in terms of cost and scheduling advertisements. Sometimes, the media-buying services work for smaller agencies in addition to servicing their accounts.

### IN-HOUSE AGENCIES

Some major manufacturers have organized their own agencies. However, if the agency is privately owned and operated for a specific business, its functions and services are the same as those available via the full-service entry. Staffing is kept to a minimum with the various services needed purchased from experts outside of the organization. When time or space is needed, a media-buying service is utilized, as is a creative agency when the actual advertisement is being developed. In this way, they gain the necessary expertise at a fraction of the cost of maintaining a full-time staff.

# Functions and Services of Advertising Agencies

As already noted, the functions and services provided by advertising agencies differ according to their types. The following is an overview of the principal ones offered.

### CREATIVE SERVICES

The key to the success of the agencies, other than those exclusively designed to purchase media time and space, is creativity. While advertisements are developed to sell products and services, the philosophies of how to accomplish this are different from one agency to the next. How the appeals should be addressed in terms of copy, artwork, and layout is the responsibility of the agency's creative director. He or she plans an approach based upon a set of standards and principles, and passes them on to those who produce the creative elements.

While most agencies employ specialists such as copywriters and artists to produce a particular aspect of the advertisement, most often, the individuals form a team or partnership to develop the project.

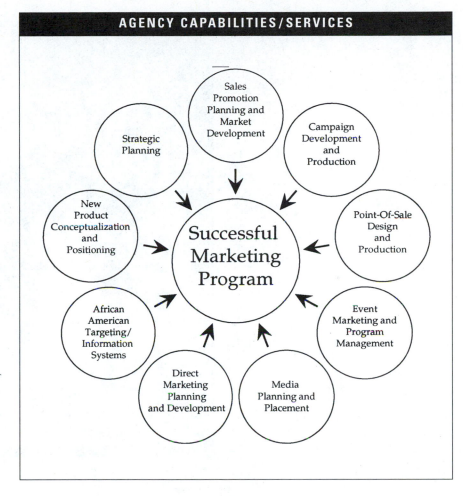

**AGENCY CAPABILITIES/SERVICES**

Sales Promotion Planning and Market Development

Strategic Planning

Campaign Development and Production

New Product Conceptualization and Positioning

Point-Of-Sale Design and Production

Successful Marketing Program

African American Targeting/ Information Systems

Event Marketing and Program Management

Direct Marketing Planning and Development

Media Planning and Placement

**FIGURE 4-2**

*Agencies offer a variety of*

*services to their accounts.*

*(Courtesy of Lockhart &*

*Pettus Advertising)*

Through a series of preliminary discussions, the team is apprised of the client's goal and offers suggestions for achieving them. The ideas that are put forth at this point might center upon a particular approach to the artwork and whether it would best be served through photography, line drawings, or perhaps, an unusual use of copy. Ultimately, each member is given his or her assignment that will fit into the scheme that has been approved.

As we examine print advertisements and television commercials, we are drawn to certain ones that are specifically unique and memorable. It is the creative team that has the expertise to design the concept and carry it out in a meaningful way.

**Figure 4-3**

*The advertising creative*

*team at work*

*(Courtesy of Johnson*

*Publishing Co., Inc.)*

## TRAFFIC CONTROL

If the best produced advertisement fails to reach the medium for which it has been developed in a timely manner, there will be no need to run the advertisement. Newspapers, magazines, radio, and television each have schedules that must be met to guarantee publication or airing. The function of traffic control is to make certain that the pieces of the puzzle are put together properly so that the finished product can reach the media on time. While performing their jobs, people in traffic control must interface not only with those on their own staff, such as writers and artists, but also with people in production and those at the publications or in the broadcast studios. Time changes are constantly being made for last-minute editing and other emergencies, requiring the speeding up of one aspect of the project to allocate additional time for another. No matter how carefully the initial plan is scheduled, those in traffic control are always challenged to make sure schedules are met.

## PRODUCTION

Once the print advertisement has been created, it is the production people who translate it into the finished product. They follow the directions laid out by the creative director and his or her team, supplying the right typefaces, refining the artwork, applying the layout to the predetermined space, and so on. They too are responsible for producing their part of the job in time for media usage.

## ACCOUNT MANAGEMENT

Each client's account is managed by an account executive. His or her function is to learn all about the client's business and provide the agency's advertising strategy that will accomplish the required goals. The account executive has the responsibility of overseeing the entire project, beginning with the presentation of the proposal. He or she selects the media to be used in a campaign and arranges for the scheduling of the advertisements, supplies the budget figures necessary to carry forth the project, presents thumbnails or roughs of proposed print advertisements, and prepares storyboards for television commercials. Once the client has given approval to move ahead, the account executive sees to it that the project is completed to specification and makes certain that it gets to the media for insertion.

Account executives are in continuous communication with their clients not only to keep them abreast of the status of current projects, but to address any changes in their businesses or product lines that must be considered for future campaigns.

## MEDIA SELECTION

In some industries, one medium may be better suited than another for a campaign. Fashion retailers, for example, make more use of newspapers than any of the other media. Apparel designers turn most often to the magazines for their spreads. Many advertisers use a multi-media approach for their campaigns.

Within each area of the media, there are choices that must be made. Would advertising in *Elle* magazine be better than advertising in *Vogue* or would a shot at television be the better choice? Perhaps, a billboard campaign might best provide the coverage needed. Agencies have experts who not only have the expertise needed to suggest the best media approach, but also are totally knowledgeable about purchasing time and space. They are able to negotiate the purchases, while keeping in mind the best way the client can spend his or her budget.

## RESEARCH

Before an agency embarks upon a particular campaign, it should have an understanding of what is happening in the client's marketplace. What is happening in terms of consumer behavior or attitudes will certainly contribute to the creation of the advertisement. In fashion today, there is more and more expression of sexual freedom. An examination of many fragrance advertisements shows that the advertisements depict sexual freedom with the use of partially clad human figures. Research has uncovered this new freedom and translated it into provocative advertising.

Everything that the marketing research organization studies such as lifestyles, income, employment trends, households, and so on, are of interest to advertising researchers so they can make the account executive's and creative director's approaches more realistic.

## MARKETING

Many of the major agencies provide marketing services for their clients. They explore the client's existing markets to learn if new products or services will provide additional business for them. They also investigate potential new markets for currently produced merchandise lines. Not only do the marketing services help to expand the client's business, but they also provide the potential for additional advertising expenditures.

FIGURE 4-4

*The media process is a*

*major area of emphasis for*

*the advertising agency.*

*(Courtesy of Lockhart &*

*Pettus Advertising)*

## THE MEDIA PROCESS

- Plans are developed to support Brand Sales Promotion, Community Relations and Trade campaigns.

- Plan development and buy analysis/execution supported by interpretations of available research (marketing and media).

- Interface with media vendors.

- Utilize leverage to negotiate packages (media and added value elements).

- Assess General market plans for BCM impact.

- Monitor new media.

- Determine application of General market techniques for BCM planning, buying and research.

- Serve as advisor to media trade.

- Use of all available research sources: Arbitron, Nielsen, Mediamark Research, Inc., Standard Rate and Data, Simmons, Independent Studies, Census Data, Media Vendors.

## SALES PROMOTION

Most businesses use a variety of promotional techniques to gain customer attention. They might be in the form of contests, premiums, special events, and personal appearances. For fashion retail clients, the agency might design a point-of-purchase (P-O-P) display that dovetails with an advertising campaign or shopping bags that spell out a store's special event. For the introduction of a new import apparel collection, the airline of the country in which the merchandise is produced and

**SALES PROMOTION CAPABILITIES**

- Concept is developed which addresses awareness, trial and target audience objectives.

- Present concept to client for input and approval.

- Explore entertainment tie-ins.

- Investigate premiums.

- Include contests/sweepstakes (where appropriate).

- Coordinate trade shows.

- Create/produce sales kits and/or collateral materials.

- Design P-O-P displays.

**FIGURE 4-5**

*Promotional tie-ins*

*enhance an*

*advertising campaign.*

*(Courtesy of Lockhart*

*& Pettus Advertising)*

the retailer who will feature it might create a cooperative promotion for the designer. Since the success of any promotion depends on an advertising campaign to get the message across, the more ideas they provide, the greater the need for additional advertising.

# Agency Remuneration

Compensation for the work provided by the agency is either based upon commission or a fee.

## COMMISSIONS

Traditionally, the advertising agency is paid a commission from the media for the advertising it places. The standard rate in the industry is 15 percent. If, for example, a magazine advertisement is billed to the client for $100,000, then the publication receives $85,000 and the agency receives $15,000. Today, the rates are negotiable. Some clients, especially those with enormous advertising expenditures, contract with agencies to get back a part of the 15 percent for themselves. Some contracts call for sliding-scale commission schedules in which the commission changes as certain advertising levels are reached.

### FEES

Sometimes the agency and client enter into an arrangement in which a fee is charged based upon an hourly rate. This is often the case when the account is small, and the revenue its advertising would generate from the commission rate is insufficient for the agency. The fee is based on the services it provides for the client such as creation of the advertising, management of the account, media negotiation, and so on.

## Selecting an Agency

With the wealth of advertising agencies available to businesses, choosing the right one is a matter of following a plan. Each stage in the selection process should address the advertising and promotional needs of the client and how each individual agency would best serve the client's needs.

### ASSESSMENT OF NEEDS

Each business has established goals that it would like to achieve. Advertising most often plays a vital role in achieving its goals. The advertiser should prepare a list of their needs so that the choice they ultimately make will then be realized.

There might be a need for exclusivity in representation; for example, the advertiser might want to use the services of a group that does not work for a competitor. Fashion retailers would probably not want their competition to be managed by the same agency since it might result in campaigns with similar images or leaks of information as to what types of campaigns are in the planning and when they will be run.

**STRATEGIC PROCESS**

- **INFORMATION**
  Collect any and all available information.

- **ANALYSIS, ASSESSMENT**
  Report key findings, implications and recommendation for Client input and approval.

- **STRATEGY DEVELOPMENT**
  Develop strategic approaches to solve problems or capitalize on specific opportunities.

- **CREATIVE/ADVERTISING/COMMUNICATIONS**
  Create campaign/execution to address overall psychographic and demographic target profile which speak to the strategic approach.

- **EXECUTION**
  Implement advertising, sales promotion and PR efforts.

- **EVALUATION**
  Evaluate program, assess growth in Client's business.

**FIGURE 4-6**

*In selecting an agency,*

*their strategic process*

*must be examined.*

*(Courtesy of Lockhart*

*& Pettus Advertising)*

## EXAMINATION OF CAMPAIGNS

One of the simplest ways to learn about advertising agencies and their creative abilities is to examine the campaigns that they have already mounted for other companies. This is easily accomplished by closely inspecting newspapers, magazines, television, and any other media that the advertiser wants to use.

Once the types of print advertisements and broadcast commercials of interest have been noted, finding the agency that created them is a simple matter. A call to the store's advertising department or designer's publicist often quickly produces the name of the agency.

Those advertisers who subscribe to outdoor and transit advertising can get a quick overview of the most recognized entries by studying that medium's Obie Awards. Each year, a book is published that features the winning advertisements, the agency of record, and the names of the individuals responsible for the artwork and copy. Since the winners are categorized according to specific classifications, those of interest are easily found. In fashion, for example, there are categories for retail—traditional and nontraditional—and clothing and accessories manufacturers.

## DEVELOPMENT OF AN AGENCY LIST

In addition to gathering names from campaigns of interest, examining the *Standard Directory of Advertising Agencies* will be very helpful. This directory features a listing of the world's top fifty agencies, the top ten agencies by United States media billings, and an alphabetical list of more than 5,000 agencies, from the smallest to the largest.

Each agency listing in the directory includes information that is essential to understand before any direct contacts, such as their areas of

**FIGURE 4-7**

*A typical advertising*

*agency listing in an*

*industry directory*

**ADVERTISING AGENCY LISTING**

FAVARA, SKAHAN, RAFFLE ADVERTISING
560 Broadway, New York, N.Y.
212-431-5827

| | |
|---|---|
| Specialization: | Upscale Products, Fashion, Beauty, Travel. |
| Employees: | 8 |
| Accounts: | American Legend Mink Co., Seattle Wash. |
| | La Prairie Skin Care & Cosmetics, N.Y. |
| | Steven Corn Furs, N.Y. |
| | Judith Leiber Handbags and Accessories, N.Y. |
| | New York Merchandise Mart, N.Y. |
| | Erwin Pearl, Inc., Jewelry, N.Y. |
| | Givenchy Hosiery, N.Y. |
| | Spring Industries, Ultrasuede Fabrics, N.Y. |

specialization, media billings, employees, and accounts represented, are warranted. The following figure is an excerpted listing that would be of interest to a potential fashion advertiser.

Not only can a potential advertiser get an overview of the company, but this enables them to get further information from the agency and from clients who are on their roster.

## VISITING THE AGENCIES

Once the list of agencies being considered has been drawn, it should be narrowed down to the few that seem worth a visitation. This decision should be based upon some preliminary research to determine whom they represent, whether any of the existing clients are competitors, the types of supportive services they offer, and anything else that would be important for the advertiser's needs.

Prior to the first appointment, a list of questions should be developed that will assist in the preliminary evaluation of the prospects. They should center upon such areas as compensation, past campaigns, services, personal interaction, and organizational structure.

**COMPENSATION.** As previously discussed in this chapter, compensation is usually in the form of a commission or on a fee basis. If it is a commission rate, the percentage should be determined. If the fee method is used, questions regarding what the fee covers should be addressed. This way, there will either be a need to continue the interview if the remuneration arrangement is satisfactory for the client, or terminate it if it does not fit the client's plan.

**PAST CAMPAIGNS.** Every agency maintains a portfolio of its past campaigns. Examining them is one sure way of knowing whether or not their work included any projects similar to the needs of the potential new client. Evaluation should involve analysis of the artwork and copy to determine whether the style fits the prospect's own company or product image, the media used, and the agency's degree of specialization. If, for example, the agency's forte seems to be newspaper, and the client is looking specifically at transit for its main medium, then this might be the time to move on.

**CREATIVE SERVICES.** Without question, creative services are of paramount concern. The client will have already evaluated this aspect during the examination of the agency's portfolio. Some fashion clients, however, have the need to dovetail special promotions with their advertising campaigns and require that an agency be equipped to provide this direction. Others might want a publicist to call on for the preparation of press kits or point-of-purchase display designers to create props that would be used for visual merchandising. Whatever the requirements are, they should be discussed carefully to make certain the agency can provide them.

**PERSONAL INTERACTION.** Any good client-agency relationship is built on the ability to communicate with each other. It is an ongoing process that continues throughout the term of the contract. During the preliminary meeting, an assessment of the principals involved, such as the account manager, art director, or staff supervisors should be made in terms of their approachability, receptiveness to ideas and suggestions, and their general manner. If there is any evidence, for example, that questions are handled in a casual manner, and the prospect's approach is more formal, then it might be the wrong partnership.

**ORGANIZATIONAL STRUCTURE.** The number of people in the organization is often a consideration. It must have the sufficient number of people to provide all of the services sought by a potential client. If an organization chart is available, as in the case of the larger agencies, it should be explored to determine the roles played by the people in it, and which ones would be servicing the client.

## MAKING THE DECISION

The initial process of elimination may take several months. This is an important time for the client to carefully compare the positives and the negatives of each agency. The ultimate winner will be charged with the responsibility for spending the client's advertising budget in a way that will maximize sales potential.

The list of the agencies visited should be narrowed to just a few finalists. At that time, they should be seen again to clarify any areas of uncertainty, to determine how specifically a particular campaign might be mounted, to visit the creative and production departments, and to again evaluate if lines and methods of communication are compatible between agency and client.

With the significant expense attributed to advertising, mistakes will be costly. There is no room for error.

# Maximizing the Agency's Role

The selection of the agency is only the beginning of a long-lasting relationship. After the contractual arrangements have been finalized and the goals have been established, much of the future success will depend on the client's ability and willingness to work side-by-side with the agency. Some of the areas that the client will need to pay attention to are: information sharing; staying with a specific advertising direction; direct communication; the approval process; satisfaction with the team's effort; and evaluation of the completed product.

## INFORMATION SHARING

In order to plan and execute campaigns of significance the agency should regularly be apprised of such matters as the success, as well as the failures, of some of the company's products, changes in market share, sales increases and declines, and anything that will help them understand the strengths and weaknesses of the company. An apparel manufacturer, for example, might discover from the sales representatives that a particular segment of the market is becoming more and more important in terms of overall product distribution. The copywriters might then want to concentrate on this segment, directing appropriate messages to make the advertising even more productive.

## STAYING WITH A SPECIFIC ADVERTISING DIRECTION

Often, the nature of the fashion industry, with its constant changes, confuses the client's thoughts in terms of the direction the advertising program should take. Although fashion changes, a store's image or a designer's approach to creating the lines do not. If an agency is challenged to bring the client's company and/or collection to the forefront, it must stay on an established path or direction. In this way, customers and potential purchasers will become familiar with the advertiser and more easily recognize what is being promoted. Lord & Taylor, for example, often uses advertisements that feature delicate line drawings for the artwork. Without even looking for the store's name in the advertisement the reader will be able to quickly recognize it as Lord & Taylor. The continuity of the effort creates interest that carries over from one advertisement to the next.

## DIRECT COMMUNICATION

All too often, either because of other responsibilities or time constraints, people at the top of the organizational chart communicate with the agency by way of assistants or people at lower levels. By doing this, the decision-makers may not be getting their own thoughts to the agency. When a planning session is held between the client and agency, for example, the principals should be involved. If they come in at a later stage of the project's development, their own thinking might warrant changes. These charges could be costly in terms of actual dollars spent or time lost while the adjustments are being incorporated.

## THE APPROVAL PROCESS

Depending on the nature of the project, whether it is a one-shot advertisement or a full-scale campaign, there will be meetings to examine what has been accomplished by the creative team. A process should be in place that simplifies the manner in which the advertising is approved. This process should require that all of those involved in the business that is purchasing the advertising, as well as the agency team responsible for its development, such as the account executive, copywriter, illustrator, layout artist, and production director, be present. In this way, new ideas may be initiated and evaluated by everyone in the room. This will eliminate the necessity for many individual meetings and will cut down on the time it takes to get the project off the ground.

## SATISFACTION WITH THE TEAM'S EFFORT

All of the preliminary planning in the world does not guarantee a good working relationship with the people assigned to carry out an advertising program. To go forth with a team that does not fulfill the advertiser's expectations is impractical. It could hamper the effectiveness of a campaign and result in less-than-anticipated results.

Advertising agencies, unless they are exceptionally small, have more than one person responsible for a set of tasks. That is, there might be several copywriters or artists on staff. It is wise to make your dissatisfaction known and ask for changes in personnel. In this way, the agency-client relationship need not be aborted, just amended.

## EVALUATION OF THE COMPLETED PRODUCT

As each project is completed, the client should carefully examine its every aspect to make certain the results are what was expected. Letting the creative team know what was considered to be excellent and what could be improved will make the next program even better. Like any other creative group of people, those in advertising are motivated with applause. Acknowledging good copy or artwork will often lead to an even better performance the next time. However, if there is something that does not sit right, the client should offer those criticisms too. Most creative people will accept well-founded suggestions and use them for the client's future work.

## REVIEW QUESTIONS

1. How many advertising agencies are there? Where are they geographically based?

2. What information does the *Standard Directory of Advertising Agencies* provide?

3. In addition to advertising development, what do some full-service agencies provide for their clients?

4. Define what is meant by the term *advertising boutique.*

5. What is a rolodex agency?

6. Why is it important to use a team effort in the development of an advertisement?

7. At the agency level, what role does traffic control play?

8. Describe the job of an account executive.

9. List some of the sales promotional devices that some agencies provide for their clients.

10. What is the typical method of remuneration for the agency?

11. How may a prospective client evaluate an agency's efforts without directly approaching them?

12. Where might a prospective client look to get an overview of an agency?

13. What are some of the topics to discuss when visiting an agency under consideration?

14. What type of information should the client provide the agency so that their creative efforts will be on target?

15. If a client is dissatisfied with a particular advertisement or campaign, is it always the time to move on?

## EXERCISES

1. Using the *Standard Directory of Advertising Agencies* as your resource, develop a chart that lists five agencies that would suit the needs of a fashion advertiser.

   The chart should include the following:
   - agency names;
   - locations;
   - number of employees;
   - specializations;
   - current accounts; and
   - media specialties.

2. Pretend that you are a principal in a fashion-oriented company and you are considering making a change from your present agency to another. Develop a list of questions that could be used during an interview with the prospective agency to determine whether or not they will be able to satisfy your needs.

3. Contact an advertising agency in your general geographical area for the purpose of interviewing an account executive. From the information you gathered, prepare an oral report that outlines the duties and responsibilities of the executive and how he or she specifically helps clients achieve their advertising goals.

# Advertising Media and the Fashion Segments They Serve

SECTION 3

*Magazines have come to the forefront for fashion advertisers. (Courtesy of Johnson Publishing Co., Inc.)*

# Magazines

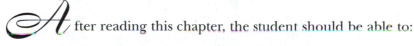

fter reading this chapter, the student should be able to:

1. Discuss why the magazine, the leading national advertising medium, experienced failure in the late 1950s and eventually returned as a formidable player of mass communication.

2. Explain the various advantages and disadvantages of magazine advertising.

3. Describe the various types of magazines used by fashion advertisers.

4. Describe the costs of magazine advertising.

5. Differentiate between consumer magazines and those that are classified as trade or business-to-business publications.

# Introduction

Early in the twentieth century, when designers and manufacturers of fashion merchandise wanted to reach their markets, the only choice was with magazine advertising. Men and women who wanted to learn about the latest in apparel and accessories trends and innovation, headed for the newsstand. There, famous publications such as *Vogue* and *Harper's Bazaar*, filled with creative designs, were snatched up by an audience waiting to learn about what it would wear in the coming season. Page after page of advertisements, editorial commentary on hemlines, silhouettes and color, fashion trends, and the like, were presented to the readers. The critics of fashion, who were employed by these periodicals had a great deal of power to determine which style would prosper and which would fail.

The competition for the advertising dollar was not very keen until television reared its head in the late 1950s and helped to cause the general demise of the magazine. It was not that the audiences abandoned the magazine, but advertisers began to spend significant amounts on the new, "live" medium. A visit to the newsstand revealed slim pickings in terms of magazine offerings. While the standard bearers such as *Vogue, Harper's*, and *Glamour* held fast and continued to publish, there was little new on the fashion magazine horizon.

In the 1980s, the industry began to revitalize its efforts and new periodicals appeared. Along with the standard bearers, the shelves of the newsstands began to fill with publications that were more clearly targeted to specific segments, such as *Ebony* and others that were imported from fashion capitals of the world—*Italian Vogue, Linea Italiana*, and *L'Official de la Couture et de la mode de Paris*.

Although television's popularity with advertisers continued to spiral, its impact on the world of fashion paled by comparison to the print media. It was more the medium for the automobile and food industries than one that dealt with fashion merchandise.

Today, row upon row of fashion magazines line the newsstand racks. The titles directed at the consumer include *Elle, Vogue Homme, Vogue Bambini, Gentlemen's Quarterly, Brigitte, Depeche Mode, L'Officiel—USA, Femme Pratique du Pret-a-Porter*, and a host of others from around the world.

The trade, or business-to-business, classification, which is aimed at the professional in the industry, includes *W, Style, California Apparel News, American Fabrics and Fashion, Women's Wear Daily,* and

*DNR.* Each plays a significant role in bringing the fashion world and its creations to life.

## Types of Magazines

There are two major magazine classifications. One classification is the consumer type that is directed toward the household purchaser. Although these publications are also read by the professionals in the industry, the primary target is the consumer. The other classification is trade magazines, or business-to-business periodicals. These are targeted to buyers, designers, manufacturers, retail executives, fashion consultants, and market representatives who work in the industry.

Complimentary magazines are also directed toward the consumer. However, unlike the traditional classifications, they are distributed without cost to the reader.

### CONSUMER MAGAZINES

The wealth of magazines available to the consumer today is greater than any other period in the history of this segment of the print media. Hundreds upon hundreds are readily available in both general formats and very narrowly focused editions. The fashion advertisers use both formats for reaching their potential markets.

Retailers like Sears and J.C. Penney, who try to capture a very broad segment of the market for their fashion offerings, generally elect the use of the general-interest format since their inventories are directed to every family member in a variety of price points. The Gap organization also advertises in general audience publications. On the other hand, when a designer or manufacturer tries to reach a narrow market segment for his or her collections, the special-interest magazine is generally the choice. Donna Karan, Ralph Lauren, and Calvin Klein would more likely expend advertising dollars in *Vogue* or *Harper's,* where the subscribers are likely to be motivated to purchase their items, than in *Family Circle,* where the readership possesses different characteristics.

**FIGURE 5-1**

*A wealth of consumer magazines have helped promote fashion merchandise.*

Since the fashion industry enjoys such a global audience, the magazines used to promote its products are internationally based. That is, the American designer or manufacturer with intentions to address foreign audiences might choose magazines that are published in different parts of the globe. Similarly, the famous French design houses like Dior, LaCroix, and Lagerfeld target American audiences with advertisements in the pages of *Harper's Bazaar*, *Vogue*, and other "bibles" of fashion.

## BUSINESS-TO-BUSINESS MAGAZINES

In order for the the textiles producers to reach the apparel manufacturers, the trimmings suppliers to entice the clothing and accessories designers, and the wholesale marketers to appeal to the retailers, they generally utilize a great abundance of business-to-business magazine advertising.

Each segment of the fashion industry boasts a number of periodicals that are read religiously as soon as they are delivered. Some, such as *Women's Wear Daily*, are a little more generalized than others

**FIGURE 5-2**

*Lycra magazine helps spread*

*the fiber's uses to apparel*

*designers and manufacturers.*

and appeal to most levels of the fashion trade. Others narrowly restrict their emphasis to capture the attention of a more specialized market segment. *Kids Fashions* and *Earnshaw's* are earmarked for the children's market; *FFANY* is used in the footwear industry; *Lycra* magazine is used by the manufacturers who might use the stretch material in their products; and *Visual Merchandising and Store Design* are used by those involved in display and environment layouts.

Unlike the readers of consumer publications who generally frequent the newsstands for their favorite magazines, the distribution of the trade-oriented periodicals is primarily by way of subscription. These publications are also available at the newsstands in the nation's wholesale fashion centers for those who are away from their headquarters and are unable to easily get their subscription copies.

## COMPLIMENTARY MAGAZINES

In the aforementioned discussion on consumer magazines, it was stated that the targeted readers are the subscribers. These individuals pay for the publications in which they are interested. There are, however, a host of magazines that are offered, without cost, to a large segment of the population. They are the people who use air travel, stay at hotels, and attend entertainment performances. In all of these arenas, the wealth of complimentary periodicals offered has significantly increased.

One of the major advantages of this publication classification is that it appeals to many people who are on vacation. Since tourists often spend more than they would at home, it holds the promise that if the appropriate motivation is applied, the purchases resulting from these advertisements will be easier to accomplish.

**AIRLINE PUBLICATIONS.** Today, the number of people using air transportation for business and pleasure continues to grow. The passengers on the flights often look for ways to pass the time. After the obligatory meal and the reading of a newspaper, there generally is time left before the flight terminates.

Every airline today takes advantage of this free time by distributing complimentary magazines. They rival the typical consumer publication in both format and quality. In addition to features that range from travel destinations to general newsworthy items, there is a wealth of advertising interspersed throughout the pages. Some of it is fashion-oriented, such as the advertisements of fashion retailers.

The number of issues produced is similar to the traditional consumer magazines. In this means of advertising, the frequent flier gets to see a new publication once a month and new advertisements each time.

**FIGURE 5-3**

*A variety of magazines, offered free of charge, are full of fashion advertisements.*

**HOTEL MAGAZINES.**   Most major hotels and resorts place copies of magazines that focus on the areas in which they are located. In addition to the standard features, such as recommended restaurants and tourist attractions, a variety of advertisements are found in the pages. Often, fashion retailers advertise in them.

One such major publication that features some fashion advertisements is the *Guest Informant*. It publishes regional editions of its magazine for distribution in thirty-nine cities across the United States. Each periodical includes an insert about the hotel in which it has been placed. However, all area hotels use the same magazine, giving the advertiser wide exposure. In *Guest Informant's* Gold Coast edition, which concentrates on Broward and Palm Beach Counties in southern Florida where a significant amount of the tourist trade is affluent, the advertising usually features high-fashion apparel and accessories.

The advantage to the advertiser is that it can capture the attention of the visitors to the area and motivate them to shop during their stays. Since many of the readers are first-time tourists to the region, this might be their only source of shopping information.

**ENTERTAINMENT PROGRAMS.** Many theatrical productions provide attendees with programs that feature both information on the performance and advertising. They are given to each individual to read before the show begins, during an intermission, and at the conclusion.

One of the more well-known publications is the *Playbill*, published for Broadway productions. In approximately fifty pages, the audience is shown numerous advertisements, many of which are fashion-oriented. Regular advertisers in these pages are Macy's, Bloomingdales, designers such as Calvin Klein, and fragrance companies such as Lancôme.

A major advantage of this type of magazine is that it is often kept as a memento, providing the advertiser extra exposure to the reader.

## Advantages and Disadvantages of Magazines

While the magazine might not be the most popular medium for all advertisers, it still ranks as the first choice of those in the fashion industry. The advantages afforded those who choose magazines to advertise their company's products include the following:

1. *The Life of the Message.* Those of us who watch television recognize that the time allocated for the sponsor or advertiser to get the message across is extremely brief. A trip to the refrigerator generally takes place during the time the commercial is being shown. On the other hand, the magazine offers the longest life of all media. Most people keep their issues for long periods of time, often as long as a year, and even then pass them on to other households. In this way, the advertisement will be experienced not only by the purchaser of

the publication and family members, but friends and relatives who often become the recipients of the discarded periodicals.

2. *Audience Selectivity.* More and more magazines are directed toward special-interest audiences. Thus, fashion advertisers are able to reach vary narrow target markets. *Gentlemen's Quarterly*, for example, has a readership core that boasts fashion-conscious, affluent males who are always eager to learn about current fashion trends. *Seventeen* is another example of a magazine that makes use of audience selectivity. While the manufacturers and designers of teen-wear might choose a general purpose magazine for some of its messages, the choice of *Seventeen* guarantees an audience that is exclusively geared for readers and potential customers of that age category.

3. *Geographical Editions.* Fashion retailers, such as Macy's, with an extensive chain of stores throughout the country, might benefit from advertisements that appear everywhere the magazine is distributed. Smaller fashion organizations generally have units in a narrower geographic area. In order to cut costs and reach only those people who could possibly patronize their stores, they often opt for a partial circulation. It would be wasteful, for example, for a southern chain of stores to choose national circulation since it is unlikely that the households outside of the trading area could become purchasers. Of course, if the advertisement concentrates on telephone or mail ordering, the need to limit circulation becomes less important.

4. *Image and Prestige.* Certain fashion magazines, because of their importance to the industry and the social classes to whom they appeal, provide prestige to the advertisers. *Harper's Bazaar* and *Vogue*, for example, have maintained fashion images that help to boost the desirability of the products featured in them.

5. *Reproductive Quality.* When compared to the other giant of the print media, the newspaper, in terms of advertising quality, the magazine is the winner. The grade of the stock used for its pages, the clarity and excitement of the colors achieved, and the sharpness of the written messages defies competition. Research shows that four-color, full-page advertisements, the forte of magazine advertising, is at least 30 percent more effective than black and white.

6. *Editorial Commentary.* Many fashion magazines have editorial staffs that are capable of excellently critiquing the styles of the times,

offering predictions on trends, and providing an analysis of the industry. Those consumers who are fashion enthusiasts often purchase these publications for the expert advice their editorial pages offer. The advertisers of fashion thus have an audience that is tuned into the field and will benefit from this informed readership who will be able to examine their wares.

7. *Audit Verification.* As will be discussed later in the chapter, the magazine's advertising cost is based substantially on circulation figures. The Audit Bureau of Circulation (ABC) is one of the agencies that verifies circulation figures.

Although it is obvious that the magazine has a wealth of benefits for its users, there are, nonetheless, some disadvantages of this advertising medium. The disadvantages of primary importance follow:

a. *Cost.* The cost per thousand or CPM as it is referred to in the field, is significantly greater for magazines than that of any of the other media. Although some advertisers argue that this amount is justified because of the long life of such publications and their ability to target very specific audiences, the initial dollar outlay is far greater than many companies can afford. When "walking" through the pages of a fashion magazine, it is quite obvious that only the giants of the fashion industry fill their pages. As discussed earlier, the cost can be somewhat minimized with the use of regional editions.

b. *Lead Time.* Unlike the newspaper, which enables the user to insert advertisements as late as the day before the edition will reach the stands, the magazine requires a significant amount of time between the order and the publication date. Most fashion magazines require two months for the process to be completed. Thus, a company that is eager to promote something very quickly is out of luck.

# Costs of Magazine Space

The rates for magazine advertising space is primarily based on circulation, with other considerations such as **partial-runs** factored in. A partial-run is an advertisement that does not appear in every distributed issue. Some retailers opt for regional editions, since their potential markets may only be in a specific locale of the publication's circulation. These limited placements result in lower costs for advertisements.

Following is a list of Audit Bureau of Circulation figures for leading fashion magazines.

*The Standard Rate and Data Service (SRDS)* as we have discussed earlier in the text, is an excellent place to determine the costs of magazine advertising. This source publishes the current full-page rates along with circulation figures. Once the advertiser has decided on the magazines of interest, a more detailed account of other charges and discounts are best obtained directly from rate cards of those publications.

On the following page an example of the four-page color rates for selected magazines appears as shown in the *Standard Rate and Data.*

**FIGURE 5-4**

*Leading fashion*

*magazines' circulation*

*(Courtesy of* SRDS*)*

## MAGAZINE CIRCULATIONS

| Magazine | Circulation* |
| --- | --- |
| *Vogue* | 331,718 |
| *Mirabella* | 618,760 |
| *Mademoiselle* | 1,268,697 |
| *Elle* | 882,767 |
| *Essence* | 970,343 |
| *Glamour* | 2,186,214 |
| *Seventeen* | 1,923,830 |
| *Teen* | 1,184,799 |
| *Harper's Bazaar* | 738,647 |
| *Allure* | 705,666 |

*Paid subscriptions plus single issues, total (1995)

| COSTS OF MAGAZINE SPACE | |
| --- | --- |
| **Magazine** | **Rate*** |
| *Vogue* | $28,210 |
| *Mirabella* | 37,310 |
| *Mademoiselle* | 41,640 |
| *Elle* | 48,980 |
| *Essence* | 32,730 |
| *Glamour* | 71,470 |
| *Seventeen* | 52,590 |
| *Teen* | 30,940 |
| *Harper's Bazaar* | 45,350 |
| *Allure* | 33,550 |

*One time, single page (1995)

**FIGURE 5-5**

*Four-color page rates*

*for selected magazines*

*(Courtesy of* SRDS)

## DISCOUNTS

The published cost of a magazine advertisement is based on what is known as its **open-rate**. It is actually the price paid for a one-time, full-page insertion. Depending on volume and frequency of advertising, the publisher offers discounts that are taken from the open-rate.

The amount of the discounts varies according to the actual frequency of placement and the volume incurred over a twelve-month period. Thus, a company that runs, for example, thirty advertisements during the year will receive a greater discount than one that contracts for only six advertisements. Similarly, the greater the dollar outlay, the greater the discount.

Some advertisers avail themselves of special discounts when the edition is ready to go to press and all of the space has not been sold. Publishers are often willing to give last-minute, money-saving considerations to those who will help fill these otherwise blank pages. Of course, the companies who take advantage of these situations must be prepared with advertisements that will be ready for immediate insertion. The last-minute available space is known as **remnant space**.

## NEGOTIATED RATE REDUCTIONS

While the standard rates are published, as we have discussed, and the discounts are available for significant usage, there is a trend in the magazine medium to stray from these established costs. **Off-the-card** rates are becoming commonplace. The phrase refers to the advertiser's ability to negotiate with the publisher for a reduction of the published rates.

There are no rules governing this procedure, except to say that in the competitive climate of the magazine industry, with more and more fashion publications being born, publishers are sometimes willing to make advertising in their pages more attractive. The reduced costs might be based on the insertion of a minimum number of pages in a particular issue or an increase in contracted space from the previous year.

## SHORT RATES

In trying to cut costs, advertisers often enter into contractual agreements that guarantee the use of a certain number of advertisements and space. While this arrangement initially benefits both the magazine and the advertiser, occasionally the specific requirements of the contract are not fulfilled. Businesses might find it necessary to cut back on their original commitments. In this case, the publisher has the right to make adjustments in rates offered in the contract.

Either at the end of the contractual period or at a time when it is conceived that less advertising will be used, an adjustment, at a higher rate, will be determined. This is known as the short rate.

It should be understood that sometimes an advertiser will use more space than initially contracted for. In such cases, an adjustment might be made that will lower the advertising rates.

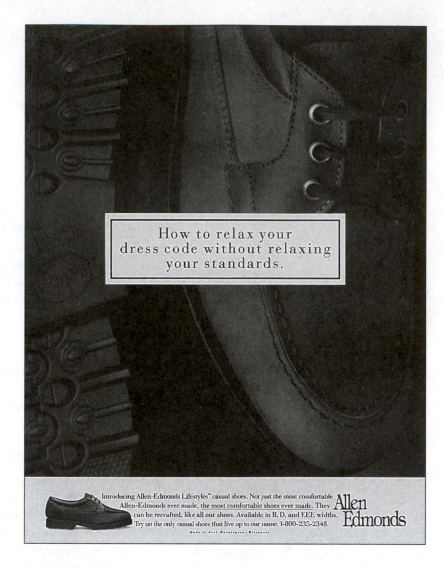

**FIGURE 5-6**

*The photograph covers the entire page, lending a dramatic enhancement. It is called a* bleed *advertisement.*

*(Courtesy of Allen Edmonds)*

## POSITION PREFERENCE

Generally, specific magazine spaces do not require additional expense to the advertiser. Unlike the newspaper, which charges premiums for such considerations as placement near the front of the edition or adjacency to a particular column, the magazine considers almost every space equally important. The exceptions, however, are for such placement as inside the front cover or the back cover. These locations get the greatest immediate attention of the reader, making some companies willing to pay extra for them.

### FOLDOUTS

In order to give more clout to the magazine advertisement, some companies choose foldouts for their advertisements. That is, the advertisement is comprised of two or more pages that are seen by the reader when they are unfolded. While this does make for a greater impact than the typically used full-page advertisement, the inherent expenses of such advertising are considerable. When the foldout is placed on the inside front cover (known as second cover in the industry), the costs are even greater.

### BLEEDS

A dramatic and often effective way to call greater attention to the advertisement is to have it cover the entire page of the publication, without the benefit of a border. The advertisement, thus, "bleeds" over the edges, eliminating the standard margins. Bleed advertisements usually cost about an additonal 15 percent above the normal one-page layouts.

## Circulation Considerations

Today's fashion designers, manufacturers, retailers, and public relations branches of the industry have a vast number of magazines to choose from for their advertising needs. Not only must they consider the costs of the advertisements, but also the number of households that will be reached. The rates that are applied are based on the number of readers who subscribe to the publication.

Each publisher guarantees to its advertiser's specific circulation numbers. A failure to meet this established minimum results in rate reductions. While this means an overall cost reduction to the advertiser, it brings with it a negative impact. Fewer consumers will see the advertisements, which would probably result in a decrease in sales volume. If these shortfalls continue, advertisers are likely to opt for other competing publications in which to display their offerings.

## CIRCULATION MEASUREMENT

The word of the publisher alone on circulation figures will generally not satisfy the potential space purchaser. Since the costs are so high and the results of the advertising often so crucial to the success of the company, independent organizations are used for the verification of the figures.

The leading auditing operation is the Audit Bureau of Circulations (ABC). Their procedure is to annually check the data provided by the publishers in their statements. In addition to verifying the numbers, ABC explores how circulation was achieved and if discounts were offered to subscribers.

In addition to ABC, there are research organizations such as Mediamark Research, Inc. that surveys readership. Through personal interviews, assessments can be made concerning demographic characteristics such as income, size of family, occupations, and the use of products.

By using both the ABC figures and the information generated from the marketing researchers, the advertiser may make a more educated selection for his or her advertising commitments.

# Merchandising Support for Advertisers

In addition to providing the space to show a company's products, the magazine may offer a host of support and services to their customers. While these are not without cost, they do provide benefits to the users.

## POINT-OF-PURCHASE DISPLAY MATERIALS

The magazine is supposed to sufficiently whet the appetites of potential customers so they will be curious enough to seek out the advertised merchandise. One tool that fashion retailers often use in their stores to

**FIGURE 5-7**

*The point-of-purchase display is meant to reunite the shopper with the magazine advertisement. (Courtesy of Ruth Scharf Industries, A Division of Bryan*

attract shopper attention is the point-of-purchase counter card that features advertisements that have been published in magazines. For a fee, the magazine reprints the advertisement, with the words *as seen in* added to the copy. In this way, the in-store shopper is reunited with the advertisement that motivated him or her to visit the store.

## DIRECTORIES AND SHOPPING GUIDES

As a means of generating business for their advertisers, both business-to-business and consumer magazines feature lists for readers to use to quickly locate certain advertisements.

*Modern Jeweler*, a trade periodical, for example, offers an index of the manufacturers advertising in their pages, the location of their

**FIGURE 5-8**

Kids Fashion

*magazine offers a list*

*of resource locations*

*at trade fairs.*

insertions, and an information request form that serves as a convenient way for the reader to secure more information from the companies that advertise. *Kids Fashion*, an industry magazine published by the Larkin Group, which sponsors trade shows for the children's wear industry, lists each advertiser's booth number for the upcoming trade events, as well as an advertisement index and reader inquiry service similar to the one featured in *Modern Jeweler*.

Consumer fashion magazines also feature directories as to where the advertised items may be purchased. This not only directs the shopper to the appropriate retailer, but also helps the advertiser generate sales.

### SPECIAL EVENTS

As a means of promoting their own publications and helping to increase sales for retailers, some fashion magazines sponsor in-store fashion shows. During the back-to-school selling period, *Seventeen* magazine offers fashion shows for teens and their parents.

In the shows, the magazine makes certain to feature the apparel and accessories available in the stores they are serving. Other events include the appearance of a publication's fashion spokesperson to discuss such topics as trends for the new season and appropriate career dressing.

### SALES BROCHURES

With direct mail being such an important manner in which to communicate with customers, the use of sales brochures has steadily increased. Some fashion magazines assist retailers with the design of these brochures, often utilizing the same artwork that is appearing in the print advertisements. In this way, the advertisement's message will be reinforced with the mailed brochures.

## Classification of Magazine Advertisements

If you examine all of the advertisements in a fashion magazine, you will come to notice that there are several different messages that are designed to appeal to the reader. While each advertisement is visually different from the others, they all fit into general categories, in terms of their emphasis. The majority emphasize a particular merchandise item or group of related styles. Some emphasize the advertiser's image, while others might depict the advertiser as one with concern for its citizens. Those that fashion companies use in both consumer and business-to-business publications are product, promotional, institutional, combination, and indirect advertising.

## PRODUCT ADVERTISEMENTS

By far, magazine product advertising is most important to the fashion industry. In advertisements of this nature, the manufacturers,

**FIGURE 5-9**

*A trade advertisement notifies the professional purchaser of the product's resource. (Courtesy of Ruth Scharf Industries,. A Division of Bryan Industries)*

designers, materials producers, and retailers feature the merchandise they want to sell to their markets.

**MANUFACTURER AND DESIGNER ADVERTISEMENTS.**   The manufacturer uses two types of magazine publications for advertising. One, the trade periodical, is used to appeal to its primary customers, the store buyers. The other, consumer publications, is used to alert the household shoppers about what they will be seeing in the stores.

Companies like Studio California, Ruth Scharf, and Peppercorns regularly opt for advertisements in trade magazines like *Earnshaw's*, to reach the retailers.

Fashion producers such as Cole of California, DKNY, Calvin Klein, Bill Blass, Guess Jeans, J.G. Hook, and Nike are regulars in the consumer fashion publications. The emphasis of their campaigns is to motivate the potential customers to buy their goods from the retailers of their choice.

**MATERIALS PRODUCERS' ADVERTISEMENTS.**   Those who produce and process the materials of fashion concentrate on three distinct groups in their advertising programs. First, the apparel and accessories creators are their main targets. These are the customers without whose business the materials producers would fail. They appeal to this segment primarily through product advertising in the business-to-business magazines such as the *California Apparel News* and *Fashion Showcase*. In these periodicals, the materials available for sale are presented by underscoring their importance to the next level of production. Companies like DuPont and Monsanto subscribe to this type of advertising.

In order to make the retailer aware of the materials used in the production of garments and accessories, the materials producers also direct their advertising efforts to this group. When the store buyers peruse both consumer and business magazines, they might become influenced by certain textiles and leathers, for example, and seek them in the finished products they will buy for their customers. Advertisements of this nature sometimes feature designer products that are manufactured with the company's basic materials.

Finally, the last group to be appealed to through product advertisements in magazines is the consumer. When the potential household cus-

**FIGURE 5-10**

*Advertisement directed at the apparel designers as well as the ultimate customer (Courtesy of DuPont)*

tomer is alerted to the advantages of specific fibers or fabrics, for example, they might be motivated to seek products in which they are utilized.

**RETAILER ADVERTISEMENTS.** Retailers need to concentrate on only one customer market, the consumer. In trying to direct the potential shopper's attention to their stores, they sometimes subscribe to magazine advertising in fashion periodicals such as *Elle*, *Vogue*, and *Glamour*. It should be understood that the wealth of retailer advertising is accomplished through newspaper insertion; only those companies with national reputations choose this medium. The advertising concentrates not only on the products offered for sale, but on the store itself. A great deal of this promotion is produced cooperatively with manufacturers and designers, where both parties share in the advertising expense.

## PROMOTIONAL ADVERTISEMENTS

When price reductions are in order or some other incentive such as "buy one and get one free" is the case, promotional advertisements are often used.

**MANUFACTURER AND DESIGNER ADVERTISEMENTS.** Price reduction is not the favorite method used by manufacturers to motivate selling. There are, however, times when nothing else works better in the disposal of unwanted merchandise.

The producers sometimes use the trade magazines, such as *DNR* or *Womens Wear Daily*, to notify their regular accounts and potential customers of the clearance prices. The emphasis in the advertisement is price and little in the way of creative artwork or layout design is utilized to attract attention. The manufacturers and designers do not use the promotional approach on a steady basis.

**MATERIALS PRODUCERS' ADVERTISEMENTS.** When an abundance of materials is in stock and a new season is rapidly approaching, which requires yet another type of fabric, the materials producer, like the garment manufacturer, opts for quick disposal via the promotional advertising route. They place advertisements announcing merchandise disposal in the trade periodical read by their customers. Again, as in the case in manufacturer and designer advertisements, this route is only addressed when quick disposal of goods is necessary.

**RETAILER ADVERTISEMENTS.** Generally, those retailers who want to run promotional advertisements, do not choose magazines. The life of the magazine is too long and reminders of sales are not exactly what is wanted by the stores. In some cases, retailers do offer extended sales periods and might choose the magazine for this type of promotion. It is the newspaper that gets the retailer's major share of promotional advertising.

## INSTITUTIONAL ADVERTISEMENTS

When the intention of the company is to promote good will, present their merchandising philosophies, or underscore their company's images, institutional advertising is the approach taken by many.

**MANUFACTURER AND DESIGNER ADVERTISEMENTS.** This approach taken by some manufacturers and designers is directed not to their customers, the store buyers, but to the end user of the product. By showing these potential customers that the company is aware of social issues and is not trying only to promote a particular style, image building might be accomplished, which could eventually translate into future sales.

At the beginning of the Clinton Presidency, for example, the YES Clothing Company ran an advertisement in *Vogue Magazine* that featured a model waving an oversized American flag accompanied by copy that merly used the word *change*.

A major approach to extensive institutional advertising was initially introduced by Ralph Lauren with his "multiple page" formats. Page after page of advertisements stressed lifestyle rather than the product line.

These advertising approaches do not generally bring an immediate sales response. However, long-range, positive results are often garnered by its users.

**MATERIALS PRODUCERS' ADVERTISEMENTS.** Like their manufacturer and designer counterparts, institutional advertising, when used, is aimed at the consumer. One of the more well-known campaigns that utilized both magazine and television was accomplished by DuPont in their Bill Demby spread. It told of the company's commitment to the welfare of paraplegics through the use of a particular fiber that was crafted into a prosthesis for the wounded. While the fiber used was not the key element of the campaign, it underscored DuPont's humanitarian efforts and captured the attention of the consumer market. The ultimate goal of the company was for the shopper to remember the DuPont label when shopping for their merchandise needs.

**RETAILER ADVERTISEMENTS.**   The major shopkeepers of America regularly subscribe to the institutional format. Lands' End regularly features magazine advertisements that concentrate on the company's attention to quality and service. Armani Exchange (A/X) often just uses its logo. Galeries Lafayette, the French-based fashion Emporium, sometimes merely features the name of the store in a European setting to bring prestige to its name.

## COMBINATION ADVERTISEMENTS

Sometimes, it is beneficial for fashion advertisers to use a combination of elements in their advertisements that touch upon more than one type. When trying to appeal to a particular market, the use of both a specific product along with some emphasis on an institutional point might make the advertisement more suitable to the company's needs.

The use of combination advertising in magazines is utilized by all levels of the fashion industry. The periodicals in which the advertisements appear is dependent upon whom the advertiser is wishing to address.

Materials producers, such as those that manufacture and process fabrics and fibers, might use a combination advertisement that features both a picture of a fabric they produce and how this material benefits the user. The photograph of the fabric constitutes the product portion of the advertisement, while the institutional aspect is achieved through the use of copy that describes the benefits. If the advertisement is geared to the wholesale market, such as designer companies, the advertisement will be placed in a trade publication. If the appeal is to the consumer, it will be found in the pages of fashion magazines such as *Harper's Bazaar* and *Elle*.

Manufacturers and designers also use the combination approach. Calvin Klein, in his fragrance campaigns, generally begins with a concept that sparks romance or love and follows with an actual display of the product. Givenchy, with its advertising campaign to promote its "eau de toilette," Amarige, follows suit with an institutional appeal that speaks of "A celebration of laughter . . . love . . . and intense happiness," and the product that is supposed to deliver these promises.

Many fashion retailers subscribe to the combination format. Lord & Taylor frequently fills its advertisements with messages about its dedication to American designers, an idea that is supposed to boost its patriotic image and couples the message with actual photographs of products it sells in its stores. Sometimes, stores use a combination of product and promotional advertising. In such cases, a particular line or item might be featured, the product component of the advertisement, and copy announcing price reductions for the depicted styles, the promotional component.

## INDIRECT ADVERTISEMENTS

In this format, the advertiser is usually a designer or manufacturer who wishes to direct the ultimate purchaser to a particular retail outlet to purchase his or her merchandise. These advertisements feature a product or product line. The focal point is generally on the specific product, the name of the resource, and a message that will enhance the advertisement's chances for success. In a less conspicuous portion of the page, words like *Exclusively at Bloomingdale's, Nordstrom, and Neiman-Marcus* are displayed, or a more complete list of the stores that feature the merchandise.

The advertisement is paid for by the designer or manufacturer, who rewards his or her most active retail accounts with the mention of their names. The term *indirect* is used to show that the retailer in the piece is indirectly afforded advertising space.

## REVIEW QUESTIONS

1. Discuss when and why magazine advertising started to decline in the twentieth century.

2. What are the two major types of magazines? In what way do the advertising messages in them differ?

3. What is meant by the term *complimentary magazine?*

4. Why do fashion designers use consumer magazine advertising when their immediate market is the retailer?

5. Differentiate between general-interest and narrowly focused magazines.

6. List three types of complimentary magazines.

7. Why is the "life" of the magazine greater than the period for which it has been published?

8. Define the term *geographical edition.*

9. What is meant by *lead time?*

10. What major service is predominantly used by magazine advertisers to determine space costs?

11. What is meant by *short rate?*

12. Describe the appearance of a bleed advertisement. How does it differ from the normal full-page format?

13. How might advertisers verify the proclaimed circulation figures of magazines?

14. Briefly discuss some of the merchandising support offered by magazines to their clients.

15. Differentiate between product and institutional advertising.

16. How does a promotional advertisement differ from one that is classified as a product advertisement?

17. Define the term *combination advertisement.*

18. Why do designers and manufacturers use indirect advertising?

## EXERCISES

1. Secure two consumer fashion advertisements, and two that are considered to be business-to-business. After each has been mounted on a foamboard, indicate the magazine in which they appeared, its classification, and an analysis of the audience to whom they are

directed. The foamboard and information should be delivered orally to the class.

2. Select five major fashion magazines and research each in terms of the costs advertising in them, their circulations, and if any discounts are available to the advertisers. Each magazine cover should be photocopied in color and placed in a folder that contains the researched information.

3. Choose one from each of the following types of magazine advertisements:

   - product ad;
   - promotional ad;
   - institutional ad;
   - combination ad; and
   - indirect ad.

Analyze the components of each that make it fit its specific classification.

*The use of the classified makes an interesting background for this advertisement. (Courtesy of Neiman-Marcus)*

# *Newspapers*

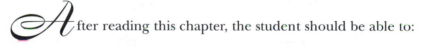

*A*fter reading this chapter, the student should be able to:

1. Discuss the numerous advantages newspaper advertising affords its users.

2. Explain why the newspaper, for all of its positive attributes, has its negative sides.

3. Determine the costs of newspaper space in relation to its circulation.

4. Describe some of the merchandising services offered by newspapers to their advertisers.

5. List and discuss the different advertising approaches found in newspapers.

## Introduction

Given all of the hoopla with television advertising, the daily newspaper continues as the leading medium in terms of advertiser's budgets. Although the number of individual publications has declined from a high of more than 2,000 in the 1920s, to approxiamtely 1,500 today, its overall dollar volume is presently at an all-time high. With a constantly expanding population, those newspapers that remain in business generally have ever-increasing circulation statistics.

A large segment of the American population either starts or concludes its day with reading the newspaper. Their motivation comes from a variety of purposes. It might be to keep abreast of the social and economic issues of the nation and their community, to learn about the newspaper's position on specific subjects through editorial comment, to read the regular columns of renowned contributors, to examine the results of sporting events, to follow the comics, or to discover what their personal horoscope is for the day. Whatever the reason for reading, it is a medium that has something for every family member.

The beneficiaries of such dedication are the advertisers. Since the various elements that comprise the newspaper are scattered from cover to cover, the reader who is looking for his or her favorite feature is confronted by a wealth of advertisements. In particular, an examination of any daily newspaper immediately reveals that a large portion of the advertising matter is fashion-oriented. Specifically, the retailers of fashion merchandise dominate the pages of most dailies.

In addition to the local dailies, such as *The Miami Herald* or *The Chicago Tribune*, which are generally distributed to their immediate geographical trading areas, others, such as *The New York Times,* enjoy national distribution. In these pages, advertisers who have national reputations are able to focus their offerings on more than just the local markets.

In 1983, the national newspaper took on new importance with the introduction of *USA Today.* Although it does have a circulation of more than one million, its advertising revenues remain weak. Few advertisers, particularly those in the fashion industry, see this type of publication as a viable means of promoting their products.

## Types of Newspapers

As was briefly stated in the opening remarks of this chapter, there are different classifications of newspapers. Each will be explored to show how it serves the fashion advertiser's needs.

## DAILIES

Most appropriate for fashion-oriented advertisements are the dailies that are published every day of the week. These are the newspapers that serve a particular trading area and assist the advertiser in getting their message across.

The primary segment of the fashion industry that uses this paper is the retailer. Since the vast majority of the retailers who subscribe to newspaper advertising are located in a specific trading area, the best way to reach their audience is through the dailies, which are distributed to those in the general area. Marshall Field, for example, with a preponderance of stores in the Chicago area, uses papers like *The Chicago Tribune* for its promotional purposes. The use of national newspapers, or magazines with much broader geographical areas of distribution, would be wasteful, since a significant number of subscribers are too far from the retail outlets to become regular customers.

In some cases where the potential market is even narrower than the markets served by the dailies, regional or zoned editions are offered to the advertisers.

**ZONED EDITIONS.** There are two types of zoned editions that retailers of fashion merchandise utilize if their trading area is localized. *Newsday*, for example, a newspaper that is targeted at shoppers on Long Island in New York State, enjoys one of the largest circulations in the country. The geographical area in which it is distributed covers several thousand square miles. Many of the retailers who use this vehicle as their main advertising source are small and do not have the potential to appeal to all of the newspaper's readers. For this reason, *Newsday* produces several variations of its publication. Its Suffolk edition is geared to the people in that county and enables advertisers to limit their advertisements to that edition. By doing so, there is considerable savings on the cost of the advertisement.

Another type of zoned edition is actually a mininewspaper within the newspaper that is inserted only in those papers that will reach a certain area. *The New York Times*, for example, publishes these zoned editions for each of the suburban areas it serves. New York's Long Island residents receive a section that exclusively features stories and advertisements of interest to that narrow segment of the *Times'* readership. A small suburban fashion operation on Long Island is thus able to zero in on a specific market and cut advertising expenses since this type of space is less costly than the full-run version.

## NATIONAL NEWSPAPERS

Unlike the dailies, which restrict distribution to narrow markets, the national newspapers reach out across the United States. *The Wall Street Journal* and *USA Today*, two of the more well-known dailies, serve little purpose for fashion advertisers.

The vast majority of the design and manufacturing segments opt for the pages of magazines, where national exposure may be accomplished in superior, quality pages. Few fashion retailers have outlets in all of the regions served by these editions, thus finding such usage wasteful. They too, if interested in national attention, opt for the magazine format.

## WEEKLY NEWSPAPERS

There are approximately 7,000 newspapers in the United States that are published on a weekly basis. Their readership is usually restricted to a very narrow geographic segment of the population. It may be a metropolitan area of a city or one that is specifically suburban. The news is locally oriented, occasionally addressing interests of national concern. The advertising concentrates on businesses in those regions. The fashion advertising emphasis is on the small retailer who, because of comparatively low costs, is able to communicate its fashion messages to an audience of potential customers. The vast majority of those who advertise in the weeklies are too small to make use of the dailies.

## SUNDAY SUPPLEMENTS

Most major daily newspapers include in their Sunday editions sections that feature four-color advertisements. Some, like the one published by *The New York Times*, rival the best magazines in the country in terms of content and quality reproduction. The supplements, sometimes called magazines, are significantly used by fashion advertisers who feel that this segment of the paper can more creatively depict the merchandise they offer for sale.

**FIGURE 6-1**

*A high-quality*

*newspaper*

*supplement with*

*magazine quality*

*(Courtesy of*

*Dayton's)*

In addition to those that are the exclusive domain of the newspapers in which they appear, there are syndicated supplements, such as *Parade,* that are found in more than 300 Sunday editions from coast to coast. Advertisers such as Sears and J. C. Penney, with large networks of stores that serve almost every part of the country, use this type of publication. Dayton's inserts its own *Today* supplement in newspapers twenty-five times a year.

# Advantages and Disadvantages of Newspapers

The newspaper is the most important media for fashion advertisers in terms of the total dollars expended for its use. Its advantages indicate the reasons why it continues to enjoy its position as favorite medium:

1. *Diversified Appeal.* The newspaper offers something for every member of the family. Not only does the seriousness of the news capture one's attention, but it might command regular daily attention to a specific column, the sports pages, horoscope predictions, and even the comics. While seeking the pages in the publication that initially motivate a person to read, there is the potential to discover eye-catching advertisements.

2. *Low Readership Costs.* Although the cost of a newspaper advertisement may be considered substantial to the advertiser, its cost per consumer is lower than any of the other media.

3. *Ease in Reaching a Market.* Newspapers are distributed by way of the newsstand or home delivery to subscribers. With these simple means of reaching the household, it is likely that most targeted shoppers will come by their favorite newspaper with minimal effort.

4. *Comparative Life of the Message.* Unlike radio and television, which afford the sponsors as little time as fifteen seconds to get the message across in a prescribed time period, the newspaper may be examined at any time of the day or evening, as determined by the reader. In this way, the advertiser does not have to decide when it is better to reach a particular audience segment.

5. *Timeliness.* Because the newspaper is offered on a daily basis, users of newspaper advertising may adapt their plans to fit any situation that arises that might benefit the sale of their products. When a snowstorm, for example, is being predicted by the weather forecasters, fashion retailers might find it advantageous to alert the public to their storm coat and boot selections. Similarly, a sudden burst of a heat wave could spell success for the swimsuit retailer who can quickly address the readers with appropriate advertisements that feature merchandise for the beach.

6. *Lead Time.* Users of magazines, television, and direct mail must plan as far as two or three months in advance of the promotion to satisfy the needs of those media. In newspaper advertising, the "lead time" is drastically reduced to as little as the day before the insertion

is to take place. In this way, advertisers can make adjustments to their advertising schedules on very short notice.

7. *Campaign Effectiveness.* In cases in which frequent exposure is necessary to capture a market's attention, the newspaper is an excellent

**FIGURE 6-2**

*A cooperative advertisement*

*features the manufacturer's*

*name along with the store's*

*name. (Courtesy of Ruth*

*Scharf Industries, A Division*

*of Bryan Industries)*

choice. Printed on a daily basis, the advertiser is able to gain a great deal of continuous exposure in a short period of time. Even the most frequently published magazines are not available more than once a week, necessitating less exposure over a short period.

8. *Geographic Concentration.* Unless it is of the national type, the daily newspaper is designed to reach an audience that is confined to one geographic area. In this way, the advertisements can be tailored to that group. When the general readership of the paper is too geographically dispersed, many offer regional editions that zero in on a more segmented market. In this way, an even smaller concentration of potential shoppers can be reached.

9. *Cooperative Advertising Potential.* The newspaper is by and large the medium of the retailer and more specifically the retailer that deals significantly in fashion merchandise. Designers and manufacturers are prone to spend their promotional dollars primarily on magazine advertising and, to a lesser extent, on television campaigns. They do, however, find it advantageous to have their collections featured in newspapers. To avail themselves of newspaper advertising at lower costs, many enter into cooperative advertising arrangements in which they and the retailer share equally in the advertisement's insertion costs. Since most retailers shy away from magazine or television advertising, the newspaper is the major medium that affords the advantages of the cooperative arrangement.

As advantageous as the newspaper is for fashion advertising, there are some negatives or disadvantages associated with it. Among them are the following:

1. *Travel Distance of Potential Customers.* Many newspapers reach out to consumers who are often too far from the merchandise source to make the shopping trip possible. If, for example, an exciting advertisement catches the attention of a consumer who is two hours away from the retailer featuring the item, it is unlikely that the consumer would visit the store. If such an advertisement features mail or phone ordering, the disadvantage could be somewhat alleviated. With the use of the regional editions, the problem could also be resolved.

2. *Message Life.* Although the life of the message when compared to the broadcast media is considered long, it is extremely brief when

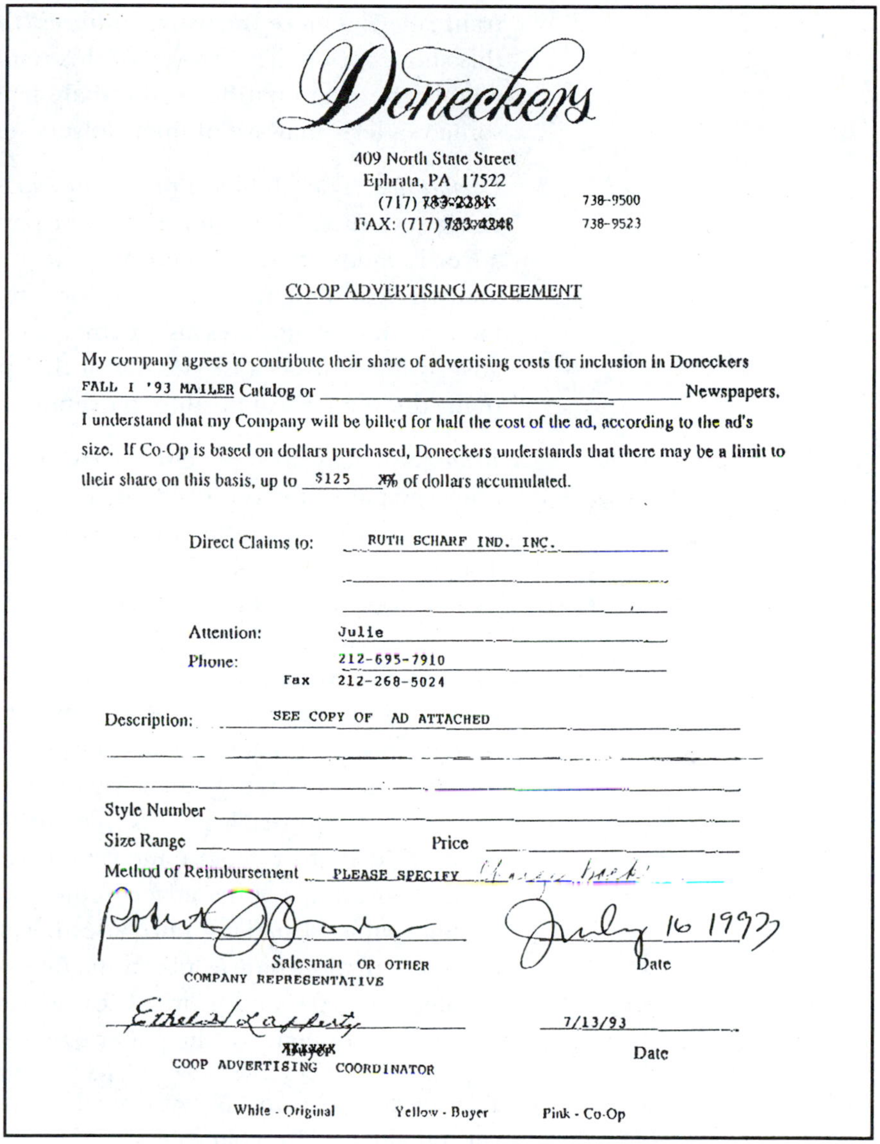

## Doneckers

409 North State Street
Ephrata, PA 17522
(717) 733-9500
FAX: (717) 738-9523

### CO-OP ADVERTISING AGREEMENT

My company agrees to contribute their share of advertising costs for inclusion in Doneckers
FALL I '93 MAILER Catalog or _____ Newspapers.
I understand that my Company will be billed for half the cost of the ad, according to the ad's
size.  If Co-Op is based on dollars purchased, Doneckers understands that there may be a limit to
their share on this basis, up to __$125__ % of dollars accumulated.

Direct Claims to:   RUTH SCHARF IND. INC. _____

_____

Attention:   Julie _____
Phone:       212-695-7910
      Fax    212-268-5024

Description:   SEE COPY OF AD ATTACHED _____

_____

Style Number _____
Size Range _____          Price _____
Method of Reimbursement   PLEASE SPECIFY _____

_____
Salesman OR OTHER                    July 16 1993
COMPANY REPRESENTATIVE                      Date

_____             7/13/93
COOP ADVERTISING  COORDINATOR               Date

White - Original     Yellow - Buyer     Pink - Co-Op

**FIGURE 6-3**

*A cooperative agreement between a vendor and a retailer (Courtesy of Ruth Scharf Industries, A Division of Bryan Industries)*

compared to the magazine. At best, for the daily editions, it will last
twenty-four hours until the next day's paper arrives. A large number
of readers, however, do not make use of the newspaper for more
than the time of the daily commute. Often, train riders will be seen
discarding them once they have arrived at their destinations. If the

train ride is a mere thirty-five minutes, the paper might "die" after this short period. The brevity of this reading time does not usually enable the examination of the daily from cover to cover, leaving some readers unaware of many advertisements.

3. *Competition.* The lifeblood of any newspaper comes from its advertising revenues. This often results in papers that are chock full of advertisements that compete for the reader's attention. With so many advertisements competing for attention, many may be overlooked. Many magazines also feature significant amounts of fashion advertising, but because the life of that periodical is so long, eventually the reader will be able to examine all of them.

4. *Reader Selectivity.* In some cities across the United Sates there is only one newspaper for the residents to read. Even the largest cities in the country do not offer as many different ones as they used to. Today, for example, New York City provides only four major dailies to a market that in the 1950s had more than ten newspapers. When there are many papers in publication, there is a tendency to market each to a more defined socioeconomic segment. When the numbers decline, there is less room to tailor the newspaper to a more specific group of readers. Thus, advertisers are less likely to be able to focus their messages to clearly delineated audiences. A fashion retailer trying to reach the upscale, affluent shopper, for example, would find that in geographic regions where there is but a single paper in print, his or her advertisement would be seen by many who are incapable of making purchases because of income limitations. Since circulation figures play a major part in advertising costs, the retailer often pays high prices for advertisements that will not be meaningful to many of the paper's readers.

5. *Reproduction Quality.* Newsprint does not allow for high-quality reproduction. The coarseness of the stock that is used diminishes the advertisement's appearance. Color is rarely seen in newspaper advertisements and when it is used, it does not provide the clarity and brilliance of the smooth paper used in magazines. The only part of the newspaper that does enable the publisher to produce quality advertisements is in the magazine supplements. The stock is finer and the reproduction techniques are more sophisticated.

*Magazine covers send the newest fashion ideas to the consumer.*

A pair of Lee Jeans for those days when all you want on your legs is sunscreen.

Give your legs a little air, with Lee Relaxed Fit Shorts. They fit you just as comfortably as your favorite Lee Jeans do, and you'll never have to roll them up when you go to the beach.

R E L A X E D · F I T · S H O R T S

*The brand that fits.*

*P*rint ads enable advertisers to effectively balance text and images in promoting their latest lines.

*S*pecial events and unique packaging are an excellent way of promoting a major store line.

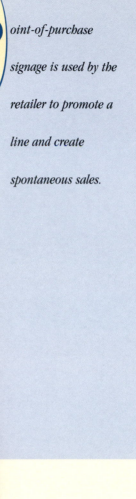

*Point-of-purchase signage is used by the retailer to promote a line and create spontaneous sales.*

*R*unway shows

introduce the

newest fashions

to the industry.

*Designer collections are promoted with personal appearances, window displays, and interior displays.*

*A*nimation can be an exciting, creative, and successful part of visual merchandising.

6. *Television Competition.* Although the newspaper is an excellent medium for bringing the reader's attention to national and local news, more and more people are choosing television as their means of enlightenment. The high cost of living has motivated wage earners to take second jobs, leaving less time for newspaper reading. Due to these factors, advertisers have lost a number of readers who would have seen their advertisements alongside the news stories.

# Cost of Newspaper Advertising Space

In addition to the costs involved in the creation of the advertisement's layout that includes artwork such as photography or line drawings and copy preparation, there are the costs that are based upon the rates charged for the space that the advertisement will occupy.

## THE RATE STRUCTURE

Newspaper fashion advertising is generally utilized by retailers. Manufacturers and designers usually opt for magazine or television and only get into the newspaper advertising pages as a result of cooperative advertising. The advertisement may be of a local nature where, perhaps, the choice is one or two publications or national advertising where papers all over the country may be considered for placement.

The national fashion newspaper endeavors are generally limited to retail organizations with stores located in many different geographical regions. Sears and J.C. Penney, for example, with hundreds of units throughout the United States, might utilize this avenue to get their fashion messages to the consumer.

Space purchases of a national nature are more complicated than when only one or two papers must be considered, as is the case with local advertising. There are many options available to these advertisers in terms of price structures, discounts, color utilization, placement positions, and regional editions.

The specific rates charged may be obtained from the rate cards of the individual newspapers, or when many are being considered, it is more appropriate to use the Standard Rate and Data Service where quick comparisons may be made.

**FLAT RATES.**   The costs for newspaper space is based upon the number of **agate lines** the advertisement comprises. The agate line is one column wide (approximately two inches) and one line deep. Basically, if a fixed rate is charged by the newspaper, without regard to the amount of space the advertisement occupies or the frequency of the insertions, it is called the flat rate.

**DISCOUNTED RATES.**   While some newspapers utilize the standard flat rate for their space, others offer discounts based upon a variety of circumstances. When rates are discounted, the initial cost begins with the open rate, which is the price of a one-time insertion, and is reduced either because of the frequency of the insertions or bulk purchases. With bulk discounts, the user is charged according to a predetermined sliding scale that reduces the actual space cost as more advertising is bought.

**POSITION RATES.**   When the newspaper charges a basic rate for an insertion, the advertisement is positioned anywhere there is available space. This is known as **run-of-paper** (ROP) placement. While this is the least costly way to buy advertising space, it does not enable the advertiser to select a place in the paper that might be more beneficial to his or her needs.

Fashion retailers, for example, might want their advertisements to appear on a page that is sure to be seen by the fashion enthusiast. The location might be on the page that feature's the fashion editor's column or in special sections. *The New York Times*, for example, publishes a section called Style, which offers commentary on fashion news. Placement in such a section would guarantee that the reader interested in fashion would certainly see the advertisement. Those who desire such advertising locations are charged **preferred position** rates, which are higher than ROP.

If the location of choice is at the top of a column or directly alongside news matter, then an additional cost is charged that is known as **full position rate.**

Sometimes, fashion advertisers are even willing to pay more for specific space on a regular basis. By using this approach, a fashion retailer's faithful clientele will immediately know where to find his or her favorite store's advertisements. This is referred to as **regular preferred position**.

**COMBINATION RATES.**    A variety of combinations is available to advertisers that significantly reduces the costs of the advertisements. It might be the use of space in both a publisher's morning and evening newspapers or several newspapers in which space is purchased on a national basis. In either case, the advertiser may pay as little as one-half of the initial paper's costs for the remainder of the papers used.

## RATE COMPARISONS

While it is very important to select newspapers for advertising purposes on the basis of the characteristics of the readers, sometimes more than one paper could supply subscribers with the same socioeconomic backgrounds and other pertinent qualities. If there are two or more such papers in a geographic trading area, the advertiser would be wise to assess the expense of space in each one in terms of costs per reader.

There is a measurement tool used in the industry that is called the **milline rate** for this purpose. First, it should be understood that this is not an actual rate charged by any publication, just a means of comparing costs. Actual space costs are determined by the number of **agate lines**, the technical term for lines in a newspaper.

The formula for the milline rate is:

$$\frac{1,000,000 \times \text{rate per line}}{\text{circulation}} = \text{milline rate}$$

Thus, if the line rates for two papers are $1.80 and $2.00, respectively, and the first has a circulation of 1,800,000 and the second 4,000,000, the milline rate formula should be used to determine which newspaper has a better cost-per-reader ratio for the advertiser.

Newspaper 1

$$\frac{1,000,000 \times \$1.80}{1,800,000} = \$1.00$$

Newspaper 2

$$\frac{1,000,000 \times \$2.00}{4,000,000} = \$.50$$

Although the second newspaper's advertisement costs more than the first, the use of the milline rate shows that the second paper is a better choice in terms of cost per reader. It must be stressed that all reader characteristics must be the same if this formula is to be applied as a means of comparison!

While many advertisers use the milline rate formula, more and more are using the cost per thousand (CPM) method for comparison purposes. Instead of focusing on the agate line as a base, it uses the open-rate page cost and addresses purchases of full or fractional pages.

If the open-rate page costs of two newspapers are $9,000 and $6,000 and the first has a circulation figure of 300,000 and the second 400,000, their CPMs would be calculated as follows:

Newspaper 1

$$\frac{\$9,000 \times 1,000}{300,000} = \$30 \text{ CPM}$$

Newspaper 2

$$\frac{\$6,000 \times 1,000}{400,000} = \$15 \text{ CPM}$$

The use of this formula tells the potential advertiser that, in terms of potential customers reached, the second paper is a much better choice.

# Newspaper Services Provided to Advertisers

In addition to providing the space necessary for the placement of advertising, the newspaper offers a number of different services to their clients. The following are some of those offered.

## CREATION OF THE ADVERTISEMENT

While the vast majority of fashion advertisers use in-house staffs or advertising agencies, or a combination of both, for their advertisement preparation, the smaller companies have neither the need nor the ability to pay the expenses of advertising professionals. For businesses at that level, the medium provides, without cost, a service that advises on copy (the written message), illustrations, and helps to arrange the advertisement's physical layout. In this way, the advertiser only needs to consider the costs of space in the paper.

## PLANNING AND BUDGETING

Again, it is the smaller user that has neither the resources necessary for professional advice nor the knowledge necessary to satisfactorily make planning and budgeting decisions. The newspaper staff will make suggestions about the best way in which to maximize the amounts earmarked for advertising and how to go about the possibility of obtaining cooperative dollars from vendors.

Too often, the inexperienced fashion advertiser inappropriately uses up all of the dollars allocated for advertising space by placing fewer advertisements that are larger than necessary to attract attention or by inserting advertisements at intervals that are too far apart to impact the market.

## ANALYSIS OF DEMOGRAPHIC CHARACTERISTICS

Demographics is a term that refers to the various characteristics of the population, such as the size of the family; age, occupation, and level of education of the inhabitants; household income; ethnicity; the number of women working outside of the home; and home ownership. Newspapers conduct studies of their readers and potential subscribers so they can inform their advertisers of the nature of the markets they serve.

The analysis of these characteristics is extremely important for the fashion advertisers since most offer a restrictive merchandise assortment. By knowing the specific demographic characteristics of each newspaper in their trading area, the advertiser can make a better judgment as to which paper would best serve their needs.

## DEVELOPMENT AND INSERTION OF ADVERTISING SUPPLEMENTS

The purchase of a daily newspaper brings news and advertising to the readers in the body of the publication. Along with these features, most newspapers offer advertising inserts. These sections are similar to the direct advertisements that are either separately hand delivered to households or make their way to consumers through the mail.

The newspaper helps to develop these pieces for retailers, many of whom are in the fashion business. The major advantage afforded to the user of these supplements is that it guarantees delivery to households that have specific characteristics.

In terms of use by the fashion advertiser, the Sunday editions generally offer the major portion of these insertions. A look at most papers quickly reveals the faith that the advertisers have in using this form of promotion.

## PROMOTING THE MEDIUM TO INCREASE READERSHIP

To motivate current advertisers to continue to utilize the medium and to attract new users, most newspapers participate in a variety of endeavors to promote themselves and increase readership. Some use other media such as radio and television to increase circulation. *New York Newsday*, a major New York City daily newspaper, regularly advertises on television to capture the attention of the viewer and to describe the features of that publication.

Many newspapers run special price promotions that are intended to appeal to new subscribers. It might be a week of free delivery, or a greatly reduced cost for a trial period. *The Sun Sentinel*, a Fort Lauderdale daily, often features free delivery for periods as long as one month to motivate future purchases. Other promotional tools include contests with cash rewards to the winners and sweepstakes.

# Newspaper Space Contracts

The major newspaper advertisers use the medium on a regular basis to keep their names, images, and merchandising offerings in the public's eye. Those whose usage is significant generally opt for a space contract that reduces the amount they pay for the amount of space they use for a stated time. Most contracts are written for annual usage.

The newspaper provides the advertiser with a list of prices that are based either on cost per line or inches. Each advertiser estimates the anticipated amount of space that will be utilized for the year. Using this figure, the newspaper then bills the advertisers for the yearly rate. If, at the end of the contract, the account used all of the lines agreed to in the contract, no adjustments to the bill will be necessary. When less than the contracted amount was used, the advertiser will have to pay a higher rate, known as the **short rate.** The following example illustrates how the final payment is determined.

Newspaper open rate per line . . . . . . . . . . . . $1.00
2,000–3,999 lines . . . . . . . . . . . . . . . . . . . . . . .$.90
4,000–9,999 lines . . . . . . . . . . . . . . . . . . . . . . .$.80

The advertiser anticipates his or her needs to be 5,000 lines for the year at $ .80 per line. At the end of the year, however, only 3,500 lines were used. The bill will have to be settled as follows:

Earned rate . . . . . . . . . . . .$.90  3,500 lines = $3,150
Rate paid . . . . . . . . . . . . . .$.80 × 3,500 lines = 2,800
Short rate due . . . . . . . . . . . . . . . . . . . . . . . . . . . . . . . . . . . . .$350

# Classifications of Newspaper Advertisements

Fashion retailers make use of the major types of newspaper advertisements: classified and display. The smaller of the two types is **classified advertising**. It is primarily used by the fashion industry segments to attract the attention of individuals who are looking for jobs. Want ads are usually small messages that give information, such as job titles, salaries, and anything else that would motivate prospective employees to contact the companies. Some newspapers feature special sections of classified advertising that are directed to those seeking upper-level employment. In *The New York Times* Sunday Business Section, for example, advertisements as large as a one-quarter of a page or more are used to attract those seeking fashion careers, such as buyers, managers, designers, sales managers, and marketing directors.

The lion's share of the newspaper's advertisements are called display advertisements. These are the advertisements that try to sell a company's products or foster a positive image so shoppers will be attracted to the store.

The display advertisements may be further categorized according to the intent of the message being delivered to the reader. These categories are product, promotional, institutional, or combination advertisements. They are the same as the ones used in magazines (see Chapter 5).

It is important to note, however, that unlike magazine usage where all of the industry's components such as materials producers, designers, manufacturers, and retailers utilize that medium, the newspaper's chief fashion advertiser is the retailer. The other levels of the industry may participate in the promotions via the cooperative route, which enables them to get exposure in the retailer's advertisements by paying for half the cost.

Fashion retailers must make steady use of newspaper advertising as a means of reminding their customers of their existence. They regularly use a variety of the types referred to in this section.

The **product advertisements** are used to tell the consumer about the various styles available in the store's inventory. They might feature a particular designer or manufacturer label if the producer's name is one that will help capture the reader's attention. When this approach is used, there is an investment made by the designer or manufacturer for as much as 50 percent of the advertisement, which helps the retailer stretch his or her advertising dollars.

At times when merchandise must be quickly disposed of, such as at the end of a season, or price reductions are being taken for a special sales event, the use of **promotional advertising** is appropriate. In advertisements of this nature, the stress is on price, and terms such as "clearance" and "closeout" dominate the copy.

Many retailers, especially those who are service-oriented and cater to a fashion-forward clientele, find that the occasional use of the

**FIGURE 6-4**

*Product advertisements center on particular styles in a store's inventory. (Courtesy of Ruth Scharf Industries, A Division of Bryan Industries)*

**institutional format** is beneficial. These advertisements focus on topics such as the store's awareness of social issues, services they feature, and the prestigious collections they stock exclusively for their customers. Advertisements of this category do not bring the immediate sales results as do those that are promotionally or product-oriented. Their value to the advertiser is maintaining long-term, positive relationships with the consumer.

**FIGURE 6-5**

*An institutional advertisement that focuses on patriotism (Courtesy of Ann Taylor)*

Sometimes, a blending of two types of messages are used in a single advertisement, which is known as the **combination approach**. The fashion retailer might wish to announce the opening of a new branch, the institutional portion of the advertisement, and combine it with a particular designer's collection, the product component.

# Ethnic Newspapers

All across the country, there is significant growth in the area of newspaper publications that are targeted toward a specific ethnic group. Papers that are directed toward African Americans are the most prominent, with the Hispanic variety the second.

Newspapers with this type of orientation allow the fashion retailer to reach an audience that might otherwise be unaware of the store's offerings. With more and more groups subscribing to these publications, it is often beneficial to make use of them.

The largest of the African-American papers is New York City's *Amsterdam News*. The next largest is *The Los Angeles Sentinel*. Los Angeles and Miami, with ever-increasing numbers of Hispanics in the population, are home to *La Opinions* and *Diarias Las Americas,* respectively. They are printed in Spanish, thus giving the retail user a market that might not have the facility to read English.

Newspapers directed at many different ethnicities are also available. It is up to each fashion retailer to explore the trading area of his or her company to determine which would be most useful in attracting these customers.

## REVIEW QUESTIONS

1. Compare the number of newspapers being published today with the number produced in the 1920s.

2. How do local dailies differ from their nationally published counterparts?

3. Does the daily or national newspaper have greater potential for the fashion advertiser?

4. Define the term *zoned edition*.

5. What is the difference in distribution between the weekly newspaper and the daily?

6. What is meant by the term *syndicated newspaper supplement?*

7. Describe some of the advantages of newspaper advertising.

8. How does the lead time for newspaper insertions differ from what is required of magazines?

9. Define the term *cooperative advertising*.

10. How does the life of the newspaper message compare to that of the magazine?

11. Compare the quality of newspaper reproduction to that of the magazine.

12. How might a potential newspaper advertiser learn about a specific publication's rates without going directly to the publication?

13. What is meant by the term *flat rate?*

14. Define the term *open rate.*

15. What is meant by ROP placement in the newspaper?

16. If an advertiser wishes to have his or her advertisement appear in a specific location of the newspaper, what type of placement must be requested?

17. How does an advertiser compare the rates of circulation of two papers?

18. Discuss some of the services that the newspaper provides for the advertiser.

19. Define the term *short rate.*

20. Discuss the value of using ethnic newspapers for fashion advertisers.

## EXERCISES

1. Purchase one daily and one national newspaper and compare each publication in terms of use by fashion advertisers.

2. Select two Sunday newspaper supplements, one that is published by a specific paper and another that is of the syndicated variety. Compare the advertisements of each in terms of the following:
   - the audiences targetted
   - the nature of the messages

3. Either through the use of the Standard Rate and Data Service or through direct newspaper contact, determine the following information on two competing newspapers:

- the basic rate per line
- discounts
- circulation figures
- special supplements
- the milline rate

*Fashion designer,*

*Maria Snyder,*

*discussing her*

*new collection*

*with the media*

# Television
# and Radio

fter reading this chapter, the student should be able to:

1. Assess the importance of television and radio to the various participants in the fashion industry.

2. Discuss the advantages and disadvantages of the broadcast media for fashion advertising.

3. Explain the use of rating methods and how they affect the cost of television usage by advertisers.

4. Differentiate between network and local television advertising.

5. Describe the role played by cable television and how it is used by the world of fashion.

6. Distinguish between network and local radio.

7. Explain how the various radio rating services work.

8. Discuss how broadcast time is purchased.

# Introduction

Television and radio are the easiest of the media for consumers to use. With the mere flick of a switch, push of a button, or manipulation of a remote control device, the consumer is quickly and effortlessly able to learn about the news of the day, tune into a favorite program or sporting event, and catch a wealth of commentary from many sources. The diversity of the programming enables advertisers to select from this wealth of formats and choose those that have the most potential appeal for the audiences they would like to target. While there is some similarity in both segments of the broadcast media, a term often used when describing both television and radio, there are significant differences that warrant separate examination of each.

Ever since Milton Berle invaded the airwaves of television during the 1950s, the public has fervently embraced the medium. Mr. Television, a title lovingly endeared to Berle, was responsible for a quick decline in Tuesday evening retail sales, the time when the famous show appeared. The vast number of viewers kept that time slot free to watch the comedian and his well-known guests. It was a time when the receiver screens were but a mere nine inches and the programming was in basic black and white. At the time, few advertisers, except for Texaco, which sponsored *The Milton Berle Show,* chose the medium for its promotions. Fashion advertising on television was nonexistent during that period.

Today, we are fed the news by such well-known anchors as Tom Brokaw, invited to watch our favorite sports events such as Monday night football and The World Series, entertained by a host of different situation comedies, and privy to musical entertainment that runs the gamut from classical to pop. To make the medium even more pleasurable, it is broadcast in full color.

A look at some of television's statistics reveals the reasons why fashion advertisers, once neglectful of the medium, now pay greater attention to it. More than 95 percent of the households in America have at least one color television set, about half have VCRs to record programs that they are unable to watch at the time of broadcast or to keep for future viewing, and approximately 50 percent are recipients of cable stations.

The availability of different types of programming continues to soar. What was once a limited medium with the three networks—CBS, NBC, and ABC—has now grown to 100 different stations. Within the next few years, audiences have been promised that this number will soar to 500!

With the ever-increasing expansion, more and more fashion advertisers are joining the bandwagon and using the medium to introduce the world to their products.

Radio, the medium that was here long before television, has had its share of ups and downs. A favored entertainment outlet for family listening, audiences were mesmerized with the antics of Bob Hope, the endless sagas of the soap operas, and dramatizations of stories that let the audience's imagination fill in the details. When television reared its head, it seemed as though radio was doomed forever. In reality, from the sixties to the early eighties, it was not considered a viable medium for advertisers, especially those in fashion.

During the early 1980s, radio was about to make a brilliant comeback. With programs that were specifically earmarked for narrow segments of the population, the advertiser was able to communicate with finely delineated markets. The conservative audience could be easily reached by purchasing time on the *Rush Limbaugh Show*, while the younger, avante-garde fun seeker could be addressed with advertising segments on the *Howard Stern Show*. There are great numbers of programs, by virtue of their concepts and formats, that reach other clearly defined listeners.

## Television

The excitement of full-color and live-action presentation makes television the perfect medium for fashion advertisers to get their messages across. No other medium generates the excitement that television is able to with visual formats that are enhanced with dialogue and music. Most of us are able to recall memorable television commercials that captivated and held our attention. It is unlikely that any of the other media can capture our attention in such dramatic ways.

A look at the screens reveals that most of advertising surrounds the food-producing, automobile, and communications industries. Michael Jackson's Pepsi commercials and Candice Bergen's pitch for Sprint are just two that are seen over and over again all across the country.

The fashion industry, on the other hand, does not generally undertake such extravagant campaigns. They are often more regionally oriented, with advertisements being targeted to more specific groups.

## TELEVISION ADVERTISING ARRANGEMENTS

The fashion advertiser has a number of different ways in which to use television as a means of reaching appropriate markets. Those chosen depend on the available budgets of the company, the size of the audience to be reached, and the level of fashion in which the advertiser participates.

**PROGRAM SPONSORSHIP.**   When an advertiser sponsors a television show, he or she must provide the monies for the program content as well as the production of the commercials. In a show's infancy, the vast majority of programs are exclusively sponsored by one company. As costs began to upwardly spiral, cosponsorship was a way in which costs can be shared by two or more companies. While the sponsorship arrangement provides for the greatest television exposure for businesses and their products, the costs have become prohibitive for all but a few major companies to use. Fashion companies rarely use this type of television advertising.

**PARTICIPATION ADVERTISING.**   In order to gain regular use of the medium without the enormous costs of sponsorship, some companies opt for the participation route. In this arrangement, each company purchases a number of minutes for a particular program in which its commercials are played. While this does not provide the exclusive viewing of one product or product line, it does open the doors to businesses that have smaller advertising budgets.

**NETWORK ADVERTISING.**   A television network is comprised of two or more stations that broadcast programs  originating from one location. Nationally, there are four major networks, CBS, NBC, ABC, and Fox, each with more than 200 stations or **affiliates.**

This arrangement allows the advertiser to pay a specified amount for a commercial to be shown on every affiliated station in the network. Companies like General Foods and the Ford Motor Company spend millions of dollars on this type of advertising annually. Except for a very few fashion-oriented organizations, such as DuPont, Inc., network advertising is not the choice of fashion advertisers.

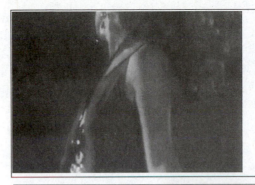

*"Ends of The Earth"
Image-building advertising,
run in conjunction with our
"Ends of the Earth" print
campaign, helped remind
viewers that we're always
pushing the borders of
fashion.*

*After we ran these
image-building TV spots,
each featuring a famous
designer talking about
his or her philosophy of
design, we heard a lot
of favorable talk around
town.*

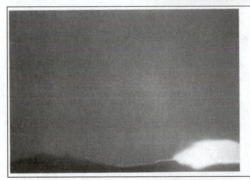

*"Thirteen Hour Sale"
This commercial demon-
strated both the power
of television and our ability
to use it effectively:
regional markets running
this spot dramatically
out-performed those
that didn't.*

**FIGURE 7-1**

*Four local television*

*campaigns targeted to a*

*narrow, regional audience*

*(Courtesy of Dayton's)*

*Our "Intimate Apparel
Sale" had been flat for
several years. Then we
ran this commercial.
Sales shot up 33%.*

**SPOT ADVERTISING.** Spot advertising is used to describe spot purchases by national advertisers. That is, instead of purchasing a time slot for every area of the country, the advertiser is able to choose the spots or locations in which to have his or her commercial aired. It enables the company to target those areas that have the greatest potential for sales. Thus, an advertiser that wishes to focus on the Southern states need only pay for exposure to those areas. Fashion designers and materials producers wishing to address particular geographic areas would find this approach more practical for their needs.

**LOCAL ADVERTISING.** This type of advertising is best suited to the needs of the fashion retailer. With all but a few companies confined to a more localized region, the stores are able to communicate with the customers who are able to frequent their premises in this manner. During a program, when a commercial break is taken, a company like New York based A & S can reach its local viewers, while, Marshall Field in Chicago, for example, may feature an advertisement that comes into the homes of viewers in its trading area. Through this arrangement, fashion retailers do not waste the dollars spent on reaching consumers who are too far from the stores to warrant a shopping trip.

## ADVANTAGES AND DISADVANTAGES OF TELEVISION

The very excitement of the medium makes it an excellent communication outlet to reach potential markets. It has many advantages, especially when it is compared with the other media. Some of the benefits derived by users, most notably the world of fashion, will be explored.

1. *Creative Flexibility.* No other medium gives as much flexibility to the advertiser as television. Fashion industry users, in particular, deal with merchandise that is best appreciated when it is witnessed in a live presentation. The movement of models wearing apparel, the vivid color harmonies employed, the messages that are spoken rather than written, the drama of visual effects, and the employment of music that enhances the advertisement all make this medium one that has little competition in terms of audience arousal.

2. *Audience Penetration.* With but a single showing, a television commercial can reach an untold number of people. Since more than 95 percent of the households have at least one receiver, the viewers are easily reached. Not only are the numbers significant, but every segment of the population is within reach via this medium. With magazine and newspaper readership limited to those who must purchase the periodicals to read the contents, television simply and almost automatically comes into the home.

3. *Audience Segmentation.* In addition to the vast numbers of viewers, television advertising may be focused on particular groups. A manufacturer of fashion merchandise with a teenage emphasis, for example, is sure to get the message across to the youth of America by promoting its wares on programs such as *American Bandstand, Beverly Hills 90210,* and the soap operas. Similarly, those in search of younger audiences might choose to run commercials during the Saturday morning cartoons.

4. *Cost Per Viewer.* Although television advertising requires a significant dollar investment, the costs per viewer are relatively modest. The costs are also minimized by the fact that the same commercial can be repeated again and again, saving the user the expense involved of creating many different presentations.

5. *Lack of Competition.* When the programs move to their advertising periods, the screens are filled only with the commercials that the users have prepared. Unlike newspapers, which generally feature news stories or competing advertisements on the same pages, the television screen features only the single advertisement. Even when viewers move from channel to channel during these promotional periods, the other stations are likely to feature their advertisements. Many major users of television advertising contract for their commercials to have simultaneous runs on all of the networks so that only their messages will be aired.

6. *Multiple Simultaneous Viewing.* Like radio, television is a medium that enables many people to watch it at the same time. Newspapers and magazines, on the other hand, are solely used by one reader at a time. This multiple-viewing advantage enables the advertiser to reach many people with the same message at one time. When a fashion retailer, such as Burlington Coat Factory, uses a format that

features men's, women's, and children's apparel during a program of general interest, all of the family members might be motivated by the single advertisement.

7. *Cooperative Involvement.* Since television has the ability to bring quick sales results, many companies are willing to cosponsor television advertisements. Fashion retailers, for example, sometimes have about 50 percent of their costs picked up by designers and manufacturers who are eager to alert potential to customers where their products may be purchased.

As is the case with any of the other media, television also has its limitations. Some of the more prominent limitations follow.

1. *Cost.* Without question, the costs of producing a commercial and the monies spent for the time it is being shown make the medium primarily available to the giants of the industry. A spot during the prime time viewing period may cost the advertiser more than $100,000. Even less desirable periods cost considerable sums. Few fashion organizations have the resources necessary for such endeavors, even though this medium gets the message across to large audiences very quickly.

   The nature of fashion with its ever-changing styles and colors necessitates the continuous development of new commercials. Where the cereal industry may run the same message over and over again for very long durations, fashion promoters must always be ready to present what is new and current in the marketplace. Although the spot costs do not change, the production costs for fashion promotions contribute significant expense.

2. *The Life of the Message.* In comparison with the print media, the television message is extremely brief. With costs continuing to escalate, many advertisers have opted for fifteen-minute spots, instead of the once-common one-minute entries. The brevity does not allow for the viewer to grasp the advertisement's message unless it is shown again and again. A newspaper's advertisements, on the other hand, last at least until the next day's edition is available.

3. *Clutter.* More and more television advertisers are using the aforementioned, briefer advertisements. Because of this trend, a television viewer may be bombarded with four commercials during a

break in programming. This adds a great deal of clutter and tends to make the impact of each message  less meaningful.

4. *Channel Switching.* Many Americans are annoyed with the commercial interruptions and "channel-hop" to avoid them. The invention of the remote control has made such commercial avoidance easier to accomplish.

5. *Limited Viewing Time.* When one wants to read a paper or magazine, he or she may do so at any time. Since programs are aired at specific times, viewers may not always be available to watch. With the number of women returning to the work force and more and more workers involved in second jobs, the viewing times are even more limited. Even the three prime time evening hours that focus on the largest audiences are not available to those with these lengthened workdays.

6. *VCR Selectivity.* The video cassette recorder (VCR) has negatively impacted  television advertising. Although viewers who are preoccupied with other responsibilities are able to record their favorite shows for watching at other times, the commercials fall victim. The use of the fast forward control enables programs to be seen without commercial interruption. Thus, the sponsor who has spent enormous sums on advertising does not have the advantage of having his promotion seen.

## TELEVISION AND ADVERTISING RATES

Although the size of the viewing audience has significantly increased over the years, making it an excellent medium to quickly reach large numbers, so have the costs. Those who sponsor entire programs, as we have already learned, are responsible for the costs of the program's production as well as the advertisements. For the most part, however, such undertakings are not generally within the budget constraints of those in the fashion industry. The more likely approach used by these participants is to purchase particular spots.

In the early years of television, it was commonplace to have rates quoted for hourly, half-hour, quarter-hour, and five- or ten-minute announcements. Today's rates are usually quoted for thirty-second segments, with two different announcements sometimes filling that brief time span.

## SAMPLE TELEVISION ADVERTISING FEES

### WCBS-TV, CHANNEL 2, NEW YORK

| Time Period | Program | Cost |
| --- | --- | --- |
| 7:00 A.M.–9:00 A.M. | *CBS This Morning* | $ 350 |
| 9:00 A.M.–4:00 P.M. | Rotation of Programs | 700 |
| 4:00 P.M.–5:00 P.M. | Afternoon Programming | 700 |
| 5:00 P.M.–6:00 P.M. | News | 850 |
| 6:00 P.M.–7:00 P.M. | News | 1,350 |
| 7:00 P.M.–7:30 P.M. | *Hard Copy* (a.t.)* | 2,000 |
| 7:30 P.M.–8:00 P.M. | *Entertainment Tonight* (a.t.) | 4,250 |
| 8:00 P.M.–11:00 P.M. | Prime Time Periods | 4,000-24,000 |
| | *Murphy Brown* | 24,000 |
| | *Knots Landing* | 12,000 |
| | *Top Cops* | 4,250 |
| 11:00 P.M.– 11:35 P.M. | News | 4,400 |
| 11:35 P.M.–12:35 A.M. | Late Night I | 1,500 |
| 12:35 A.M. –2:00 A.M. | Late Night II | 250 |
| 2:00 A.M. –6:00 A.M. | Overnight | 50 |

* Access Time

**FIGURE 7–2**

*Thirty-second spot*

*advertising rates*

Specifically, the rates are based upon a number of factors. They include:

1. *Time Period.* Different time periods account for considerable price differential. Prime time, for example, is the period from 8:00 P.M. to 11:00 P.M. and has the greatest number of viewers. Thus, commercials shown during this time cost considerably more than any other. Access time is the slot just before prime time and thus because of its comparatively large audience, commands prices that are almost as high as the peak prime times. At the other end of the

spectrum,the overnight times, enormously reduced costs are instituted because of the sparsity of the viewing audience.

2. *Size of Viewing Audience.* There is a great deal of disparity among rates, even for those programs in identical time slots. If the audiences measured are the highest for the time period, the costs for advertising time will substantially increase.

3. *Popularity of Program.* Long before a program is initially aired, its advertising costs often are determined by its potential for success. When a station features a famous personality in a new series, it automatically increases its charges for advertising. However if the show does not live up to its advance notices and promotion, the rates are eventually scaled down.

The following rate schedule for local advertising on WCBS-TV, Channel 2 New York, in March 1993 demonstrates the costs and the variables that determine rates.

## RATING SYSTEMS

The size and characteristics of the viewing audience are extremely important to television advertisers. If they can predetermine which programs provide the most appropriate viewers as potential purchasers of their products, they can more efficiently use their promotional budgets.

There are several different systems and companies involved in determining these ratings. The formats used range from those that require hand-recorded information to the type that are automated.

**THE DIARY METHOD.**    During the formative years of the industry, the diary method was the mainstay of television ratings. It requires that a member of a household records which programs are being watched. It also provides beneficial information about the characteristics of the family.

Arbitron, a syndicated television and radio ratings company, uses the diary method. Participants in their surveys receive preprinted diaries that require hand-recorded entries and a page of instructions for recording. The participants need to include information such as the channels received by the television set, the names, the sex, and ages of the people in the household, the programs watched, and those in the family that actually viewed the programs. All of this information is then used to produce a profile of the viewers as well as to show the popularity of the programs offered.

Proponents of this methodology conclude that this technique affords economical, meaningful data collection for potential advertisers. Those who argue against its use suggest that while it is cost-effective, it may be at the expense of accuracy. Some participants, for example, may not immediately record the required information. By entering it at a later time, the data may be inaccurate. Some even rely upon other household members to provide the necessary information in their absence.

**THE HOUSEHOLD RECORDER.** In 1950, the A.C. Nielsen Company, a name that has become synonymous with television ratings, introduced the Audimeter. The device is attached to the receiver and provides the company with the names of the programs the sets are tuned to. Although this mechanical device automatically delivers this information accurately, it does not have the ability to determine if anyone is actually watching the program.

**PEOPLE METERS.** The next generation of measurement devices combines the advantages provided by the diary and mechanical methodology of the household recorder. Using a sample of 4,000 households, Nielsen provides pertinent television ratings with the installation of a sophisticated mechanical recorder. Not only does it record what is being watched, but the information is further augmented by a preselected viewer who indicates his or her presence with use of a series of illuminated buttons.

The major argument against the Nielsen rating is the size of the sample that is used. Some believe it is too small to use for accurate forecasting. On the other hand, those who favor this technique argue that its size is greater than that used for political polling and that larger numbers will be too costly.

**TELEPHONE INTERVIEWS.** Companies such as Birch collect information from television and radio audiences via the telephone interview. Although this technique involves direct contact with the audience, it has some limitations. The most notable, perhaps, is the amount of time individuals must spend answering questions. Birch interviews last nine minutes, an amount of time considered to be lengthy for today's households. Many participants simply do not have the time to spend answering questions. Other negatives include people's reluctance to converse with individuals they do not know or cannot see, which makes the sample unreliable.

**COMBINATION TECHNIQUES.** One of the most innovative techniques was introduced by Arbitron. It combines the methodology of the people meter with a system that records products purchased by the household. Not only does it provide potential advertisers with information about who the television watchers are of a particular program, their ages and sex and the time of the viewing, it also analyzes the purchases they make. Through the use of a scanning device that reads the universal product codes on packages, it can tell exactly which products the viewers purchased. In this way, the advertisers can determine whether or not the products shown in the commercials are actually purchased.

**MAIL QUESTIONNAIRES.** Marketing research companies have used the mail to gather information on a variety of topics. Sometimes, questionnaires are mailed to people to learn about their programming likes and dislikes. While this is an appropriate method of data collection, it does have its limitations. For example, only a small number of questionnaire recipients complete and return the forms. The rate of return is often just 1 percent. Another disadvantage is the inability to verify if the submitted information is accurate. However, the expense of such methodology is relatively modest.

## CIRCULATION MEASUREMENT

As was discussed earlier, newspaper and magazine circulation figures are easy to access. Using these numbers, advertisers can assess each periodical and determine if its circulation warrants expenditures for promotional dollars. Under the watchful eye of independent agencies such as the Audit Bureau of Circulations, these numbers are verified.

The television medium relies upon a rating system that provides the advertiser with a number indicating the percentage of the viewing audience that watches a particular program. For example, if a specific market has 100,000 homes that receive a broadcast signal and 10,000 television sets are tuned into a specific program, that program's rating is 10 percent.

Further circulation information provides the advertiser with figures on a program's audience share. To determine the share, the program rating is divided by the number of sets in use. Using the 10 percent in the previous example as the program rating and the sets-in-use were found to be 40 percent (the number determined by various ratings techniques previously discussed), the share would be 25 percent.

Naturally, the greater the share, the more desirable the program is for advertising purposes.

In the world of television advertising, the percentage is dropped, and the share is simply stated as a number. In the previous illustration, the share would merely be classified as 25.

## ALTERNATIVES TO TRADITIONAL TELEVISION

In addition to the regular network and local programming, other television systems are making an impact on the viewing audience. The most popular is cable television. Others, such as subscription television, are gaining in importance.

There are more than 50 million cable subscribers in the United States. The programming is often unique and unavailable on the networks. Specific audiences are more easily targeted, making this communication system a natural for many advertisers. Programs like Elsa Klench's *Style*, for example, make it the perfect place for fashion advertisers to promote their wares. At this point in time, however, the fashion industry is making only modest use of cable television.

Subscription services such as Pay Per View, charge additional fees for program viewing. Currently the major features are movies. Advertising has not yet impacted on it.

# Radio

The scenes of joggers going through their daily rituals with headsets attached to their ears listening to radio and highways full of automobiles stalled in traffic with captive audiences passing the time tuned into their favorite talk shows are just two indications that radio is back in town as an important communication outlet. Radio stations have changed their formats from the earlier days by specializing in programming that captures the attention of specific segments of the consumer market. Some outlets are all music, for example, featuring one type such as country-western or light rock; others feature a twenty-four-hour news format and still others emphasize the talk shows. The listening

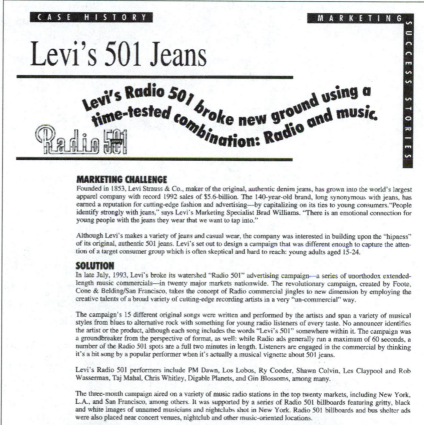

**CASE HISTORY** — **MARKETING SUCCESS STORIES**

# Levi's 501 Jeans

**Levi's Radio 501 broke new ground using a time-tested combination: Radio and music.**

Radio 501

**MARKETING CHALLENGE**

Founded in 1853, Levi Strauss & Co., maker of the original, authentic denim jeans, has grown into the world's largest apparel company with record 1992 sales of $5.6 billion. The 140-year-old brand, long synonymous with jeans, has earned a reputation for cutting-edge fashion and advertising—by capitalizing on its ties to young consumers. "People identify strongly with jeans," says Levi's Marketing Specialist Brad Williams. "There is an emotional connection for young people with the jeans they wear that we want to tap into."

Although Levi's makes a variety of jeans and casual wear, the company was interested in building upon the "hipness" of its original, authentic 501 jeans. Levi's set out to design a campaign that was different enough to capture the attention of a target consumer group which is often skeptical and hard to reach: young adults aged 15-24.

**SOLUTION**

In late July, 1993, Levi's broke its watershed "Radio 501" advertising campaign—a series of unorthodox extended-length music commercials—in twenty major markets nationwide. The revolutionary campaign, created by Foote, Cone & Belding/San Francisco, takes the concept of Radio commercial jingles to new dimension by employing the creative talents of a broad variety of cutting-edge recording artists in a very "un-commercial" way.

The campaign's 15 different original songs were written and performed by the artists and span a variety of musical styles from blues to alternative rock with something for young radio listeners of every taste. No announcer identifies the artist or the product, although each song includes the words "Levi's 501" somewhere within it. The campaign was a groundbreaker from the perspective of format, as well: while Radio ads generally run a maximum of 60 seconds, a number of the Radio 501 spots are a full two minutes in length. Listeners are engaged in the commercial by thinking it's a hit song by a popular performer when it's actually a musical vignette about 501 jeans.

Levi's Radio 501 performers include PM Dawn, Los Lobos, Ry Cooder, Shawn Colvin, Les Claypool and Rob Wasserman, Taj Mahal, Chris Whitley, Digable Planets, and Gin Blossoms, among many.

The three-month campaign aired on a variety of music radio stations in the top twenty markets, including New York, L.A., and San Francisco, among others. It was supported by a series of Radio 501 billboards featuring gritty, black and white images of unnamed musicians and nightclubs shot in New York. Radio 501 billboards and bus shelter ads were also placed near concert venues, nightclub and other music-oriented locations.

**RESULTS**

The combined Levi's Radio 501 advertising effort reached an estimated 97% of the target audience an average of 40 times. But Radio's flexibility and unique programming environment allowed the unique creative approach to work effectively. Even though Generation Xers are marked by the diversity of their beliefs and lifestyles, Levi's believes that music is the basic thread that connects them as a group—and that Radio is the way to communicate via that shared language.

"The age group we're targeting listens to Radio to hear music. It can be very difficult speaking to this age group because their tastes vary so widely," says Williams. "Music is the most universal means of reaching them and obviously Radio, through its wide variety of formats, offers a strong vehicle to get the message to many consumers within that age group."

10/93

**RADIO ADVERTISING BUREAU INC., 304 PARK AVENUE SOUTH, NEW YORK, NY 10010**

**FIGURE 7-3**

*Levi's 501 Jeans case*

*history for radio usage*

*(Courtesy of Radio*

*Advertising Bureau)*

audience is thus able to tune into the station that peaks his or her interests without having to move the dial.

Through this specialization, advertisers may easily reach the segments of the market that they think are the most likely purchasers of their products. This, coupled with the fact that radio is a relatively inexpensive medium to capture consumer attention, makes it worthwhile for many advertisers to use.

The fashion industry, most notably the retailing segment, makes considerable use of radio. When sales events are being promoted, radio can quickly alert its target market. Manufacturers and retailers who merchandise active sportswear and footwear also are using radio a great deal. The runner, listening to his or her Sony Walkman as the miles are being covered, will certainly pay attention to any products that will enhance the aerobic activity.

## ADVANTAGES AND DISADVANTAGES OF RADIO

Although radio is not one of the media used by all components of the fashion world, it does provide an effective method for the retail segment. Some of the advantages of radio follow:

1. *Mobility.* Unlike television, which is generally restricted to the places where the sets are stationed, except for the transportable types, which are sparsely used, radios are easily mobile. Listeners may use them in their homes, at the office, in cars, and during exercising. The listener need not be away from hearing his or her favorite programs when leaving their residences.

2. *Immediate, Personal Communication.* At any time of the day or night, individuals may immediately become in touch with the world by turning on the radio. By and large, it provides a personal avenue to hear about sports, news, weather, music, and talk shows. Many people find solace in radio listening because they feel they are being directly addressed by the program hosts. Listeners are often invited to request their favorite tunes or call in to have their personal problems considered by advice experts.

3. *Selectivity.* Advertisers are given a wide range of programs and markets to chose from in order to sell their products. A fashion retailer specializing in women's apparel, for example, might opt for commercial

time during a talk show that centers on women's problems. Men's shops might use the time during a sports event to capture the attention of the male market. With more than 10,000 commercial radio stations on the air, there are scores of programs to select from.

4. *Costs Per Listener.* In comparison to television, radio is considerably less expensive for the advertiser. The competition for the large

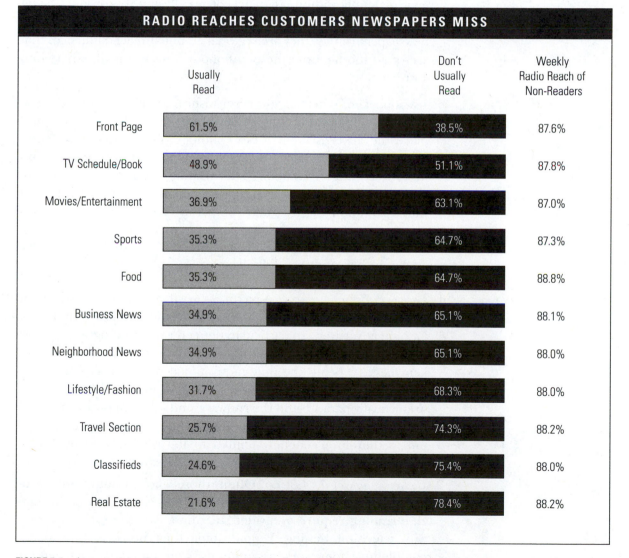

## RADIO REACHES CUSTOMERS NEWSPAPERS MISS

| | Usually Read | Don't Usually Read | Weekly Radio Reach of Non-Readers |
|---|---|---|---|
| Front Page | 61.5% | 38.5% | 87.6% |
| TV Schedule/Book | 48.9% | 51.1% | 87.8% |
| Movies/Entertainment | 36.9% | 63.1% | 87.0% |
| Sports | 35.3% | 64.7% | 87.3% |
| Food | 35.3% | 64.7% | 88.8% |
| Business News | 34.9% | 65.1% | 88.1% |
| Neighborhood News | 34.9% | 65.1% | 88.0% |
| Lifestyle/Fashion | 31.7% | 68.3% | 88.0% |
| Travel Section | 25.7% | 74.3% | 88.2% |
| Classifieds | 24.6% | 75.4% | 88.0% |
| Real Estate | 21.6% | 78.4% | 88.2% |

**FIGURE 7-4**   *A comparision between the reach of radio and newspaper audiences (Courtesy of Radio Advertising Bureau)*

number of available outlets keeps the costs down. In addition to the price paid for air time, the production of a radio commercial is considerably less costly than that of television advertising, which requires significant expenditures for the visual aspects of the promotion. When compared to the other media, the cost per thousand (CPM) is considerably less, except for the outdoor advertising format.

5. *Audience Reach.* With the local nature of radio advertising, the listener is generally within easy reach of purchasing the product being promoted. The other media, most notably television, magazines, and newspapers (unless they are regional editions) reach audiences that are often too far from the point-of-purchase to turn listeners into customers.

6. *Late Insertions.* When an advertiser wishes to use television or magazines, there is a significant amount of time needed to create and place the advertisement. Color photography sessions, live-action shoots, and special effects require a great deal of planning, executing, and editing. A fashion retailer wishing to quickly advise its customers of a special sale can create the message and have it aired with a minimum of effort and comparatively short notice.

Given its low cost and ease of production, the radio, like all other media, has its limitations and disadvantages.

1. *Lack of the Visual Element.* "A picture is worth a thousand words" is an old cliche that adequately describes one of radio's major drawbacks. Fashion advertisers, in particular, depend upon photographs, drawings, and live-action to best dramatize their offerings. With the spoken message being the only motivational device, it is difficult to relay the product's appearance. Television may show the models dramatically parading on the runways, and magazines can use color to show designs to their best advantage. Radio, as a fashion medium, is therefore generally limited to the retailer who uses it to announce sales and other promotional endeavors.

2. *Concentration of the Listener.* Often, those who are tuned into programs are busily engaged in other activities. Newspaper and magazine reading require undivided attention, as is generally the case with television viewing. People doing their housework, students completing homework assignments, and motorists engaged in

conversation with passengers do not always pay strict attention to every spoken word. Even when there is little interference from other chores, commercial time may be appropriate for getting a snack in another room.

3. *The Life of the Message.* Newspapers and magazines may be read at times convenient to the user, thus providing a number of opportunities for the advertising messages to be seen. The radio is a medium in which the life of the message is but for a few moments, and when it is gone, it is gone. Users of radio run the same commercials again and again in hopes of getting the message to be heard.

4. *Retention of Pertinent Information.* Newspaper and magazine advertisements sometimes use coupons to motivate readers to buy. In order to receive a special discount, an advertisement must be presented at the time of purchase. The radio, without benefit of being able to place something in someone's hands, does not aid in this retention power. For example, if a phone number or address is mentioned, the motorist has no way of jotting down these numbers, making the commercial worthless.

## THE RATE STRUCTURE

Each radio station determines the different rates they charge. The specific costs are usually based on the time of the day, the length of the commercial, and the number of times it will be aired per week. Many stations price the peak driving times of its potential audiences at the highest levels. Costs of air time are available to advertisers on station rate cards and through examination of the *Standard Rate and Data Service.* The latter provides a quick means of comparing one station's rates to another. On the following page is an excerpt of a typical rate structure for a radio station.

### ANALYSIS OF RATE CARD.

1. The rates vary according to the desirability of the time period. That is, AA times are considered more valuable to advertisers than A periods because of the potential size of the listening audience.

2. The rates for thirty seconds are not one-half of the minute rate.

3. There is a premium for the most desirable times, such as the drives to and from work.

4. As the number of times the advertisement placement per week is increased, the time costs, per airing, are reduced.

5. The greater the number of weeks the announcement is aired, the lower the cost per announcement.

## SAMPLE RADIO RATES

KVEN, Ventura County, California

### TIME RATES

AA—Monday through Saturday, 5:00–10:00 A.M. & 3:00–8:00 P.M.
  A—Monday through Saturday, 10:00 A.M.–3:00 P.M. & 8:00 P.M.–midnight,
    Sunday 6:00 A.M.–midnight

### Spot Announcements
#### One Minute

| per week | 1 wk | | 13 wks | | 26 wks | | 52 wks | |
|---|---|---|---|---|---|---|---|---|
| | AA | A | AA | A | AA | A | AA | A |
| 6 times | 44 | 33 | 37 | 30 | 34 | 28 | 33 | 26 |
| 12 times | 39 | 30 | 36 | 29 | 33 | 26 | 30 | 25 |
| 18 times | 36 | 29 | 33 | 26 | 30 | 25 | 29 | 24 |
| 24 times | 34 | 28 | 30 | 25 | 29 | 24 | 26 | 22 |
| 30 times | 33 | 26 | 29 | 24 | 26 | 22 | 25 | 21 |

#### Thirty Seconds

| per week | 1 wk | | 13 wks | | 26 wks | | 52 wks | |
|---|---|---|---|---|---|---|---|---|
| 6 times | 34 | 28 | 30 | 26 | 29 | 25 | 29 | 24 |
| 12 times | 33 | 26 | 29 | 25 | 26 | 24 | 25 | 21 |
| 18 times | 30 | 25 | 26 | 24 | 25 | 22 | 24 | 18 |
| 24 times | 27 | 24 | 25 | 22 | 24 | 21 | 22 | 17 |
| 30 times | 26 | 23 | 24 | 21 | 22 | 18 | 21 | 16 |

A.M. Drive: AA rate plus 20 percent, Midday: A rate plus 20 percent

**FIGURE 7–5**

*Typical rate structure*

*for a radio station*

**OTHER RATE CARD INFORMATION.**   Each station's rate card features information, in addition to rates, that helps the potential advertiser make a decision about using the particular outlet.

1. The nature of the programming is indicated. In the prior example, the station noted its emphasis on news, sports, and talk shows.
2. The facilities of the station, area coverage, and hours of broadcasting are indicated.
3. The target audience is indicated.
4. Payment requirements are indicated.
5. Combination rates, if any, with other outlets are indicated. Station KVEN, as featured earlier, is an AM facility. It offers its users a rate if they combine the spot announcements with air time on an affiliate FM station, KHAY.

## RADIO RATING SERVICES

Like television, radio has its rating services. Two rating services dominate local radio. The largest of these services is the Arbitron, which uses the diary method, as described in the television section, to collect data. Its major competitor is Birch, which primarily relies upon telephone interviewing.

In the area of network ratings, Radio All Dimension Audience Research, or RADAR as it is referred to in the industry, is the major service. Those in the sample are contacted via telephone over a forty-eight-week period, with each survey participant called as often as nine times. The information provided by these services primarily centers upon circulation figures.

## REVIEW QUESTIONS

1. What term is used to collectively describe the media of radio and television?
2. During the 1950s, which television personality accounted for a serious curtailing of Tuesday evening business in retailing?

3. What percentage of the population in the United States has at least one color television set?

4. Discuss the major advantage that television advertising affords the fashion world.

5. Define the term *program sponsorship*. Why has it declined in recent years?

6. Discuss the term *television network*.

7. Which type of advertising arrangement is best suited to the needs of fashion retailers?

8. Compare the cost per television viewer to that of the other media.

9. Why do many of the fashion world's components shy away from television for their advertising endeavors?

10. How does the use of the VCR affect the user of television advertising?

11. On what factors are television rates based?

12. Discuss the diary system for television ratings.

13. Which company introduced the Audimeter to television? How does it work?

14. In what way does the Birch organization gather its information for ratings?

15. In addition to listening to the radio at home, in what other places do people listen to the radio?

16. In terms of overall cost per listener, how does radio compare to the other media?

17. What is the major disadvantage of radio for fashion advertising?

18. Discuss some of the factors that enter into the rates charged by radio stations.

**EXERCISES**

1. Call or write to five radio stations within one geographical area and ask for a copy of their rate cards. The names, addresses, and telephone numbers of each station are available in SRDS. Once the cards have been received, prepare a comparative chart with the following information:

   - the targeted audience;
   - program emphasis; and
   - rates.

2. Contact an affiliate of a television network that serves your area for the purpose of interviewing the station manager. The following information should be obtained during the interview:

   - the audience to whom it is targeted;
   - the major programs in its schedule;
   - the cost for spot announcements; and
   - the types of fashion advertisers who use their services.

   Once the interview has been completed, an oral report should be prepared and delivered to the class.

3. Contact one of the major radio and television services to learn about the methods they use to gather data for ratings. Make certain that you ask for the various forms that they use in their approaches. Prepare a written report, accompanied by the forms, outlining the services the company provides.

destination ANN TAYLOR.

spring 1994

*Fashion catalogs have*

*made shopping easier.*

*(Courtesy of Ann Taylor)*

# Direct
# Advertising

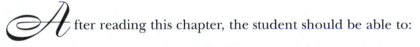fter reading this chapter, the student should be able to:

1. Describe the different types of pieces that are used to gain customer attention and motivate purchasing.

2. Discuss the advantages of using direct advertising for fashion-oriented products.

3. List the various segments of the fashion industry that use direct advertising and the audiences they target for their programs.

4. Explain how the users of direct advertising secure the names of potential customers for the distribution of their advertising pieces.

5. Compile a list indicating the various components of a direct advertising program.

## Introduction

On a typical day, household consumers and businesses alike are inundated with a rash of advertising pieces that virtually clog their mailboxes. Relegated to a somewhat obscure position in the overall marketing of fashion merchandise as recently as twenty years ago, few companies shun the medium today. While the newspaper gets the lion's share of the advertising budgets from the retailing industry and television and magazines the bulk of the designer's and manufacturers promotional expenditures, it is unusual for any segment of the fashion world to disregard the use of some form of direct advertising. Usage may involve direct mail, the largest method of direct advertising, hand-delivered advertisements, or stacking countertops with brochures for the customer's taking.

In the past, direct advertising was the only medium that enabled the retailing industry to motivate consumers to become customers. With many people living too far from the traditional retail arenas, access to stores was often a difficult task. Although today most people are within easy reach of a shopping mall or other retail center, the need for direct mail has resurfaced because of the vast numbers of women who work outside of the home. Other components of the fashion industry have also embraced one form or another of direct advertising to reach their targeted markets. Designers wishing to announce the opening of their new collections, resident buying offices trying to motivate interest in their private label collections, and trade associations trying to increase attendance at an upcoming exposition, are just some users of the direct advertising medium.

It is at the retail level, however, that direct advertising is emerging as the leading medium for some fashion merchants. Aside from the abundance of pamphlets, brochures, and catalogs that are regularly delivered through the mail, one need only to enter a department store to observe the numbers of advertising pieces that fill cosmetics areas. Most every major fragrance and cosmetics producer makes available colorful advertising pieces that notify shoppers about new products in their lines and special promotions. With the enormous increase in the use of direct advertising by the fashion industry, it seems that the results are worth the investment.

# Advantages of Direct Advertising

Fashion organizations are extensively using direct mail and hand delivery as a means of communicating with their clientele and selling them their wares. It is a medium that offers numerous advantages that the others—such as the print and broadcast media—do not.

## UNDIVIDED READER ATTENTION

When a manufacturer or designer wishes to reach a significant audience for his or her product line and newspapers, magazines, radio, and television are the choices, exposure is, of course, to a large group. There is, however, the distinct disadvantage of competition from all of the other advertisers using the same publication or air time. The newspaper, for example, with its host of advertisements and short life, is often discarded before a company's advertisement may be seen. On television, where the life of the message is even briefer, leaving the room during the commercial time results in missing the message.

When a brochure, catalog, or any other advertising piece is mailed or hand-delivered, the potential customer's undivided attention is more likely to be achieved.

## COST EFFICIENCY

Although mail rates continue to increase, the sender has a number of options to use. If time is of the essence and specific delivery is a requirement, first-class postage, the highest rate except for overnight delivery and other special handling, is necessary. However, if the company carefully plans its mailings, and the timeframe is not a rigid requirement, third-class mailings can be substituted at a lower cost.

Some fashion industry segments such as retailers and resident buying offices make use of direct mail without incurring any additional expense. When retailers mail the monthly charge statements to their customers, they generally include pamphlets that announce special merchandise offerings and sales. Resident buying offices, who also send regular end-of-month statements to their accounts, also make use of enclosures that tell of special purchase inducements, private label products, and so forth.

In both of these situations, the postage is already necessitated because of the billing, so an additional piece might not even increase the cost of the postage.

## SELECTIVITY

If narrowing the market to a specific group of individuals is the goal, then direct advertising is the best medium to use. While the typical broadcast and print media are nonselective, that is, they reach vast audiences, many of whom have neither the desire nor the need for the product, direct mailings and hand distribution allow for selectivity.

Mailing lists may be generated that carefully consider such factors as age, sex, income, occupation, educational background, and religion. The compilation and acquisition of mailing lists will be discussed later in the chapter.

## SIMPLICITY OF RESPONSE

Many advertising pieces that are directed to a consumer's home or to the business professional are replete with order forms and envelopes for customer response. This eliminates the amount of effort required by the respondent to accept the advertiser's offer. The other media generally require phone responses or store visits, both of which may be time consuming and often unacceptable by the targeted audience.

## FORMAT FLEXIBILITY

A host of different advertising pieces are used by direct advertisers. They range from the simple one-page, letter-type announcement to a wide variety of catalogs. Each company uses the format that will best accomplish its tasks. The various types of mailers will be discussed later in the chapter, with an emphasis on catalog development.

## SUCCESS MEASUREMENT

When a customer comes to the store and makes a purchase or a retailer makes an inquiry to a designer about a collection, there is no

Crate and Barrel
P.O. Box 9059
Wheeling, IL 60090-9059

If purchaser's name or address is missing or incorrect print
corrections here. No P.O. Boxes, please.

To place an order, call 24 hours toll free **1 (800) 323-5461**
Fax orders: 1 (708) 215-0482, please include your return fax number.

**Payment Information:**

Telephone Number: Day (    )                Evening (    )

☐ Check (No cash, C.O.D. or money orders accepted.)   Fax No. (    )

☐ Visa   ☐ MasterCard   ☐ American Express   ☐ Discover        Card Expires

Signature (if charging)

Use this section for items being shipped to the above address.

| Catalogue number | Qty. 1 Set = 1 Qty. | Description or name of item | Color | For sheets: Flat or Fitted | Price each | Price total |
|---|---|---|---|---|---|---|
| | | | | | | |
| | | | | | | |
| | | | | | | |
| | | | | | | |
| | | | | | | |

Use this section for items shipped to an address *other* than above.        Gift message:

Name

Address (No P.O. Boxes.)

City, State, Zip

Use this section for items shipped to an address *other* than above.        Gift message:

Name

Address (No P.O. Boxes.)

City, State, Zip

**Important Ordering Information:**
**1.** We ship U.P.S. whenever possible. Delivery
charges are indicated below.
**2.** You will be notified of any delay of over 20 days
in shipping items.
**3.** Orders to APO and FPO addresses are shipped
via Parcel Post.
**4.** For orders to U.S. territories, please add $5.00
to the regular shipping charges. These orders
are shipped via Parcel Post. Some heavy or bulky
items may not qualify. Sorry, no foreign deliveries.
**5.** Items ordered together will not necessarily be
shipped together. Sorry, we cannot gift wrap.
**6.** Because of the fluctuating monetary situation,
some prices may be subject to change.
**7.** For Customer Service please call 1 (800)
237-5672. Monday-Friday, 9:00 am-4:30 pm C.S.T.

**Gift Certificates:**
If, after looking through this catalogue, you are
undecided about what to give someone, you
could give a Crate and Barrel Gift Certificate.
Gift Certificates are issued in any amount and
may be used for catalogue orders or in any of our
California, Florida, Georgia, Illinois, Indiana,
Maine, Massachusetts, Michigan, Minnesota,
Texas, and D.C. area stores. #9999.

**Phone Orders:**
For your convenience, you can shop by phone
24 hours a day. To place your order, simply call
Toll Free 1 (800) 323-5461. If the number is busy
call Toll Free 1 (800) 843-2334. Or if you prefer,
fax your order, 1 (708) 215-0482.

**FEDERAL EXPRESS** Most of our products can be received
within 2-3 business days from receipt
of your order via Federal Express for an additional
$5.00. Please call 1 (800) 451-8217 between
8:30 am-5:00 pm CST, Monday through Friday,
request Federal Express delivery and we will
confirm item availability. Heavy or bulky items
may not qualify.

**Customer Satisfaction Guarantee:**
We stand behind the quality of our products. If at
any time you are displeased with your purchase,
simply return it and we will refund, replace or
exchange it for you.

**Delivery Charges:**

| Total merchandise | Delivery charges |
|---|---|
| Up to $15.99 | $3.80 |
| $16.00-$30.99 | $4.80 |
| $31.00-$40.99 | $5.75 |
| $41.00-$50.99 | $6.90 |
| $51.00-$75.99 | $8.90 |
| $76.00-$100.99 | $10.75 |
| $101.00-$150.99 | $13.90 |
| $151.00-Above | 10% of merchandise |

Merchandise total

Sales tax total (see below)

Delivery total (see chart at left)

Add additional delivery cost:
Some heavy items require additional charges. These
are indicated in parentheses following the item price.

Grand total

**Sales Tax for Deliveries to:**
California 7¾%*, Florida 6%, Georgia 6%, Illinois 7½%, Indiana 5%, Maine 6%, Maryland 5%, Texas 7¾%,
Massachusetts 5%, Michigan 4%, Minnesota 6½%*, Virginia 4½%*. *Please include local taxes.

**FIGURE 8-1**

*Mail ordering is made*

*easy with a standardized*

*order form. (Courtesy of*

*Crate & Barrel)*

reliable way to measure whether the action was due to advertising or
chance. Was it a clever television commercial or a print advertisement
that prompted the customer's attention? In the case of direct advertising, the results of a campaign's success are measurable. Either with the
receipt of an order written on a mailing form or the use of a response
coupon, the advertiser can determine the advertisement's effectiveness.

# Types of Direct Advertising Pieces

Those who use direct advertising for reaching their customers and potential purchasers have a host of pieces from which they may choose. The choice might be as simple as a letter announcing a special incentive program or as complex as the video format that some in the fashion industry are using. The type selected is based on a number of factors, including the magnitude of the promotion, available funding, and the number of people the advertiser hopes to reach.

Sometimes the direct advertising approach that is hand-delivered or sent through the mail is coupled with another medium. A simple announcement card might be used by a manufacturer's representative who is planning a visit to his or her territory with a follow-up telephone call to try to arrange for an appointment with the buyer.

One of the most important aspects of the direct medium is the envelope or package that contains the advertisement. Some are straightforward and simply designed, while others employ a more intricate package or outside message that will capture the attention of the recipient. Considering the competition of direct advertising and the large number of pieces that might be received at the same time, the sender is more likely to have his or her message read if the envelope or package bears a motivational message. The retailer might use a "teaser" statement such as "It's Easy to Save 25 percent on Your Next Purchase." With the industry reporting that about 75 percent of the pieces are not read, the chances might improve if the recipient's attention is captured. Following are some of the direct advertising pieces used by the fashion industry.

## LETTERS

The simplest and least expensive direct advertising pieces available are letters. A letter may be used by the retailer to inform the charge customer of a special private sale that will not be announced to the general public, a special offer for a specific selling period, or any message that might benefit from the personalized letter format. Designers and manufacturers often communicate with buyers and merchandisers via the letter format to notify them of an upcoming season opening or special closeout promotion. Resident buying offices and other market consultants regularly use a letter to communicate promotions of interest, such as vendor promotional deals.

Depending on the message, the familiarity of the direct mail receiver with the company, and the complexity of the offer different approaches to letters might be used. When the targeted audience is made up exclusively of a manufacturer representative's steady customers, the approach might best be informal. The tone of a message that is being sent to a potential clientele list, on the other hand, might use a more formal approach.

In addition to style, the length of the piece should always be considered when it is being written. If should be long enough to include all of the elements necessary to pique interest but not too long that the reader will never have the time to finish reading it. Typically, letters are about two or three pages in length. Remember that the end-result of a successful letter campaign is sales! Often, letters are supplemented with brochures, order forms, or other types of direct mail pieces.

## BROCHURES

While the letter is generally used to deliver a more complete message, it is often the wrong tool to use. It is an informative device that concentrates on words to get a point across. Brochures, on the other hand, are generally four-color advertisements that might be one-page designs or extravagant foldouts called **broadsheets** that open up to pages that are sometimes larger than double-spread newspaper advertisements.

The Fashion Association is a trade organization that uses the broadsheet format as a direct mail piece to communicate with the industry. Its *Currents* newsletter features a foldout that includes photographs of various industry promotions and announcements of events of potential interest to its membership.

A fashion retailer might use a single-page brochure as a supplement to a charge customer's statement enclosure. It might advertise a particular manufacturer's item, in which case the cost of the piece might be supplied free of charge by the producer. Very often, hosiery, cosmetics, and fragrance promotions are handled in this manner.

Textile mills such as DuPont use a wide variety of brochures of every size to alert potential fabric purchasers of new materials in the marketplace, product care, new directions for the company, and so forth. Some are produced to motivate professional purchasers, while others are developed as informative pieces for the consumer.

Resident buying offices make significant use of brochures to directly advertise merchandise to their accounts. Henry Doneger Associates, the largest of these fashion consulting organizations, regularly uses brochures that feature trends for the upcoming season, style forecasts, introduction of new vendors, and hot item notices for immediate purchases.

## CATALOGS

While catalogs are used by the manufacturing segment of the industry to reach potential accounts, it is the retailer that makes the most significant use, by far, of this advertising piece. The catalogs are publications that range from the giant varieties used by such companies as Spiegel and J.C. Penney, in which a host of products are featured, to the more specialized, smaller types that exclusively merchandise one product segment such as apparel or home fashions

No matter of what magnitude the catalog is, the main feature of any one publication is the graphic presentation. The pictures must be attractively presented with a minimum amount of copy. Once the eye has focused on specific merchandise, details such as size and color availability and price are important to feature. Some catalogs, such as the one produced by Spiegel, include a page on size and measuring information to guide the purchaser when ordering and to reduce the number of returns due to improper fit.

Originally, the catalog was developed to reach those people who were not close enough to stores to do their shopping. With the great number of women working, the catalog has become the only way many can satisfy their shopping needs and take care of other responsibilities. Selling via the catalog is done by retailers that have traditional store outlets and by others that are simply mail order operations.

**DIVISIONS OF STORE ORGANIZATIONS.**   To supplement their in-store sales volume, most major retailers have entered the direct mail arena with catalog divisions. Generally, the catalog operations are separate and apart from the store's traditional operations and are managed by different staffs.

For many years, the use of the catalog was relegated to Christmastime, when retailers presented a publication to their customers that

**FIGURE 8-2**

*The department store uses the catalog to motivate buyers who cannot visit the store.*

*(Courtesy of Dayton's)*

featured a host of gift items. The most famous of these was—and still is—the *Neiman-Marcus Christmas Book.* Since its inception, it featured a variety of unique gifts for the affluent household and some of an extravagant nature such as the "his and her" selections that were among the priciest offered in any catalog. Neiman-Marcus, like other full-line and specialized department stores, expanded the mail order concept to extend far past the holiday season. Neiman's features Neiman-Marcus By Mail, which contains a host of apparel and accessories unavailable in their store units and *NM Edits,* fashion merchandise for the upcoming season. At that company and at many of the other majors, it is not unusual for as many as fifty different catalogs to be published.

In addition to the department stores, many chains also use the direct mail catalog. Some, such as Ann Taylor, feature an array of private label items that are carried in their stores as well as in the catalog and others

**FIGURE 8-3**

*Benetton used the direct mailer to invite at-home purchases. (Courtesy of O. Toscani for Benetton)*

choose to feature merchandise that is unavailable at their retail outlets. Using the latter approach, Victoria's Secret, the intimate apparel division of Limited, Inc., expands upon its store's lingerie format and offers a variety of apparel by mail in addition to its undergarments.

**CATALOG OPERATIONS.**   Companies such as Spiegel that sell primarily through catalog publications, except for unsold merchandise that is sold through a few clearance centers, have grown during the last decade. Unlike the Spiegel merchandise assortment, most in this classification resort to specialty offerings. Garnet Hill, for example, restricts its product line to goods made with natural fibers. Patagonia markets a complete line of winter-weight apparel for sports enthusiasts such as skiers, hikers, and those who merely want to dress the part of the winter athlete. If catalog planning is carefully approached, then it generally produces revenue for the company using it.

### VIDEO CATALOGS

The traditional print catalog has been joined by a contemporary direct mail partner, the video. In this age of electronics, some fashion companies are beginning to make use of the device as a means of advertising and selling its products to customers.

Price Breakers, an off-price fashion buying service, uses this format to reach its clientele. Four times a month, the company sends videos called *The Merchandise Network* that feature the highlights of numerous apparel and accessories collections of many vendors to clients. After viewing the video, the retailer is able to quickly get the feeling, in living color, of the merchandise that is currently available in the marketplace.

The advantages of the video catalog include the following:

- The merchandise presented in this format immediately gives the buyer a more accurate reading of style, material, fit, and so on, than it can in the traditional catalog.
- A voice-over may be used to describe important product features, delivery dates, prices, and terms.
- Production of the videos is relatively inexpensive.
- The finished product can be simply viewed because of the accessibility of VCRs.

At the present time, manufacturers and retailers are also beginning to investigate potential use of the electronic direct mail advertisements.

## Reaching the Appropriate Market

For any direct advertising pieces to bring positive results, they must, first and foremost, be delivered to the appropriate customers. If the recipients have neither a need for the products featured in the direct mail piece nor are sufficiently curious to explore their potential use, they will throw them away.

Direct mail is the only medium that requires the advertiser to seek his or her potential customer. The other print and broadcast media are targeted to a more general audience. To achieve a greater return on its direct mail advertising investment, the companies themselves must provide the appropriate lists.

## TYPES OF LISTS

The types of customer lists used are known as **house lists**, **compiled lists**, and **response lists**.They may be constructed by companies themselves or purchased or rented from list brokers who may recommend a variety of them.

**HOUSE LISTS.** One of the more important sources of names for future use in direct advertising comes from the company's own customers. Retailers, in particular, know the value of loyal customers in this highly competitive arena. Through the initial taking of names at the times of purchase or from the credit cards used for payment, a basic list of customers may be developed. The initial obtaining of the names is not enough to make a list complete and viable. The customers must be regularly approached via the mail with any number of different offers such as special sales "for customers only," private shopping periods, contests, free gift offerings, and so on. With each mailing, it is important to rid the list of people no longer considered excellent targets, such as those who have moved out of the trading area and to correct the addresses of those who have changed their households but are still considered potentially good customers. The latter adjustment may be made by asking the customer to indicate a change of address.

Manufacturers and designers also maintain lists of those companies who have purchased from them in the past. They might communicate via the mail with invitations to the new season's collections, end-of-season price promotions, upcoming representative visits to the client's territory, and so on. Regular retail accounts might have disbanded their businesses and no longer serve as potential purchasers. In such cases, the list should be regularly updated to remove their names. Companies may get the assistance of their credit departments in determining whether or not a store is still in business or from undelivered pieces of mail.

Market consulting organizations have their own mailing lists of businesses that pay for their services. They might expand their customer base with the use of the other types of lists that will be discussed later in this section.

**COMPILED LISTS.** When a company wishes to go beyond the confines of their house lists, which only offer information on their own customers, it often rents one from a direct mail list broker. These lists may come from someone who has his or her own in-house list that has individuals or companies with similar characteristics as those needed by the business wishing to expand its direct mail usage. The lists generally feature those with single, valuable characteristics such as recent motherhood, which would be appropriate for direct mail advertising for infant's wear, or people who subscribe to specific magazines, which could indicate preference for a particular type of product. Names of subscribers to fashion magazines, for example might be beneficial to direct mail fashion merchants such as Ann Taylor.

**RESPONSE LISTS.**   Another type of list that offers potential customer reaction is one that is developed from customer response. The names might come as a result of an advertisement that invites further inquiries on a company and its products. Lands' End, for example, in each of its print advertisements incorporates a coupon that invites readers to send for a free catalog. In this way, they acquire new names through the response system. Since the respondents have been motivated to respond in this manner, in all likelihood they are excellent candidates for inclusion on a list. These lists are not only those that come from your own compilation, they may also be rented from other advertisers.

## MERGING AND PURGING OF LISTS

When companies vigorously use direct mail solicitation, they often make use of more than one list. They might compile a great list of potential prospects through the three aforementioned techniques: in-house development and purchases of response and compiled lists. While this approach gives the greatest coverage of a market, it also may result in a major problem for the advertiser; that is, a name may appear more than one time, resulting in two or more mailings being sent to the same recipient. In addition to incurring additional, unnecessary costs to the sender, which for frequent users of direct mail could seriously hamper profits, the annoyance of receiving many of the same mailers could turn the prospective customer away from the company.

To avoid the perils and pitfalls of such duplication, computerized systems have been developed. By sending the various mailing lists to a merge/purge system, the duplication is eliminated, saving the user the expense of unneeded mailing pieces and costly postage.

# The Component Parts of a Direct Mail Program

For a direct advertising program to deliver the results for which it has been established, many different aspects of the project must be examined, developed, refined, and executed. In the case of hand-delivered pieces or those that are found on countertops for customers to take, the task is simpler than that of direct mail. While each involves planning and production of the pieces to be used, the delivery is simpler than that of direct mail. The following are some of the component parts of developing and executing the direct mail program, with some pertaining to the other types of direct advertising distribution.

## CHOSING THE ADVERTISING PIECE

As is the case with any of the advertising media, the format and message must be carefully developed. A number of different decisions will determine the choice of the piece to be transmitted to the potential customer.

Once the goals of the promotion have been established and the amount of dollars to be expended have been determined, the advertising piece is created. It might be a straightforward, simple card with a return portion that a fashion designer might use to announce the opening of a new collection and to invite potential clients to view it. In the case of a sales representative who is planning a visit to his or her territory to sell a line, the format might involve a letter and a response card with space indicating interest for an in-store preview of the merchandise. A fashion retailer wishing to offer a special incentive to its credit card customers could design a small brochure that would be used as part of a statement enclosure—one that is sufficiently lightweight so that additional postage will not be a necessity. A resident buying office wishing to offer a private label program to its customers might elect to use a broadsheet, complete with an order form, for customer use. Finally, the choice could be a substantial catalog that features a representation of a fashion retailer's merchandise mix.

## THE CONTENT OF THE ADVERTISEMENT

The elements of the advertisement may run the gamut from the sole use of a written message to one that provides full-color artwork.

**FIGURE 8-4**

*The photograph in this direct mail piece is the same as the one used on the company's magazine advertising. (Courtesy of Ruth Scharf Industries, A Division of Bryan Industries)*

The ultimate message and artwork used must be determined by the company's ultimate goals.

If the direct advertising piece is one that is part of a multimedia campaign, its content, quite often, reflects that of the other media used.

For example, it could be a duplicate of a magazine or newspaper advertisement or one that merely capitalizes on the headline and some of the artwork used. In direct advertisements that are meant to stand on their own, the only element that might be used regularly is a company style of type or its logo. This might serve as an element of recognition.

## STOCK CONSIDERATIONS

The choice of the appropriate paper or "stock," a term used in the industry, is of great importance. There are significant numbers to choose from, each providing a particular weight and appearance. Size and weight are extremely important in terms of delivery cost. Oversized pieces, as determined by the United Postal Service, require additional postage, perhaps increasing the budget past its limits.

In addition to the mailing cost, each stock type offers the user a different benefit and serves a different purpose. For a letter, **writing stock** comes in a variety of weights, finishes, and qualities. "Bond" is considered the best type and is used for the transmittal of important direct mail messages. Most of the paper used in direct advertising is known as **book stock**, which comes in a wide range of offerings. Included are antique-finished paper used for quality work; machine finish, a medium-quality choice; English finish, which provides a nonglare surface; and a coated variety that is often the one used for large catalogs. For the covers of booklets, a stronger quality is generally used that is called **cover stock**.

## PRODUCTION

Once the details of the proposed advertising piece have been determined, the actual production must be determined. The vast majority of companies use outside sources for their printing needs. In this case, a production company should be chosen that has the ability to handle the task in the time allocated by the advertiser. Once the company has been chosen, the completed work, including artwork and type selection, should be submitted. As is the case with any print media, proofs should be painstakingly checked for errors. Too often, a wrong price or caption could cause the downfall of the promotion.

It should be noted that more and more fashion retailers who rely heavily upon catalogs are using in-house production for their direct mail pieces. Fortunoff, for example, a specialized department store, operates its own department to print its catalogs. With the use of highly sophisticated software and scanners, they are able to accomplish their goals without the need to use outside sources. This saves the company money and enables them to produce last-minute mailings, often unattainable with an outside service.

## CHOOSING THE MAILING LIST

The earlier discussion on mailing lists described the different types of lists available to all of the segments of the fashion industry. Once the advertiser has made the decision to use the direct mail approach, the list or lists for each promotion must be selected.

While it seems that a house list is the best choice for a business to use, this is not always the case. If, for example, the goal is to target new customers, the house list will be inappropriate to use. Resident buying offices that try to elicit new accounts would be better served by using a list that could be rented from a broker. Retailers, attempting to capture a new credit card customer base, would also benefit from the rented list. If the intent, for either of these or other fashion companies, is to communicate or advertise with their own clientele, the house list would be the one to use.

One of the most important factors in the use of lists is its accuracy. While the merge/purge operation removes duplicate names, it does not necessarily remove the names of individuals or companies no longer at the indicated addresses. The services of a list broker usually include cleaning up the mailing list. Without constant attention to a list's refinement, it could unnecessarily increase the overall cost of the mailing. When new business is the goal, lists may be purchased at extremely affordable prices. For the fashion organization, the costs are approximately thirty-five dollars per one-thousand names.

Sometimes, when an entire geographical area is being targeted by a company, such as in the case of a new store opening, a full mailing is sent to everyone in a particular ZIP code. Instead of being selective in terms of which families are reached, the mail will be labeled "occupant." Often, this approach, while saturating an entire market, will result in the piece being thrown away without ever being opened. Each situation requires careful analysis before the final list is chosen.

### TIMING THE MAILING

Care must be exercised to make certain that the mailing will reach the desired market at the appropriate time. If third-class mail is used, the piece might not be delivered on time to maximize the promotion's effectiveness. There are always complaints from direct mail users that a percentage of third-class mailings never reach their destinations.

In terms of the specific direct mail promotion, it is imperative that the piece arrive at the most beneficial time to maximize sales. If a fashion retailer's Christmas catalog arrives days after that of its competitors, it might be too late for an order. Advice from the professionals is a must when determining the best timing of the mailing.

### THE MAILING

The actual mailing of the direct mail pieces is generally handled by a professional mailing house, sometimes referred to as a "letter house." In small companies, the procedure could be handled in-house. For the independent retailer wishing to send out a letter inviting "special customers" to take advantage of a private sale or a moderately sized manufacturing company to announce "price considerations" for its 150 accounts for a short time period, the internal staff could handle the mailing. However, when the mailing is of significantly large proportions, the use of a mailing house is a must.

With the use of computerized systems, these companies fold the pieces for mailing, automatically address the envelopes or packages, seal the contents, and perform any other activities to complete the task before delivering the package to the post office.

## Limitations of Direct Mail

As is the case with the other media, direct mail also has its limitations. There is, however, a continued increase in the responses it brings to at least one segment of the fashion industry. With the enormous increase in the number of women in the work force, it is the only way in which many may avail themselves of merchandise.

Bearing this advantage in mind, however, some fashion industry segments believe it has some disadvantages. Among those most regularly offered are:

- There is not anything that will draw attention to it such as the editorials or features of a newspaper, magazine, or television program. The package must be carefully designed to motivate its opening.
- Some people are turned off by the bulk of the direct mailings and often disregard them without reading them.
- The increase in the number of pieces received increases the competition for the recipient's attention.
- The costs continue to spiral with the improved quality of the offerings and the increase in the postal rates.

## REVIEW QUESTIONS

1. Why has the mail order business become an important method of increasing sales for the retailer when there are so many stores within easy reach?

2. In what way, in addition to direct mail, is direct advertising marketed to consumers?

3. What is meant by "undivided reader attention" as an advantage for direct mail advertising?

4. How does the sender of direct mail pieces reduce the amount spent on the actual mailing costs?

5. In what way can the direct mail advertiser measure its effectiveness?

6. What is the simplest and least expensive type of direct advertising piece?

7. Define the term *broadsheet*.

8. How does a company like Victoria's Secret expand its business via the catalog route?

9. Define the term *video catalog*. What advantage does it serve the company using it?

10. In what way may a fashion retailer develop a house list?

11. How does a compiled list differ from a house list?

12. What is meant by the term *response list?*

13. Describe the operation of merging and purging lists.

14. In what way may a direct mail piece be used in conjunction with a magazine advertisement?

15. Define the term *stock* as it applies to direct mail.

16. What is considered to be the best type of writing stock?

17. In what way does cover stock differ from writing stock?

18. Explain what is meant by cleaning up a mailing list.

19. What purpose does a list broker serve?

20. Are there any limitations of direct mail advertising? If so, what are they?

## EXERCISES

1. Write to a major fashion retailer to obtain a sampling of the different types of catalogs used by the company. When they are received, examine each and prepare a brief oral report about the different purposes served by each one.

2. Many direct mail pieces are part of an overall advertising campaign. Prepare a visual presentation for the class that features such a campaign. The following pieces should be used in the presentation:

- The direct mail piece sent to the home, such as a catalog, brochure, pamphlet, and so on
- Newspaper advertisements that feature the same merchandise or promotion
- Photographs of window and interior store displays that use the same items as the newspaper advertisements and direct mail pieces

3. Write to a resident buying office to obtain copies of direct mail pieces that they send to their clients. The task may be accomplished easily if the office is told that this is a class project! Mount each piece on foamboard and describe the role it plays for the resident office.

*Billboards*

*impact*

*downtown*

*pedestrian*

*traffic.*

# *Outdoor and Transit Advertising*

........................................................................................................................................

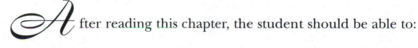

*A*fter reading this chapter, the student should be able to:

1. Describe the various formats used in both outdoor and transit locations by the segments of the fashion industry.

2. Discuss the locations where the "out-of-the-home" advertisements are placed.

3. Explain the advantages and disadvantages of the medium for fashion advertisers.

4. Discuss the role played by the federal government in controlling the use of billboard advertising.

5. List and explain the various components of an outdoor campaign.

........................................................................................................................................

# Introduction

Outdoor advertising is the oldest advertising medium. It evolved from ancient carvings in stone, bronze, and wood. In the Egyptian civilizations, which date back more than 5,000 years, the messages, or hieroglyphics, were used to direct travelers to places they were seeking. About 2,500 years later, the Egyptian merchants used stone to etch messages about their wares.

Many years later, when paper was first developed and printing presses were built, the outdoor poster became prominent. By the fifteenth century, the billboard was an accepted means of advertising in European countries. Four hundred years later the billboard became a medium that was transformed into one that featured artistic designs. Artists of significant renown tried their hands at the outdoor medium and the likes of Daumier, Manet, and Toulouse-Lautrec created masterpieces of poster artwork.

In America in the late nineteenth century, many companies began to lease wooden boards to post their advertising messages, or "bills" as they were called; hence the name billboard was born. From that time on, commercial enterprises have recognized the worth of the outdoor advertisements and have since used the medium to display their messages.

Today, a walk on the street, a drive through both suburban and downtown areas, standing on corners or in train depots, waiting for public transportation to arrive invariably attracts us to a variety of outdoor advertisements. High above the buildings of major cities, Donna Karan uses billboards to promote her DKNY collection and Giorgio Armani uses them to alert observers to his less expensive A/X designs. At bus stops, Liz Claiborne and The Gap are calling attention to their product lines and Galeries Lafayette, the American branch of the French fashion landmark, is calling our attention to their presence in this country. Even the shopping bag, initially considered to be a functional, disposable carrying device in which fashion retailers packed customer purchases, has become an important force in outdoor advertising.

Although it appears that from every indication outdoor advertising is a growing medium for fashion businesses, its use has somewhat been hurt by environmentalists and public interest groups. The particular target has been the billboard, which some say causes a blight on our highways and others indicate that their use sometimes results

**FIGURE 9-1**

*High above the*

*city billboards*

*attract attention.*

in automobile accidents when motorists glance at them and take their eyes off the road. No matter what the opponents say, those who create the various forms of outdoor and transit advertisements are constantly bringing fresh and innovative ideas to their development and are finding that more and more fashion industry segments are including them in their plans.

# Out-of-Home Formats

## BILLBOARDS

The billboard, in one form or another, is the major classification of outdoor advertising formats. It includes the traditional large-sized paper production known as a 30-sheet poster, a variation of the large size known as a bleed; its smaller counterpart, the 8-sheet poster; and the painted bulletin.

### THIRTY-SHEET POSTERS.

The standard bearer for the industry for many years has been the 30-sheet poster. It fits on the standardized panel that is used throughout the industry and provides the advertiser with printed copy that measures $9'7'' \times 21'7''$. The space between the poster's design and the panel to which it is affixed is covered with "blanking paper," which provides a border. They are generally produced by the means of silk screening or lithography, two techniques that enable the creator to use a wide range of designs and colors.

The posters are prepasted and installed in sections on billboards. They are found on primary and secondary arteries to attract motorist attention and on building tops in downtown areas where pedestrians can see them.

Their placement is done on a contract basis, with a thirty-day period being typical for a poster. Advertisers who make significant use of this format sometimes contract for space for periods up to one year. For these long-term arrangements, discounts are generally available to the users.

The life of the 30-sheet poster is generally one month, with changes made at those intervals with new entries. The fact that their production is relatively simple and their placement equally uncomplicated makes the thirty-day change a minor task.

### BLEEDS.

Also produced to fit the same panel frame as the 30-sheet poster is the **bleed**. The term signifies that there is no border around the printed matter, with all of the copy and design reaching right up to the edge of the paper. Bleeds measure $10'5'' \times 22'8''$, which provides the user a little more space for the message as well as a more artistic presentation. Bleeds are printed directly on white blanking paper, the same material that is used as a border with traditional 30-sheet posters. In terms of placement, contractual arrangements, and message life, they are the same for bleeds as for the 30-sheet variety.

**FIGURE 9-2**

*Posters are prepasted and fit standardized panels.*

**EIGHT-SHEETS.**  With measurements of 6′ × 12′, 8-sheets or junior panels as they are referred to by the industry, are primarily used in urban areas on city streets. As is the case with the larger variety of outdoor advertisements, they usually are changed every thirty days. Production techniques are also the same as the larger variety.

**PAINTED BULLETINS.**  The largest of the traditional outdoor advertisements is the painted bulletin. Typically, it measures 14′ × 48′, giving the advertiser 672 square feet of space in which to present a message.

There are two types of painted advertisements, the **rotary** and the **permanent bulletin**. The former may be dismantled for replacement at different locations. The rotational periods generally range from sixty to ninety days. By using this format, the advertiser is able to communicate the message in a variety of locations within the desired trading area. During the typical one-year life of a painted message, it can be seen by the vast majority of those to whom it would have appeal. The latter, the permanent bulletin, remains in one location. It is usually one that is heavily traveled and has the potential to reach a large number of people in the marketplace.

The painted bulletin is generally purchased on a one-unit basis, unlike the aforementioned posters, which are produced in quantities. The designs range from the traditional to three-dimensional entries, many with movable parts. Many are even extended past the regular size limits by adding top, bottom, and side extensions. The extensions used vary from design to design and must conform to the regulations established for the areas in which they will be displayed.

The painted bulletins may be produced in a number of ways. Included are those that are accomplished through means of computer technology, printed by silkscreening or lithography processes, hand-painted indoors, or on location.

## EXTERIOR TRANSIT PANELS

More and more fashion advertisers are embracing the sides of buses to advertise their names, product lines, and institutional messages. Advertisements from companies like Calvin Klein, Benetton, and John Weitz are regularly seen on buses in many major urban centers.

The panels used are similar to the traditional billboards in terms of production and contracting for the space they occupy. One major difference is that because the message is moving, it must be carefully designed to quickly capture the attention of the passersby. This is accomplished with the use of color, limited copy that can be rapidly understood, and simple design.

## CAR CARDS

Advertisements that are mounted on panels inside of buses and subway cars are called **car cards**. The typical types line the spaces over the car's windows and are usually eleven inches high and up to forty-eight inches wide. At the front and back sections of the public transportation

**FIGURE 9-3**

*Exterior transit*

*panels attract*

*pedestrian attention.*

vehicles, there are areas for advertising with varying sizes, depending upon the holders or frames that have been installed.

Where the message on the outside of a bus must be conveyed in a matter of seconds because the vehicle is moving away from the observer, the interior transit advertisement may be studied for as long as the passenger is en route to his or her destination. The riders often spend as much as forty minutes of traveling time, some of which is spent reading the car card advertisements. While there is some competition from newspapers and magazines that are being read by commuters, generally there is a period when the transit advertisements are examined. In times when the vehicles are overcrowded and the reading of newspapers and magazines is difficult, the interior advertisement becomes even more important. With this extended viewing time, the messages may be more extensive and complex.

Car cards are sold for subway use in designations called **runs**. A full-run gives the advertiser one card in each subway car; a half-run, in every other car; a double-run, two in a car; and so on.

## BACKLIT TRANSPARENCIES

What started out as signage that was used exclusively in fashion retail interiors has spread to the outdoors. Walking through some of America's fragrance and cosmetics departments in high-fashion emporiums, the shopper is quickly drawn to a new classification of signage, the backlit transparency. Companies such as Chanel, Clinique, and others place these eye-catching signs in stores such as Marshall Field, Bloomingdale's, and Macy's. They are attractive, life-like, spirited, and different from the traditional point-of-purchase advertisements that are regularly used.

Basically, a "light box" fixture is used to display color transparencies that can easily be changed to coincide with a particular promotion. The dramatic effect is achieved by using "lighting from within," instead of the conventional overhead spotlights.

Borrowing from this initial in-store use, fashion designers such as Liz Claiborne use the backlit transparency at places where shoppers are apt to stand or pass by. At the sides of bus shelters, where waiting time is often as much as twenty minutes and on busy city street corners, these advertisements are attracting customer attention. One major advantage of this type of outdoor advertisement is its illumination feature. No matter what the time of day, the public is shown whatever the fashion company wants to promote.

## BUS TAILS

In addition to the sides of buses that feature advertisements, the backs of buses are also being used for the same purpose. While the side of the bus is meant to attract the attention of the pedestrian, the back

**FIGURE 9-4**

*The backlit*

*transparency allows*

*for 24-hour viewing.*

portion is directed at automobile drivers and passengers. Since a car very often follows a bus for a few blocks and is sometimes delayed in traffic behind the vehicle, it provides yet another opportunity to feature a company advertisement. Since advertisements of this nature are observed for longer periods than those on the bus sides, the messages they bear could be more complex. Generally, they feature illustrations as well as descriptive copy.

## SHOPPING BAGS

One of the more cost-effective methods of advertising outdoors is with the use of shopping bags. Initially a functional device that was designed to carry several purchases from a store, today's versions far exceed the utilitarian purpose.

When a customer exits the store carrying a shopping bag, it has the potential to be seen by a host of people walking in the street or riding on public transportation. Whether it is merely the store's name or logo that is featured on the bag or a special retail promotion along with the store's name, they are considered to be "walking" advertisements. Stores like Bloomingdale's and Macy's often incorporate shopping bags into their multimedia advertising campaigns. Whenever Bloomingdale's presents a storewide celebration such as a salute to a particular country's

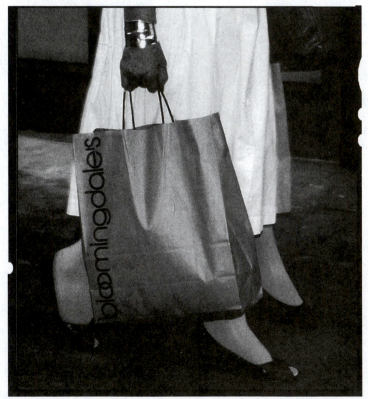

**FIGURE 9-5**

*The shopping*

*bag is a mobile*

*advertisement.*

merchandise, the shopping bag is designed to enhance the promotion. Each year when Macy's plans its Thanksgiving Day Parade, it makes certain to create a shopping bag that features the event.

A distinct advantage of today's shopping bag is that more and more people collect them and use them over and over again, and not only to transfer their purchase from the store to the home. In this way, whether it is being used to carry towels to the beach or refreshments to a picnic, for example, the store will gain additional advertising exposure.

## Advantages and Disadvantages of Outdoor Advertising

Like each of the other media discussed, outdoor and transit advertising offer the user advantages as well as some limitations. Each must be carefully considered to make certain that the pluses outweigh the minuses for the company's promotional program.

### ADVANTAGES OF OUTDOOR AND TRANSIT ADVERTISING

On the positive side, there are a number of factors that make this form of advertising exceptional for some of fashion industry's segments. They range from cost-efficiency to continuity of viewing.

**COST-EFFICIENCY.**   In the case of cost-efficiency, outdoor advertising is an excellent value. In fact, in comparison to television usage it costs seven times less and in comparison to the newspaper it is three times less expensive!

The following chart shows comparisons per thousand for outdoor, 30-sheet advertisements, and radio, magazines, television, and newspapers. The figures were supplied by the various associations that represent their specific medium. They are the Outdoor Advertising Association of America, Radio Advertising Bureau, Television Bureau of Advertising, American Newspaper Association, and The Magazine Publishers of America.

**CONTINUITY.**   Unlike television, where the message lasts but for a few seconds and is lost to the viewer if he or she leaves the room or changes the channel, the outdoor poster or panel is always there to be observed. It cannot be turned off as in the case of the radio, or discarded unopened as in the case of a direct mail piece. It is only with the outdoor variety, be it during the day or at night with proper illumination, that the medium is a twenty-four-hour salesperson.

**REACH.**   When a shopping mall wishes to reach its consumer market, the placement of outdoor advertisements in key areas such as at bus depots near the shopping center or at parking garage entrances that are also in close proximity to the facility, the outdoor advertisement  is destined to bring favorable results. The size of the larger panels and their creative designs and color usage are more than likely to improve the reach factor.

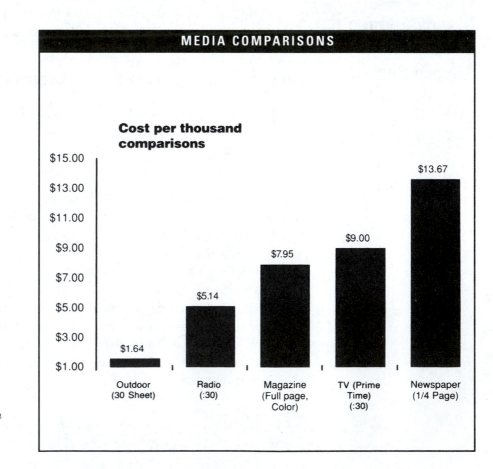

**FIGURE 9-6**

*Media comparisons in*

*cost per thousand*

**MINIMAL COMPETITION FROM OTHER ADVERTISEMENTS.**
The pages of any major newspaper are replete with scores of advertisements. Readers are given a host of choices on which to focus their attention. It might be a particular column, the editorial, the comics, horoscopes, or the multitude of advertisements that fill the pages. With the life of the paper so short, it is unlikely that every advertiser's message will be seen, let alone examined. The competition for the reader's attention is also keen in fashion magazines. However, with the longer life expectancy of the magazine, the problem is not as serious.

By comparison, much of the outdoor advertisements can be placed without the problem of competition from other advertisements. On the rear of a bus or on its sides, there is room for only one message. At bus shelters or telephone kiosks, the advertisement is for one product. Even when the large 30-sheet poster is the format, they are often placed so far from each other that exclusivity of viewing is the benefit. While some car cards in subway cars and some 8-sheet posters that line a railroad platform have some competition, the time spent in these locations gives the viewer ample time to study the advertisements, making the competitive factor less important.

## DISADVANTAGES OF OUTDOOR AND TRANSIT ADVERTISING

Included among the disadvantages or limitations afforded by the medium are those that range from restrictions on placement to the inability to actually pinpoint a targeted market.

**PLACEMENT RESTRICTIONS.**   When the Highway Beautification Act was passed in 1965, it adversely affected the use of billboards. Specifically, it imposed regulations that controlled the use of outdoor advertising along Federal-Aid Primary and Interstate highway systems. Billboards were then relegated to specific commercial and industrial zones. Thus, the retailer wishing to notify motorists in advance of their reaching the exit in which his or her store is located, may not do so if the zone does not fit the specifications of the bill.

**MARKET SELECTIVITY.**   While certain publications have targeted markets pinpointed, outdoor advertisements do not. *Brides*

*Magazine* is aimed at the bethrothed female, *The New York Times* at the more affluent segment of the population it serves, and *Gentlemen's Quarterly,* the fashion-minded, contemporary male. The best that an outdoor advertisement can hope to focus on, in terms of selectivity, is a wider audience that might include people who will be the advertiser's potential customers. The posters in airport terminals, for example, only guarantee that travelers will see the advertisements and not a specific segment of that market with regard to income and lifestyle. Placement of "aerial advertisements" on downtown rooftops appeal to everyone looking up and not a particular group, as might a specific television show or fashion publication.

**ESCALATING PRODUCTION AND RENTAL COSTS.**   Although, as previously discussed, the cost-efficiency for outdoor advertising is exceptional, the real costs, in terms of production and space, are constantly escalating. The magnitude and complexity of some of the painted billboards cost dearly for each installation. Realtors also capitalize on the best locations for the signage and continue to increase the costs of rental space, especially where there is a great deal of interest in but a few spots. All things considered, however, outdoor and transit advertising is still a bargain!

## Components of an Outdoor Campaign

If the use of an outdoor advertising promotion is to be successful, attention must be paid to specific details, which begin with the selection of the targeted audience for the product and conclude with the selection of the sites for the advertisement's placement.

### AUDIENCE SELECTION AND MEASUREMENT

Before any company decides to use some form of out-of-the-home advertising, it must determine which market it is trying to address and where to place the billboards and posters in its campaign. Among the organizations that provide this information is Harris-Donovan

Systems, a company that assesses audience delivery by key demographics for over 550 markets in the United States; MISA, a business that obtains audience demographic information by tracking license plate registrations to ZIP codes and relating them to the census information available for those areas; and Simmons Market Research Bureau, analysts for determining target markets.

## SELECTION OF AN OUTDOOR ADVERTISING COMPANY

Once it has been determined that there is an audience for the product and outdoor or transit advertising will be beneficial to position the company's products, an outdoor company representative should be contacted for information pertaining to planning the campaign and the industry's purchasing process.

One of the better ways in which to choose a company for the promotion is by examining all of the award-winning advertisements that were honored with Obies. Each year, the Outdoor Advertising Association of America publishes a book that shows the winning advertisements, by category, and lists the names of the agency, artists, and copywriters responsible for their creations.

Traditional retailers, for example, might find the appropriate company to contact that was listed in the "Retail-Traditional" category, while fashion discounters and off-pricers might be best served by those in the "Retail-Nontraditional" classification. High-fashion designers would benefit by paying attention to the agencies that were singled out for their advertisements in the "Clothing & Accessories/Manufacturer-Nontraditional" class. The right investigation will more than likely bring the advertiser together with the most appropriate agency.

## PRODUCTION CONSIDERATIONS

In addition to choosing the right agency, consideration must be given to the choice of billboards or other advertising formats and the time it takes for them to be completed and installed. The simplest method, such as the silkscreened poster, requires from one to two weeks of production time, with lithographic reproduction taking about three to four weeks. Once the works have been completed, they should be delivered to the outdoor company for installation about ten days before the time of posting. When a painted bulletin is the choice, the artwork from which the final project will be copied should be delivered to the outdoor company about a month or two prior to the contract date. Painted bulletins that have extensions or intricate three-dimensional characteristics often require additional time for completion. The specifics of the production processes will be explored in Chapter 11.

## SITE SELECTION

Along with the other considerations, attention must be paid to the locations in which the advertisements will be placed. Before the age of the computer, on-site inspection was considered the best approach to take to make certain that the chosen locations were suitable to maximize exposure. Today, the outdoor industry utilizes the computer for advertisers and agencies to inspect various locations directly from their premises. Not only does this save time for the advertisers, but it also cuts the costs of in-person observation.

## Purchasing Considerations for Outdoor Posters

As has been discussed with the other advertising media, the purchase of print space as in the case of newspapers and magazines and air time for television and radio involves different concepts and considerations. The poster, the largest of the outdoor and transit advertisement, is purchased on the basis of showings or gross rating points (GRPs), as are some of the other media. The showings are purchased in designations that range from twenty-five to 100 and increases at intervals of twenty-five. The GRP rating system measures daily audience exposure of the advertiser's posters. A fifty  GRP showing, for example, will generate duplicated exposure opportunities equal to 50 percent of the market population on a daily basis. On a monthly basis, the fifty GRP showing will reach more than three out of every four adults in a market. According to the research of the Outdoor Advertising Association of America, no other medium offers that coverage! Once the size of the showing has been determined, it is necessary to arrange for the poster's placement. Unlike placement in both the broadcast and print media which is relatively simple, the process of outdoor placement is complicated because each posting is considered to be a separate advertisement. Thus, advertisers and agencies have long found themselves dealing with a host of different companies to place each advertisement.

The industry ultimately developed **outdoor networks,** which overcame the problems associated with placement. Among the services they provide the advertisers are the analysis of space availability, cost of the specific site, reservation of the spaces, and preparation of the contracts for the entire placement. Some of the networks also provide information on production costs and handle delivery of the posters to the installing companies.

## The Future of Fashion Advertisements

Not long ago, the major fashion advertisers spent little money on out-of-the-home advertisements. The fashion designers chose magazines such as *Harper's Bazaar, Elle, Vogue, Mirabella*, and others to get their messages across to the readers. Retailers with a fashion orientation relied most heavily upon the newspaper, direct mail, and some magazine exposure for their promotions. Fashion designers and retailers also subscribed to television usage to round out their campaigns.

Billboards were generally used by hotels, restaurants, beverage companies, automobile producers, and others with an occasional investment by the fashion industry. Today, the picture has radically changed. While it is still not the major medium for fashion, posters of every format and size are regularly being used by the likes of DKNY, Bijan, Daffy's, Levi's, Jordan Marsh, Bugle Boy, Calvin Klein, The Gap, Nike, and Liz Claiborne in airline terminals, rail platforms, transit exteriors, telephone kiosks, on rooftops, in shopping malls, bus shelters, and other places where pedestrians and motorists regularly pass. From the obvious creativity of the billboards used and the recognition the fashion users have received via the multitude of Obie Awards, it seems the medium is one that has captured the attention of the fashion industry.

## REVIEW QUESTIONS

1. What was the manner in which the ancient Egyptian civilizations first expressed themselves with outdoor messages?

2. What is the major classification for outdoor advertising formats?

3. Describe the measurements of the 30-sheet poster.

4. Discuss the purpose served with blanking paper for traditional 30-sheet posters.

5. How does a bleed differ from the typical 30-sheet poster?

6. Define the term *8-sheet poster*. What are its measurements?

7. In what way does the rotary painted bulletin give the advertiser more flexibility than the permanent type?

8. Where are exterior transit panels used?

9. In what designation are car cards purchased?

10. Describe the function of the backlit transparency.

11. Why is the shopping bag considered to be a functional as well as a promotional outdoor advertisement?

12. Discuss the cost-efficiency of outdoor advertising versus television usage.

13. Define the term *continuity* as it refers to outdoor advertisements.

14. In what way has the billboard's placement been somewhat curtailed?

15. How do outdoor advertisers measure potential audiences and select those most appropriate for their campaigns?

16. How long does it take for the standard silkscreened poster to be completed?

17. On what basis are outdoor advertisements purchased?

18. What is an outdoor network? What services does it supply?

**EXERCISES**

1. Select a major site where potential consumers congregate or pass to assess the different types of outdoor and transit advertisements they might see. Each poster, bulletin, and so on, of a fashion orientation, should be photographed and mounted on foamboard to show to the class. An oral presentation discussing the types of formats used in each example should be delivered to the class.

2. Visit a fashion retailer in your community to study the image of the operation and the merchandise it sells. Using photographs, sketches, or information you have gathered from the store, create a poster that would best represent the company to their targeted clientele. Press-on letters and photographs from magazines are excellent tools to use for the creation. For those with artistic ability, original sketches might serve as some of the components of the advertisement.

# Creating Fashion Advertisements

SECTION 4

Photo P.Biasion Art.Moschino Sironi GHN

USA Agent: MODA & COMPANY - 745 Fifth Ave. - Suite 604
NEW YORK 10151

**LET'S GIVE
A HOME TO
IMMUNE DEFICIENT
CHILDREN !**

**MOSCHINO & ANLAIDS**
SMILE !

Children with immunodeficiency diseases,
including HIV positive children,
need special attention.
In Italy, project "SMILE !" is gathering
the necessary funds to establish
a vacation home where sick children will
be provided with the necessary care.

For further information 212  2233223

# MOSCHINO

# The Copy, Illustrations, and Layout

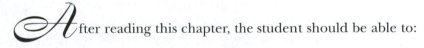

*A*fter reading this chapter, the student should be able to:

1. List and explain the various elements of an advertisement's structure.

2. Describe the different types of message approaches used to capture the intended market segment.

3. Discuss the various types of visual illustrations that are used to enhance the copy.

4. Understand the basic principles of design that are imperative to creating an appropriate layout.

5. Design a layout for a fashion print advertisement.

## Introduction

Walking through the pages of a fashion magazine immediately reveals a host of advertisements that use different approaches to capture the reader's attention. Some, such as Calvin Klein's Obsession advertisements, focus on sexuality and use photographs to set the mood; others, like Lands' End, find the informative format, primarily copy-driven, best suits their needs; and still others rely upon a consciousness-raising direction, like Moschino Jeans, that combines eye-appealing artwork and informative copy to grasp the eye of the reader.

With the wealth of fashion advertising that is being produced today, the competition becomes keener among the industry's users. Not only does magazine utilization continue in the world of fashion, so does the use of newspapers, direct mail, radio, and television. The creative teams are challenged to make the best use of the desired medium and generate sufficient sights and/or sounds that will make the viewer come one step closer to making a purchase.

Creative teams, either the in-house variety that fashions their own company advertisements or the advertising agencies that work for a host of different accounts, have the responsibity to produce an advertisement. At their head is a copywriter who provides the message and an art director who interfaces the words with artwork. The goal is to produce a layout or physical arrangement in which these basic elements enhance each other's presence. In some instances, a photograph without any message except for the company's name, or copy without any visual illustration, is an approach used. Radio, for example, by its very nature, solely relies upon the message to carry the advertisement. Utilizing all of the information that has been provided by the client, the creative team now must produce something that will result in a positive impact.

## The Advertising Team

Once the information has been supplied by the advertiser to the team that is responsible for the advertisement's creation, the tasks involved in the transformation of the facts into a viable promotional piece are assigned. The three major contributors to the process are the copywriter, art director, and layout artist.

## THE COPYWRITER

In the majority of fashion advertising, be it print or broadcast, the genesis of the advertisement rests with information that must be conveyed to the viewer of the advertisement. The producer of the words, or the copywriter, receives the facts about the product, services, or people that are to be featured in the text and develops a story that will motivate the reader to examine the advertisement.

The writer generally engages in a number of sessions with the art director so that the two can brainstorm and discover which approach might best suit the needs of the advertiser. There is no rule as to who starts the ball rolling.

## THE ART DIRECTOR

Whether it is a photograph, drawing, or some other visual device, it is the art director who has the responsibility for its selection and use. The fashion industry, in particular, uses distinctive artwork that hopefully will identify with the advertiser. It might be a particular artist's rendering ability that will capture the essence of the illustration or some imaginative photography that lends excitement to the piece. In situations where the art director is challenged with a modest campaign or series of advertisements, or an ongoing promotion, the nature of the artwork is often carried throughout the project. This continuity often results in faster recognition of the advertisement by the targeted market.

## THE LAYOUT ARTIST

The task of the layout artist is the ultimate placement or positioning of the work provided by the copywriter and art director. He or she prepares a rough layout encompassing all of the components of the advertisement such as the headline, subheadline, message, illustrations, and so forth. If changes have been suggested by a store buyer, designer, account executive for an advertising agency, or anyone with the right to suggest alterations, the rough presentation is transformed into a finished layout that is ready for production.

# The Elements of an Advertisement's Structure

Whether it is a print advertisement or broadcast commercial, there are specific elements that constitute the finished product. Within each of these general categories, the manner in which the specific elements are used is dictated by the specificity of the print or broadcast product. For example, magazine and newspaper fashion advertisements, while both are print oriented, differ because of the nature of the publications.

## MAGAZINES AND NEWSPAPERS

As mentioned earlier in the chapter, the typical print advertisement utilizes both copy and artwork in an eye-appealing format.

**COPY.**   The written portion of the text is often divided into four parts: the headline, subheadline, message or story, and the action to be taken to avail oneself of the offer. In some cases, it is not necessary to utilize all of these elements, but to chose only those that warrant inclusion. For example, a famous designer's advertisement might focus only on his or her unusual creation; in this case, it is not necessary to offer copy as an inducement to seek the product. The mention of the designer's name and perhaps a logo might suffice in the place of typical copy. The words in each of these copy components, when used, are designed to benefit the advertiser in a unique way.

*The Headline.*   The most important part of an advertisement is the headline. It is the attention-getting device that usually makes the reader stop and determine whether or not further interest is necessary. If interest is not generated with the headline, it is more than likely that the remainder of the pieces will not be seen.

There is no specific direction or foolproof formula that goes into the creation of a good headline, be it one with a fashion orientation or not. There are, however, some essential ingredients that make some better than others. When examining them, the following points should be considered:

1. Simplicity is the key. Unless an unusual situation, the number of words should be restricted to ten.

2. A good headline should make its appeal to a potential market of users, with the feature of a benefit to the ultimate purchaser, a

**FIGURE 10-1**

*The positioning of the headline and its content motivates the observer to view the entire advertisement. (Courtesy of Lee Apparel Company)*

specific label, such as a designer name, or something that will motivate further examination.

3. Generalities should be avoided, with the emphasis on attracting a particular audience.

4. There should be enough information in the headline to give an idea of what will be gained from further reading.

5. The size of the type used should be sufficiently large to attract attention.

There are many different types of headlines that the fashion industry uses for magazines and newspapers. They include those that offer a benefit, provoke curiosity, select particular readers, focus on a particular label or style, announce a claim, or announce the need for immediate attention.

The following headlines exemplify each of the types suggested:

- Rockport Is All About Ease (Rockport Shoes)—offers the benefit of comfort.

- Bring Your Own Attitude (Ellen Tracy Company)—provokes the reader's curiosity in terms of fashion individuality.

- Confessions Of A Shoe Addict (Nicole Shoes)—selects the particular customer who always seems to need another pair of shoes.

- Introducing Ralph Lauren Madras...The Classic Fabric Of The American Summer (Ralph Lauren)—focuses on both a famous label and fabric style.

- Now Your Skin Doesn't Have To Act Its Age (Revlon)—announces a claim.

- Last 4 Days...Renovation Sale...30% To 60% Off (Tourneau Corner)—calls for immediate action.

*The Subheadline.* If the headline, by virtue of its size and attention-getting message, does not seem to provide sufficient interest to motivate further inspection, a subheadline, which utilizes smaller print, can do the job. It is often longer than the headline, with the intention of further defining it.

The following example of a headline and subheadline in a fashion advertisement shows the relationship between the two.

- AMARIGE (Headline)—The name alone is used as the headline since its label is a well-known fragrance. It is displayed in bold, upper-case type.

- A celebration of laughter...love...and intense happiness (Subheadline)—The copy is significantly longer to explain the benefit or appeal, and the size of the type is considerably smaller.

*Slogans.* Fashion advertisers sometimes develop slogans that are used over and over again in their advertisements. Their use is intended to increase memorability of the company or product.

**FIGURE 10-2**

*The slogan, regularly used in conjunction with the store's name, hopes to achieve memorability. (Courtesy of Bloomingdale's)*

Although each advertisement may have its own emphasis, it is the slogan that is the connecting device.

Some slogans that have helped to increase recognition for fashion advertisers include:

"It's Like No Other Store In The World." (Bloomingdale's)

"What Becomes A Legend Most?" (Blackglama)

"It's Between Me And My Calvins." (Calvin Klein Jeans)

"Does She, or Doesn't She? (Clairol)

A slogan is difficult to create, but those that have been on target have helped generate considerable value for the advertiser.

*The Body Copy.*   With the headline and sometimes the subheadline now in place, the remainder of the copy is written into the body of the advertisement. These words are used to amplify the message. The scope and depth of the rest of the words depends upon the nature of the advertisement. In fashion print advertisements, a great deal of emphasis is placed on the artwork, often leaving full-blown amplification of the headline unnecessary.

When the body copy warrants written emphasis, it usually concentrates on selling points or features, reassurances to the potential purchaser of the advertised products, proof that any claims that are made will be delivered, and slogans or logos that give immediate recognition to the advertiser's product or name.

The Tourneau headline, which was examined earlier in the chapter, sparks interest with the announcement of a sale. The reader attracted to the headline is further assured by amplification of the message with the following body copy:

*Prices have never been lower...Your opportunities for substantial savings have never been better. Fine watches and jewelry of this quality are rarely, if ever, offered at these sale prices.*

**VISUAL ILLUSTRATIONS.**   No matter which fashion magazine or newspaper advertisements we examine, with the exception of those

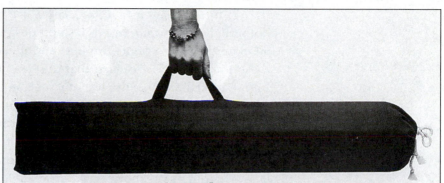

## Now there's a picnic table you can actually carry to a picnic.

Picnic blankets are romantic, but a little hard to eat from. And picnic tables are nice to eat from, but a little hard to drag out of the back yard.

Well, now you can have the convenience of a table at a picnic without needing the muscles of a Superman to get it there.

This remarkably simple idea is called the Roll-Up Table.

It begins with a washable carrying bag. Rolled up inside, a series of hardwood slats connected with thin canvas strips create a generous 30″by 30″top.

Joined to sturdy 16″legs, this top becomes a table that's perfect for picnics, camping trips, and al fresco dinners at summer concerts.

Available with either a natural finish and a forest green bag or a white lacquer finish and a marine blue bag, the Roll-Up Table is easy to assemble without tools, is just $32.95, and is available only at Crate and Barrel stores.

So whether it's a picnic table that's easy to take or a whole collection of picnic accessories that are easy to afford, if it's outdoor entertaining items you're after, the Crate and Barrel is a great place to camp out.

### Crate&Barrel

In Crate and Barrel stores at Grant Avenue in San Francisco, The Village at Corte Madera, Stanford Shopping Center, Valley Fair, and Broadway Plaza in Walnut Creek (opening June 15).

**FIGURE 10-3**

*The body copy amplifies the headline and concentrates on benefits and selling points. (Courtesy of Crate & Barrel)*

that are promotion-oriented, artwork is an essential ingredient. The use of photographs, halftones, and drawings clearly enhance any written message.

The art director is responsible for the type of graphics or illustrations that will best capture attention. However, few create their own artwork. In the fashion field, specialists are employed to produce the photograph or drawing. Just as fashion designers have their own styles and expertise, so do photographers and illustrators.

Although we have learned that the headline is the attention-getter in most advertisements, the use of visuals in the field of fashion sometimes captures the reader's eye before the headline is read. The mood of the piece can be easily accomplished with photography. Many fashion companies, from the apparel producers to the makers of cosmetics, for example, use photography to create a mood of sensuality. Instead of placing emphasis on the specific product in the advertisement, photographs of models or body parts are used to generate the sensual excitement that might encourage purchase of the product.

The fragrance and cosmetics industry exemplifies how photography can capture the hearts and minds of the customer by maximizing the use of sensuality: Max Factor, for its Impact advertisement campaign focused on a model's eyes; L'Oréal, on a model's face that imparted a sexy feeling; Laura Biagiotti perfume on a male and female embracing; Christian Dior Svelte, on a partially nude figure; and Revlon, on a seductive female.

So successful has the fragrance field been with the sensual approach, the use of similar photography has carried over into apparel. Express Jeans often uses scantily or partially clad models in their layouts, as does Giorgio Armani for Armani Exchange campaigns. So, whether it is the sophistication expected from the Ralph Lauren layouts, the elegance of the Tiffany illustrations, or the simplicity of the Gap advertisements, it is the artwork that often makes the initial impact.

**LAYOUT.**  As individual elements, the headlines, subheadlines, slogans, body copy, and illustrations do not make an entire advertisement. They must be arranged in some organization or format that makes the eye move from one component to the next, until the reader has focused attention on its entirety. The arranger for a symphonic performance knows  how to use the instruments in the orchestra in an effective manner to generate excitement; the layout artist does the same with the elements that are made available to him or her. Judgments must be made in terms of how to properly place the pieces to produce the best eye-appealing advertisement. Sound layout design involves understanding certain principles and how white or blank space interacts with the advertisement's elements.

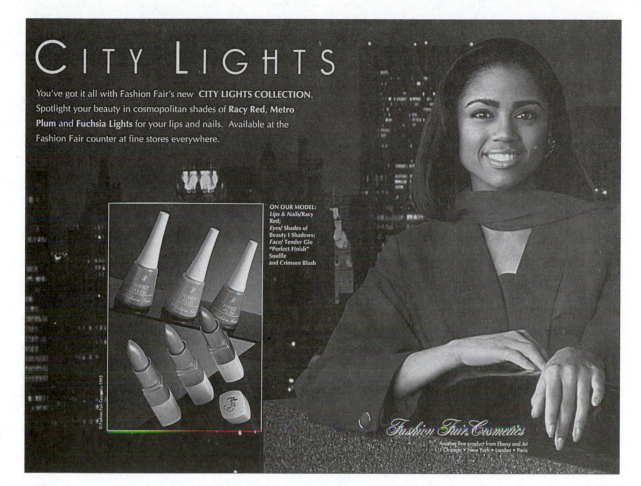

**FIGURE 10-4**

*The excitement of the photograph commands the viewer's attention. (Courtesy of Johnson Publishing Co., Inc.)*

***Principles of Design.*** The rules that govern design include balance, emphasis, proportion, contrast, harmony, and sequence.

* Balance—The concept involves the eye's impression of equal weight distribution. To test for balance, an imaginary line is drawn down the advertisement's center and a comparison is made to determine if both sides weigh the same. One side need not be a mirror image of the other to be balanced, but should provide some impression that it is similar. There are two types of balance used by layout designers, **symmetrical** and **asymmetrical**. Advertisements that are symmetrically balanced utilize the formal approach, where

both sides of the advertisement are identical to each other. While this is a safe way to achieve balance, often, its use produces an unimaginative look. On the other hand, asymmetrically balanced layouts are informal and generally more exciting. The balance is achieved through the use of different elements on either side of the advertisement's center, that when properly placed give the impression of equal weight. The latter methodology is more difficult to achieve and requires more sophisticated placement to achieve success.

- Emphasis—One element should be selected on which the eye should first focus attention. This area of interest, or focal point, may be the headline, photograph, drawing, logo, symbol, or anything else that is considered vital to the advertisement's success. If each of the elements is of similar size, stature, and importance, there will be no emphasis.

- Proportion—The size of the aforementioned elements should fit the space of the advertisement. An oversized headline in a limited amount of space not only leaves little room for the remainder of the message and the artwork, but it gives the advertisement a disproportionate appearance.

- Contrast—To bring interest to the layout, a variety of sizes, shapes, and tones should be used. Different typefaces, of which there are hundreds, may be used to achieve contrast, as can both dark and light tones. If a word or sentence in the body copy is italicized when all of the others are in block form, contrast may be achieved.

- Harmony—While contrast is important to achieve interest, the elements of the advertisement must fit together in some harmonious relationship. They must work favorably together. That is, an advertisement that is designed to give the impression of traditional fashion should make certain that the photography and type style are suited for each other. It is much the same as the apparel designer who makes certain that the garment's trimmings enhance the silhouette. Without attention to this principle, the layout might appear confusing to the observer.

- Sequence—When elements are placed in an orderly fashion, the eye will move from one element to the next until all have been examined. The best sequencing involves getting the eye to focus from left to right and from top to bottom. This is achieved by focusing attention first on

**FIGURE 10-5**

*A fashion advertisement that*

*exemplifies the principle of design*

*and white space effectiveness*

*(Courtesy of Tiffany & Co.)*

the advertisement's most important element, and from there, getting attention to move across and down.

*White Space.* To emphasize the elements chosen to be used in the advertisement, such as the artwork and copy, it is essential to leave space between them. Without attention to this detail, the various components will run into each other, causing each one's value to diminish. The amount of white or blank space to use is an arbitrary decision. Too little will cause reader confusion, while too much will result in a fragmented advertisement.

When print advertisements are examined, it is typical to see a border of white space left at the edges of the piece. This is considered to be a standard and safe layout direction. More and more fashion layout artists, however, are using bleeds, where the photograph runs to the advertisement's outside edges and gives it a more artistic flavor. It is the expertise of the layout director and the impression that needs to be made that dictates its usage.

*Layout Preparation.* Once all of the elements have been finalized, they must be set out in a drawing that will serve as the basis for the finished advertisement. Typically, three stages of development are utilized before the final print is made.

- Thumbnails—A series of miniature, rough drawings is produced, each featuring the same elements in different arrangements. After careful study, a few of them will be selected for additional refinement.

- Roughs—The thumbnails that have been chosen will be made into more detailed drawings in the same size of the finished advertisement. This will enable the decision makers to determine if any changes need to be made before the final stage is addressed.

- Comprehensives and Mechanicals—A comp, a term that is used to describe the final layout, is prepared. It is accurate in terms of size, color, type, and any other details necessary to show how the final advertisement will look.

It should be noted that the computer has become an invaluable tool in the preparation of layouts. Today's software packages provide

## PRINT ADVERTISEMENT DEVELOPMENT STAGES

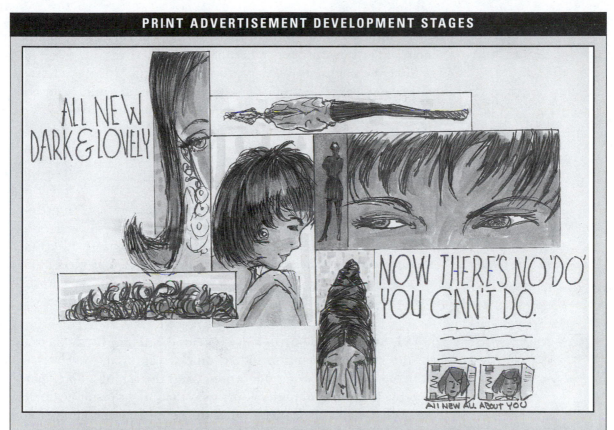

1. The Advertising agency begins working on a creative concept once the client and agency agree on a strategy. Three concepts are presented to the client. The concept pictured above was chosen by the client along with some modifications.

2. The modifications asked for by the client are incorporated into a rough layout.

3. Once the rough layout is approved, the agency selects a photographer and models. Photography is taken and shots are chosen with which to prepare a sub-mechanical. This step insures that the photography matches the concept.

4. While the sub-mechanical is worked out, the headline and body copy for the ad is typeset.

5. The final mechanical and type is shown to the client for approval before proceeding into print.

**FIGURE 10-6**   *The stages of development of a print advertisement. The finished four-color advertisement is featured in this text's color insert. (Courtesy of Lockhart & Pettus Advertising)*

sophistication that enables a wealth of type styles and sizes, illustrations, and other details to be quickly tested, reducing the amount of time spent by the artist in hand rendering the parts.

After the comp has been approved, production of the advertisement takes place. The various production techniques utilized in both the print and broadcast media will be explored in Chapter 11.

## RADIO

Unlike the print media, which uses artwork as a major component, radio relies upon words, sound, and music to create an image that impacts on the listener. Where newspaper and magazine advertising generally warrants a team to produce the promotional piece, radio commercials are usually the work of one individual. He or she is a script writer who augments the words with specific sounds and music.

**THE SCRIPT.**   Before a script is written, attention must focus on how the listener's attention will be quickly captured, what benefits will be derived from using the product and the selling points that it will provide them, and perhaps any risks that might result if the purchase is not made.The conclusion of the commercial should provide the necessary information on which the listener should act to avail himself or herself of the offer.

Since radio commercials generally run from thirty to sixty seconds, the material must be written in simple terms. Too many different areas of emphasis tend to confuse the listener, with the result being that nothing is heard at all. The words should be simple and within the scope of the audience's understanding. The use of unfamiliar or technical language tends to limit the impact of the message.

Although there are many different approaches to getting the message across, those that are fashion-oriented tend to use the straight announcement or interview. It should be noted that the segment of the fashion industry that uses radio is retailing.

The script indicates the words, who is speaking them, the music and when it is to be played, the sounds and where they are to appear, and so on. The following is typical of a thirty-second fashion retailer's radio script:

## SAMPLE RADIO COMMERCIAL

CLIENT: The Shoe Emporium

LENGTH: 30 seconds

TITLE: The Expansion Sale!

---

MUSIC:    The theme from the movie *Rocky* should be played loud and strong for about five seconds before any words are spoken. This will impart an air of excitement and urgency of the message to be spoken. Music level lowers slightly and the announcer begins...

ANNOUNCER:    Never before has The Shoe Emporium reduced its prices in the middle of the season... To commemorate the opening of our newest store, we are pleased to offer this special event... For just three days, beginning today and ending on Saturday, all the merchandise in The Shoe Emporium will be reduced 25 percent... Don't miss out on this once-in-a-lifetime opportunity to get the best in footwear at unbelievable prices at all of our locations.

MUSIC:    *Rocky* theme comes up at end of announcement and again plays loud and strong for the last five seconds.

**FIGURE 10-7**

*A thirty-second*

*radio commercial*

**DELIVERY OF THE COMMERCIAL.**   There are a number of methods used to get the commercial to the listening audience. The majority of them are delivered either by the program's host or announcer or are prerecorded.

*Live Delivery.*   There are advantages as well as disadvantages to live delivery. If the "star" of the program during which the commercial is to be aired is well-known or has a large market following, the listeners often pay a great deal of attention to the message. If the listeners like the personality's traits and manner, they could be apt to try a product that he or she personally endorses. Also, the plus side of live presentation is the spontaneity of the delivery. Of course, live performance might result in straying from the message, overrunning the time allocated for its delivery, and stumbling over words. In terms of cost, the live announcement eliminates the need of actors to do the voice-overs.

*Prerecordings.*   The canned presentation, or prerecording, protects against unexpected word blunders, time overruns, and other mistakes. They also may be used over and over again wherever the advertiser wishes to pay for air time. They do, however, often sound impersonal and unconvincing.

## TELEVISION

While the medium has taken the major portion of many advertiser's budgets, it has not yet become as significant to the fashion industry. Most rely more heavily on print for their campaigns. When it is used, however, its visual elements, enhanced with words and music, make it an exciting way to deliver a commercial message. Unlike its broadcast counterpart, radio, in which one individual is often responsible for creating the commercial, television generally uses a creative team. There are specialists who deal with the written aspects, others with the visual aspects, and still others who supply the sound and music.

**THE SCRIPT.**   The script is a relatively brief story that covers the essential selling features and benefits of the product. With thirty or sixty seconds available for the entire commercial, the words must be kept to a minimum. Today, in some television fashion advertisements, there is a tendency to minimize the spoken element and rely more heavily on the visual presentation. Calvin Klein fragrance commercials generally set a mood with sensual sight and sound and only barely mention the name of the product. These commercials use words very sparingly at their conclusion. Thus, the script writer must be able to refrain from an abundance of words, selecting only the few that will help augment the visuals.

Since the commercial is earmarked for a rather general audience, the words chosen must be easy to understand and easily remembered. While fashion has a language of its own, a word like *couture* might be lost to the population at large.

A rough script is written that features the words to be spoken and by whom, the corresponding video that will be used, music placement and notation, and any additional sounds that might be used. The visual portion of the script is roughly sketched on the script. Once this preliminary plan has been scrutinized and altered as seen fit by the creative team, it is presented in storyboard form.

**THE STORYBOARD.**   A series of sketches and accompanying words are laid out in frames or boxes. Each frame is divided in two, with the top portion showing the visual and the bottom the audio. The number of frames used depends upon the complexity of the commercial and the demands of the advertiser. Typically, the smaller storyboards feature four frames, with twenty-four generally the limit. The following page shows a sample of a fashion storyboard.

## DIRECT ADVERTISING

Unlike its other advertising counterparts, direct advertisements are two-way communication devices that often utilize some type of reply format, such as order forms to make a sale. This is the distinct difference between this medium and the newspaper and magazine.

In terms of elements, the copy and artwork are the key ingredients in direct advertising. Experts prepare the written material and enhance it with artwork, most often photography. In some circumstances, the picture is the starting point and is later augmented by a message.

Unlike newspapers and magazines, however, there are many formats of direct advertising, each requiring different attention from the creative team. Some are merely one-piece cards that are used as inserts for a store's monthly statements. At the other extreme is the catalog featuring a host of different offerings and messages, with each page individually handled as if it were a separate print advertisement.

**FIGURE 10-8**

*A sixteen-frame television storyboard (Courtesy of Lee Apparel Company)*

Where newspaper and magazine creative teams are bound by the physical sizes of the publications in which their advertisements appear, there are few boundaries that limit the size of the direct mail piece. A designer is employed to develop the right size and shape of the direct advertisement that might be more exciting than the standard fare. In the fragrance field, for example, a direct mailer that duplicates the shape of the product's bottle will prove to be more exciting than one that is typically shaped like a rectangle.

Once the format of the direct advertising piece has been developed, and the copy and artwork decided upon, they are set out in a layout

**FIGURE 10-9**

*A one-piece mailer aimed at the children's industry (Courtesy of Ruth Scharf Industries, a Division of Bryan Industries)*

called a "dummy." Actual production of the piece is the next step. This will be discussed with all other production techniques in Chapter 11.

## OUTDOOR AND TRANSIT ADVERTISING

As discussed in Chapter 9, this medium involves the use of posters and painted signs for its messages. While copy and artwork are both used, it is the visual component that is the attention-getter.

**VISUAL ILLUSTRATIONS.** In examining the Obie Awards for excellence in outdoor advertising, it is obvious that the visual element generates the excitement. Sometimes it is an artist's rendering that stops traffic, as in the case of the Levi's Jeans For Women campaign where a stylized female figure is the focus, along with the company logo. A DKNY poster features a photograph of New York City and its attractions, such as the Statue of Liberty, encased in oversized letters that spell out the company name. The illustrations are generally full-color to draw attention, with sharp, contrasting tones preferred. Since artwork of this nature is seen both day and night and will therefore be either naturally illuminated or lighted in some manner, the right color choice is necessary to maximize viewing. A very deep red against a white background, for example, would be an excellent combination. In order to achieve a degree of uniqueness and sophistication, some advertisers such as DKNY opt for a black and white presentation. In this case, the artwork must be sufficiently eye-appealing to gain attention.

Finally, confusion, in terms of artwork usage, must be avoided. If, for example, the featured product is shown in a wealth of colors or patterns, the contrasting background should be a solid color. Sporto fashion athletic wear, featured in many colors on poster, used a white background to offset the busyness of the hues.

**THE COPY.** The key to success in writing copy for outdoor and transit advertisements is brevity. The message should enhance the artwork and deliver a statement that will give the production recognition. "Our bottom line...BUGLE BOY JEANS"; "Our Prices Are Also Itsy Bitsy Teeny Weeny" (copy for a Target store campaign that features a tiny bikini swimsuit); and "Some Assembly Required" (copy used to

**FIGURE 10-10**

*A bus depot*

*advertisement*

*maximizes artwork.*

accent Levi's 501 button-fly jeans) each offer a minimal number of words in the posters.

On occasion, if the copy is the all-important ingredient, the omission of artwork is appropriate. Daffy's, an off-price high-fashion apparel chain, amplifies its image with a large billboard that reads "AT $79 IT'S SEXY. AT $320 IT'S OBSCENE. Designer clothing 40–70% off everyday. 5th Ave. & 18th St., Madison Ave. & 44th St., DAFFY'S, clothes that will make you, not break you." There is no evidence of a photograph or drawing in the piece.

**TYPOGRAPHY.**  The size and style of the type used is another important factor to consider. Because of the distance at which some outdoor advertisements are viewed and the short time they will be seen, it is necessary to use clean, sharp, simple letters and avoid the frills of showy type such as Old English. An observer should be able to appreciate the entire message with only a glance. A Levi's 501 jeans poster merely states, "Lord of the flies." This copy uses very simple letters to catch attention.

**LAYOUT.**  As is the case with any print advertisement, the artwork and the copy must be carefully integrated to provide the viewer with an eye-catching visual presentation. Each component should be an enhancement of the other.

Once all of the necessary elements have been developed and refined for use in the various media, the next stage is to put them into production for commercial use. The methodology used in each of the media will be discussed in the next chapter.

## REVIEW QUESTIONS

1. Briefly discuss the role of the copywriter for both print and broadcast advertising.

2. Once the copy and artwork have been developed, describe the function performed by the next member of the creative team.

3. What is generally considered to be the most important part of a retailer's newspaper advertisement?

4. Explain some of the essential characteristics and conponents of a headline.

5. Why do some print advertisements use a subheadline in their structure?

6. What is generally the focus in the body copy of a print advertisement?

7. Instead of directing attention toward a specific style or product, many fashion designers are creating a mood for their presentations. Discuss this approach and its appropriateness.

8. Define the term *balance* as used in advertising design.

9. What function does white space perform in print advertisements?

10. How does a thumbnail sketch differ from a mechanical?

11. In addition to the spoken message, what other element is generally necessary to achieve interest in radio advertising?

12. Does the prerecorded radio commercial have any advantages over those delivered live?

13. What is a storyboard?

14. In what way does direct advertising differ from the traditional print advertisement?

15. Discuss, in order of importance, the elements of outdoor and transit advertisements.

## EXERCISES

1. Pretend that you are the art director for a fashion designer and are working as part of the creative team to produce a magazine advertisement. The copy has already been written for the advertisement. It uses only a headline and a subheadline to enhance the

visual element. The focus of the advertisement is on the designer's latest collection.

Using your own photographs or drawings, develop a piece of artwork that will best exemplify the designer's line.

Note: If you choose to use a photograph, you might ask a friend to pose in a garment that will typify what is needed.

2. Write a thirty-second radio script for a fashion manufacturer or retailer. The format should follow that used in the text and should include all of the necessary elements and where and how they will be used.

Note: Make certain the copy does not exceed the time limit. This can be accomplished by reading the words aloud and paying attention to a clock with a second hand.

3. Develop a twelve-frame storyboard for a television commercial that is fashion-oriented. Make certain that the sketches and accompanying words are properly featured. The example in this chapter should be used as a guide.

*Quality printing*

*requires the*

*involvement of a*

*master technician.*

*(Courtesy of*

*Horan Engraving*

*Company)*

# Production: The Print and Broadcast Media

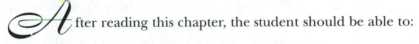

After reading this chapter, the student should be able to:

1. Explain the technical terminology used in print production.

2. Describe the various printing processes used in newspaper and magazine production.

3. Discuss how the computer has helped many fashion retailers with in-house advertising production.

4. List the advantages of videotape over film for producing television commercials.

5. List the stages of production of a television commercial.

6. Describe the production stages of a radio commercial.

## Introduction

As discussed in earlier chapters, the development of any advertisement comes at the hands of the advertising agency or in-house staff. Once the creative team has written the copy, prepared the artwork, arranged the layout, and gained approval for its production, the next step is to get it into print or on the air in a timely, well-produced fashion.

While time is generally of the essence for most advertising campaigns, it is not the only element that advertisers must address in terms of production. If the color quality of a magazine advertisement falls short of the desired mark, for example, or the sound of the voice in the radio commercial is not sharp, the success of the advertisement could be in jeopardy.

In order to guarantee that the best possible results will be achieved, it is necessary for advertisers to have a working knowledge of production principles. Knowing which printing process will best achieve the desired results, which "type font" will make the message easier to read, and whether "line art" or "halftones" will make a greater impact on the observer usually eliminates the potential for any surprises.

In the mid 1980s, computer utilization significantly impacted the advertising world with the advent of desktop publishing, which enabled segments of the fashion industry, such as retailers, to produce some of their materials in-house. Software, from the simple to the sophisticated, became available to satisfy a wealth of needs for advertisers. Not only did it enormously help those charged with the creative responsibilities of advertising design, but it also helped those who had little or no hands-on production experience gain the knowledge needed to understand the complexities and intricacies of print production.

It should be understood that the print media are not the only ones who benefit from computer utilization. Radio and television also benefit from production techniques that offer far more by way of sophistication and cost cutting than ever before achievable. As we head toward the twenty-first century, from all accounts, print and broadcast production will continue to experience positive change.

## Print Production

Fashion advertisers continue to make more use of print media than broadcast. Designers, manufacturers, retailers, marketing consultants, and trade associations use fashion magazines, newspapers, direct mail pieces, posters and bulletins, and industry periodicals to reach their targeted markets. Each task requires consideration in terms of how to best transform the creative works into good, readable pieces. Although the computer has replaced much of the work that was once accomplished by the hands of skilled artists and craftspersons, many of the basic processes are still employed in the industry.

## PRINTING PROCESSES

Each task begins with the selection of the printing process that will be used. While some media rely upon a specific process, others come at the hands of the agency or in-house team.

**LETTERPRESS PRINTING.**   The oldest form of printing is called **letterpress**. It involves the use of a raised surface, similar to the one used in a rubber stamp, to which ink is applied. The inked surface of the metal plate is then pressed against the paper, leaving the imprint of the message. Most of the printing done today is accomplished through other methods.

**FIGURE 11-1**

*Letterpress uses*

*a raised surface*

*to print.*

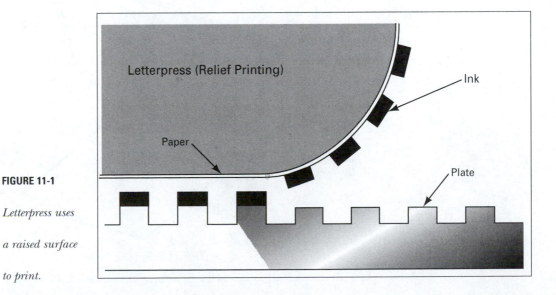

**OFFSET LITHOGRAPHY.**   **Offset lithography** is a photochemical process that involves shooting a photograph onto a thin aluminum plate. The concept uses the theory that water and oil do not mix. The plate is treated with a chemical so that the surface attracts the oil, while the rest of the plate is covered with water. The finished plate is then wrapped around a roller, which rotates through a water bath and then presses against an ink roller. The inked portion then transfers onto the paper. This process is extremely efficient and is the major printing process used in advertising.

**ROTOGRAVURE.**   The process of gravure is the exact opposite of letterpress or relief printing. The desired image is engraved or etched into the surface of a copper plate. The printing is achieved by means of tiny inkwells that fill with ink. Suction is used to pull the ink from the wells and onto the paper.

The vast majority of Sunday newspaper supplements are printed using the gravure method, as are quality magazines, catalogs, and news-

**FIGURE 11-2**

*Offset lithography is*

*the major printing*

*process used today.*

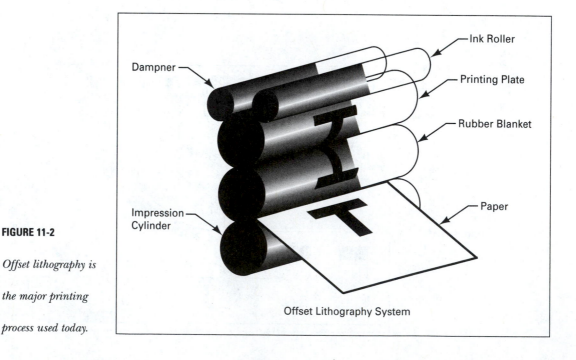

Ink Roller

Printing Plate

Rubber Blanket

Dampner

Paper

Impression Cylinder

Offset Lithography System

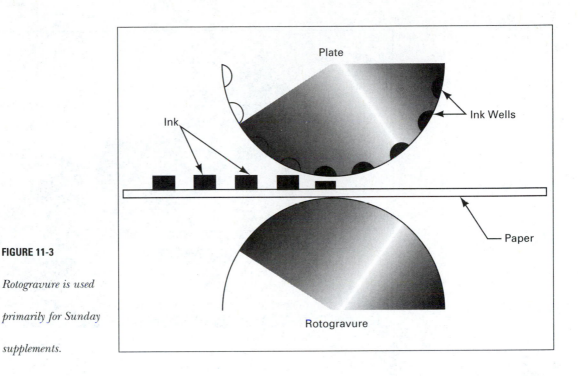

**FIGURE 11-3**

*Rotogravure is used primarily for Sunday supplements.*

paper inserts. It is extremely cost-efficient for printings of greater than 100,000 pieces; smaller quantities generally rely upon offset lithography.

**SCREEN PRINTING.**   When limited production runs are needed, as in the case of posters, screen printing is often the choice. The principle, unlike that used in the previously discussed techniques, involves the use of a silk or synthetic screen, stretched tightly on a frame, onto which a "film" or stencil is adhered. A design has first been cut from the film, creating areas that are void of the film and leaving areas in which the film will remain. Those areas that are cut away allow the color to penetrate. Inks are then spread over the screen by means of a squeegee and pushed through the stencil, printing only the unprotected surface. Each color in the advertisement requires a separate screen.

**FLEXOGRAPHY.**   Many newspapers are using flexography for their advertisements. It is similar to the offset method in that it uses a rubber plate to transfer the image to the paper. It uses water-based inks, instead of the traditional inks, making cleanup easier and faster. One of

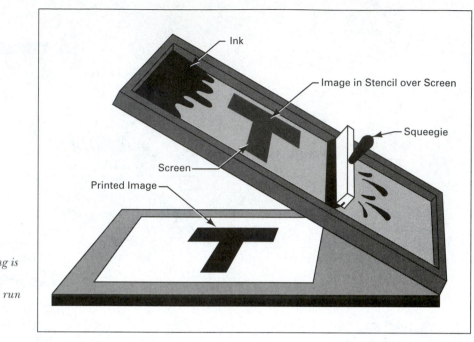

Ink

Image in Stencil over Screen

Squeegie

Screen

Printed Image

**FIGURE 11-4**

*Screen printing is*

*used for short run*

*production.*

the major assets of the process is that the results are sharper than those produced on letterpress.

## TYPE SELECTION

While the actual words deliver the message, the style of type used can significantly enhance it. A mood can be created, an image can be achieved, and readability can be improved with the appropriate selection. There are hundreds of different styles from which a type selection may be made, from the simplest to the most ornate, as well as a wealth of sizes.

The first step is to choose the **typeface** or style of the type that will serve the advertisement best. Two commonly used typefaces are Sans Serif and Old Roman. Each typeface offers a basic set of letters, numerals, and punctuations called a **font.** The letters are shown in both capitals, known as uppercase, and small letters, called lowercase. When two or more series of types have variations on one design, they are part of a **type family**. The following features some of the most commonly used advertising types.

## SAMPLE TYPEFACE SELECTIONS

| | |
|---|---|
| **Acchen** | Journal |
| Antique Olive | LITHOS |
| Berkley | **Madrone** |
| Berhnard | *Medici Script* |
| *Boulevard* | *Mistral* |
| Cassandra Condensed | New Baskerville |
| CHARLEMAGNE | Novarese |
| Cochin | Officina Sans |
| **Doric** | **Onyx** |
| FAJITA | Palatino |
| Futura | *Shelley* |
| Garamond | Stone Informal |
| Gills Sans | Stone Serif |
| Helvetica | Tekton |
| Hiroshige | Univers Condensed |
| Industria | Walbaum |
| **Insignia** | Weiss |
| Janson | *Zaph Chancery* |

**FIGURE 11-5**

*A variety of typefaces*

*used in printing*

## TYPE MEASUREMENT

There is a standard measurement system that typographers use to mark the copy being prepared for typesetting. The units are measured in points and picas.

**FIGURE 11-6**

*The size of type is*

*measured by point.*

> ### TYPEFACE SIZES
>
> FASHION (6 point)
>
> FASHION (8 point)
>
> FASHION (10 point)
>
> FASHION (12 point)
>
> FASHION (14 point)
>
> FASHION (18 point)
>
> FASHION (24 point)
>
> # FASHION (36 point)

**POINT.**    **Point** is the unit for measuring the size of type in terms of height. Each point is 1/72 of an inch. Thus, 72 point type is one inch in size; 36 point, 1/2 inch; 18 point, 1/4 inch; and so on. Type may be set at any point; however, anything less than 6 points is difficult to read.

The space between the lines of type, known as **leading**, is also measured in points. Typically, 1 or 2 points are used to separate the body copy in an advertisement.

**PICA.**    The width of type is measured in picas. There are six picas to the inch. Thus, copy that features forty-eight picas is eight inches wide.

## ARTWORK

As has been already noted in Chapter 10, fashion advertising relies heavily on the use of artwork to deliver a message. The art that is used may be a line drawing or photograph that must be transformed into a **photoengraving** for use in production.

**LINE ART.**   Drawings produced with black ink on white paper are known as **line art**. There may be only solid areas, with no changes in tones or values. The drawing is then made into a photoplate that is appropriate for the printing process.

**HALFTONES.**   The use of photographs requires a different procedure. Since photographs are made up of a range of gray tones between black and white, halftone plates must be prepared. Reproduction of the photograph requires that it be broken up into dots. The differently sized dots convey different values of grays to the eye. In the process, the original photograph is covered with a fine screen and shot with another camera. The quality that is ultimately achieved is dependent upon the fineness of the screens. Rough stock, such as that used in newspapers, uses a coarse screen for reproduction, while magazines use finer screens.

**COLOR ART.**   In fashion advertisements, color is often a very important element. In order to reproduce color, another printing system is required. Known as **four-color process**, it involves the use of red, yellow, blue, and black to achieve an infinite number of colors. Since printing inks are transparent, laying one over the other produces different colors. Laying yellow on blue, for example, produces green.

The production involves the reduction of the original piece of colored artwork, such as a slide or transparency, into four halftone negatives. This procedure is known as **color separation**, in which individual negatives of red, yellow, blue, and black are produced photographically or with the use of laser scanners. Once the four-color halftone negatives are achieved, they are used to create the color advertisements.

The following steps are used in the transformation of the original piece of art to the final plate that will be used in printing:

1. The slide or transparency is cleaned with a solvent and taped down onto the drum of a mounting device. The scanner operator must make certain that there are no bubbles on the slide so that the final piece will be perfectly produced.

2. On a machine such as a Magnascan 646, the slide is magnified anywhere from 300 to 2,000 percent to pick the grain. It is then placed onto a dotted screen by a laser scanner and transformed into a film of the slide.

A

**FIGURE 11-7A-C**

*The technician carefully cleans slide or transparency, tapes it to drum, and inspects it for bubbles. (Courtesy of Horan Engraving Company)*

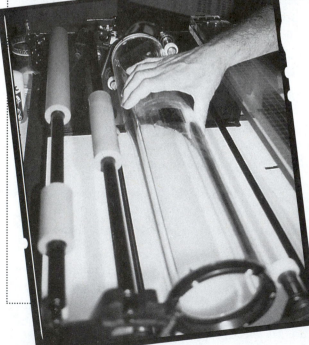

B

C

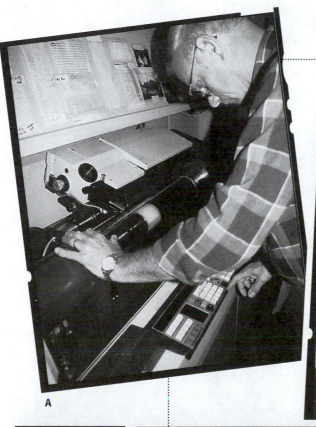

A

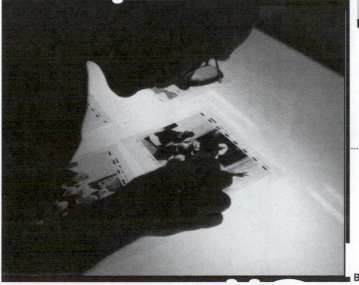

B

C

**FIGURE 11-8 A-C**

*The slide is magnified to pick up grain, transformed into a film of the slide, and reproduced on a scanner in sizes up to 30 × 40 inches. (Courtesy of Horan Engraving Company)*

**A**

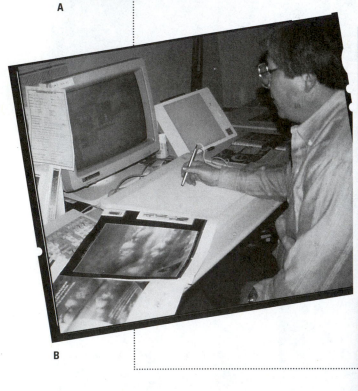

**B**

**C**

**FIGURE 11-9 A-C**

*A stripping technician makes changes by inserting elements or removing some from the original slide after which another technician makes color corrections. After plates are made, the final pieces are produced. (Courtesy of Horan Engraving Company)*

**FIGURE 11-10**

*The finished advertisement*

*(Courtesy of Horan*

*Engraving Company)*

3. The film exits on an output scanner such as a Magnascan 636E, from which a print can be produced in sizes up to thirty by forty inches.

4. The film is then developed in halftone form. Separate films are produced for yellow, red, blue, and black.

5. The films then go to a stripping technician, who, with the use of a computer, "strips" the piece. Stripping involves the insertion of any artwork that might be warranted for the final advertisement that was not present in the original slide. If, for example, there is a need to add a flower to the model's hair, it can be accomplished at this point. In the past, additions to the artwork required an artist's hand that would paste the new pieces into place. The computerized stripping procedure has eliminated the need for the traditional "paste-up."

6. Color corrections and refinements are then made at the next computer station. The slightest imperfections or adjustments can be quickly made. Heretofore, the use of an airbrush might have been used for the color corrections.

7. Once the problems have been eliminated, individual plates are then made for each color's film.

8. The plates go to press, with each color being overlayed, one at a time, until the final piece is produced.

## Desktop Publishing

Before 1985, desktop publishing, a term coined to describe computers and software applications to produce copy that is ready for production, did not exist. Since then, more and more companies have developed in-house facilities that enable the user to compose a complete publication, including copy and illustrations and viewing it on a screen, before it is printed. Fashion retailers, in particular, are making significant use of the desktop publishing programs to produce everything from posters to catalogs. Major department stores such as Dayton Hudson, A & S, and Macy's complete total projects such as catalogs with such software as QuarkXPress and PageMaker. When it comes to newspaper and magazine advertising, however, the software is generally used for creative purposes, with the production left to the publications in which the advertisements will run. Not only does desktop publishing enable the user to create his or her advertisement from start to finish, but it does so while cutting down on cost and production time.

It should be understood that whether production is achieved in some traditional manner, accomplished via computer utilization at a production house, or with in-house desktop publishing, the stages of the projects are all similar.

## Television Production

The use of the television commercial continues to increase for the fashion industry. Textile producers such as DuPont, designers such as Donna Karan and Calvin Klein, and fashion retailers from the upscale

Bloomingdale's to the off-price companies such as Marshalls are regularly using the medium to attract customers to their merchandise.

While more and more segments of the fashion industry produce their own print advertisements in-house through the advent of desktop publishing, the same is not true of television. Advertisers hire a producer for each commercial. A producer has the responsibility of coordinating all of the activities from preproduction to postproduction. Once the script has been written and the storyboard has been created, as discussed in Chapter 10, production is ready to begin.

## SHOOTING THE COMMERCIAL

After the actors or models have sufficiently rehearsed, the commercial is ready to shoot. The arena used may be a studio replete with a stage set that was specifically created for the piece, an outdoor environment, or a combination of both. Typically, a director is responsible for setting up the appropriate shots to be taken by the cameraperson, making certain that the lighting is suitable for the shots, and the sound is clearly audible without distortion.

The actual recording is done on either film or tape. Most television commercials use 35 mm or 16 mm film, both of which result in fine quality production. However, more and more producers are opting for videotaping since it provides for immediate viewing of what has been captured on the tape. No matter which format is used, it should be understood that only about 1 percent of the footage is used in the actual commercial.

## EDITING

Once all of the footage has been taken, the next step is to put the pieces together. Rarely is a commercial shot in the actual order as it will appear in its final form. It is shot in sequences, which must be assembled to conform to the script and storyboard. The job of the editor at this point is to put the pieces together in a preliminary version known as a **rough cut**. The same scene usually is shot over and over again to make certain that one will feature the quality desired by the director. The editor selects from these pieces and assembles what he or she considers to be the best ones. At this stage of development, the roughs are sent to the advertising agency for viewing and approval. If changes need to be made on footage, this is the time it is done.

## RECORDING SOUND

The voices heard on the commercial may be recorded during the shooting, before or after the action is shot, or a combination of both times. If the actors or models are delivering the actual lines, then the sound is recorded simultaneously with the shoot. When **voice-overs** are used (voices heard but not seen on the commercial), they are recorded separately and inserted at a later time.

## INSERTION OF MUSIC

Music is used for various reasons and at different times during the commercial. It might be used to set a mood for the entire piece or to make a transition from one segment to the next. It can be brought up in intensity to make an impact, softened to enable the voice-over to be heard more clearly, or used as an accent for a particular part of the piece.

The music may be written especially for the commercial or taken from unpublished stock resources. The latter approach is the more economical way to produce the music portion. After the music and sound tracks have been recorded, they are then placed on a single track for later incorporation into the film or tape.

## PRODUCTION OF AN INTERLOCK

The edited picture, along with the recorded track, are then put together into a format known as an **interlock**. The interlock is then sent to the client who will be asked to review it for final approval. If any changes need to be made, they are made during the final editing.

### FINAL EDITING

It is at this point that the editor transforms the footage into a more interesting piece with the addition of different effects. Among those that are used are **dissolves**, a technique that produces an overlapping effect when one scene slowly fades from view as another fades in; **wipes**, where the new scene moves the previous one off the screen from one side to the other or from top to bottom; and **zooms**, which bring close-ups of distant shots.

### VIEWING OF ANSWER PRINT

The final version of the commercial with the sound and film intact is called the **answer print**. It is sent to the client and advertising agency for final approval.

### DUBBING

When the decision has been made to go ahead with the commercial, it must be duplicated or dubbed into as many **release prints** or copies that are needed for airing throughout the country.

## Radio Production

Once a neglected medium for the fashion industry, radio has started to play an important role for some of its segments. Retailers use it to announce special sales events and promotions and apparel manufacturers such as Levi Strauss are using it in conjunction with the print media. It has the advantage of being produced in a relatively brief period of time and at a nominal cost.

The commercial may be delivered live by an announcer, program host, or any radio show personality. When there is a need to use the same commercial again and again or on many stations simultaneously, it is prerecorded.

Once the script has been written, the following steps comprise production: casting, recording, and distribution.

## CASTING

Those whose voices will be heard on the commercial are tested to make certain that their voice qualities are appropriate for the mood of the message. Since there is no visual aspect to radio, the voice is the only means of properly communicating the words that were originally written.

## RECORDING

First the music is recorded on tape, then the sound effects are recorded on a separate tape. When they have been approved, they are then mixed with the vocal tape by the studio. The master tape is then prepared and readied for approval by the advertiser and agency.

## DISTRIBUTION

Copies of the master are made on reels or cassettes for distribution to the stations that will be playing the commercial.

# Outdoor and Transit Production

With larger-than-life canvasses available to deliver their advertising messages, more and more components of the fashion industry are turning to this medium. As discussed in Chapter 9, the use of outdoor and transit advertising, in a variety of forms, continues to increase. The interest has not only lead to more usage, but also to significant creativity in the formats used. Once the designs have been created, production may be accomplished by a number of means.

## POSTER PRODUCTION

The vast majority of posters are either silkscreened or lithographed. Smaller panels are produced in one-piece formats, while the larger entries are made into separate sections that are assembled and installed at the viewing site. They are prepasted for ease in installation.

## PAINTED BULLETINS

Where the message is of a more permanent nature, the painted bulletin is often used. It enables the advertiser to produce a unique, individual design to deliver the message. The painting is accomplished by artists either at a studio or on the site where the piece will be displayed. The artist must consider the distance from which the advertisement will be seen before beginning the project. Since most viewing is at a significant distance from the site, the actual painting must be produced with that in mind. That is, up-close inspection might reveal exaggerated dimensions that only come together when seen from the desired viewing point.

In addition to the painting of the piece, production may involve the use of extensions and embellishments with moving parts to give them extra eye appeal. This requires careful construction, since winds and rain can cause havoc with the bulletins.

The material on which most painted bulletins are created is seamless vinyl canvas. It is very flexible and resists much of its exposure to the elements. In place of the hand-rendered painting, more and more pieces are being painted with the use of new computer technology.

## BACKLIT TRANSPARENCIES

At bus depots and rail stations, a great number of advertisements are being used that are nothing more than color transparencies that are illuminated from within. The artwork is shot on film and placed inside a lightbox. The result is an exciting advertisement that comes to life after dark.

## SPECTACULARS

The most demanding production is used in the creation of the spectacular, a bulletin that features lighting as a major ingredient. Special effects may be accomplished, such as lights that blink or colors that change, panels that revolve, or messages that move. This requires special construction considerations that must live under the most adverse weather conditions.

# Direct Mail Promotion

Catalogs, pamphlets, brochures, and the host of advertising pieces that make up direct mail require production considerations that are somewhat different from the other media. While the printing techniques used are the same as those employed in the traditional print media, there are other areas of consideration that need addressing.

## PRODUCTION ALTERNATIVES

Companies have the choice of using outside resources for their production or in-house desktop publishing. More and more fashion retailers are using the latter route since it allows them to produce their own materials at lower costs. The wealth of computer software provides everything needed for production, beginning with the copy, artwork, and layout, and ending with the ultimate printing of the pieces.

## CREATION OF THE INSTRUMENT

Unlike the other media, which have certain inherent rules and regulations that govern advertisement size and time, direct mail has none. Newspapers come in one or two formats, thus limiting the size of a particular advertisement and television has its stipulations regarding the length of a commercial. While the ultimate mailing cost might be greater for oversized pieces, the postal service places no restriction in terms of weight.

Without the aforementioned limitations, producers of direct mail may develop any type of package that best serves its needs. Typically, the forms generated range from the one-page flyers to catalogs of hundreds of pages. Some advertisers, wishing to distinguish their mailings from others, are creating oddly shaped pieces **die-cut** by a machine that can produce hundreds of artistically shaped pieces in any style.

## ASSEMBLING THE PACKAGE

After the printing has been completed, the pieces may have to be collated; bound and sealed, as in the case of catalogs; inserted into appropriately sized envelopes that contain monthly statements; sealed; or just, in the case of a cardlike mailer, prepared for delivery.

## PREPARATION FOR MAILING

This final stage involves addressing the finished product. Names and addresses are affixed to the mailers either by way of labels that have been printed via a computer or typed, or by printing the delivery information directly on the package.

## REVIEW QUESTIONS

1. What advantage does desktop publishing afford the fashion retailer in terms of production?

2. What is the oldest form of printing? How does it work?

3. Briefly describe the concept of offset lithography.

4. For what type of production is the gravure method used?

5. Discuss the concept of screen printing. When is it used in advertising production?

6. What is meant by the term *typeface*?

7. How do typesetters measure the sizes of type?

8. In what way does a line drawing differ from a halftone?

9. Name the colors used in four-color processing. How are they used to produce other colors?

10. Define the term *stripping* as it applies to printing.

11. What traditional step in production has computerized stripping eliminated?

12. Describe the job of the editor in the production of a television commercial.

13. What are voice-overs?

14. Define the term *interlock*.

15. List some of the effects used in final editing to give a commercial enhanced visual impact.

16. Why is it easier to produce a radio commercial than a television commercial?

17. Why are some outdoor panels painted rather than produced as posters?

18. Describe die-cutting for direct mailers.

## EXERCISES

1. Using a traditional book on type and lettering as your resource or printouts that have been obtained from type software packages, select five typefaces that are used in *fashion* print advertisements. Each typeface selected should then be discussed in terms of the kind of advertisement in which it would be used and the impact that it is supposed to have on the reader.

   Note: Close inspection of newspapers and fashion magazines will help you to learn which styles of type are being used in fashion advertising.

2. Videotape a fashion-oriented television commercial to analyze its production elements. The commercial should be shown to the class. Stop and start at points in the production that make it an appealing advertisement. Your talk should include such elements as voice-overs, environments, music, sound, and optical effects.

# Fashion Promotion Presentations and Techniques

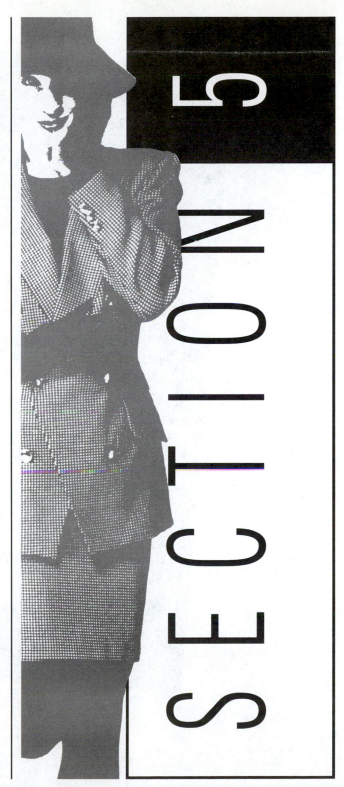

SECTION 5

*The bride*

*and groom*

*traditionally*

*signal the*

*show's end.*

# Fashion Shows

After reading this chapter, the student should be able to:

1. Discuss the various fashion industry components that produce fashion shows and the audiences they target for the presentations.

2. Describe the different fashion show formats that are used as promotional endeavors.

3. List and explain the different reasons for presenting fashion shows.

4. Develop a budget for a fashion presentation.

5. Select a facility in which the show will be presented.

6. Choose models for the presentation that are appropriate to the merchandise being featured and the invited audience.

7. Describe the integral parts of a production.

## Introduction

The lights of the arena dim and the music begins. It is the signal for one of the industry's components to make a fashion impact on the waiting audience. The audience might include the representatives of the press who have the power to extoll the virtues of a designer's newest collection, professional buyers who have the responsibility and the budgets necessary for purchasing the merchandise, or consumers who will ultimately decide which styles will be accepted and which will be ignored.

To stimulate enthusiasm and motivate purchasing, few other promotional vehicles of the fashion world can generate the sparks of excitement as quickly as the fashion show. Although the collection designers toil endlessly in their pursuit of creative originality and excellence, it is this theatrically oriented presentation that helps the collections gain their prominence.

Fashion shows do not merely parade live mannequins down the runways to feature fashion's latest endeavors that will make their way to the sales floors. They also serve as productions that are often intended to shock and entertain. The wealth of fashions that make headlines on Paris runways rarely ever translate into salable merchandise. Outrageously designed costumes displayed by wildly coiffured and accessorized models achieve more promotional notoriety for the designer than the merchandise he or she has created for the consumer to wear. How many brides will actually be convinced to wear the micro-mini bridal ensemble that concludes the couture show or the outrageous hairstyle that enhances it? Will anyone actually wear the transparent styles, void of undergarments, that have made headlines at these events? Famous designers often capitalize on the fashion show format with such offerings to publicize their names and hopefully maintain lasting prominence in the competitive world of fashion.

Thus, the show's promotional clout is more than just selling particular styles and designs. It is the ultimate, very special event that provides the fast route to make the cash registers ring!

## Sponsors of Fashion Shows

Organizations at every level of the fashion industry make use of the fashion show either on a regular basis, such as the opening of a new season, or as an occasional vehicle for events like charity fund raisers. Designers, manufacturers, trade associations, consumer publications, fashion marketing services, and retailers are some of the industry's components that subscribe to the fashion show format.

Outside of the professional arena of players, other groups often choose the fashion show format as the centerpiece of the promotions they use to call attention to themselves. Colleges and charitable groups, for example, are representative of these nonprofessional sponsors of such events. Each organization subscribes to the type of show that best represents their goals and directs its efforts to a specific audience.

## DESIGNERS OF HAUTE COUTURE

The runway shows that introduce each season's collections of couturiers such as LaCroix, Armani, Lagerfeld, and other masters of original apparel design at the highest levels of the industry, are legendary.

**FIGURE 12-1**

*The designer takes a*

*bow at the conclusion*

*of the show.*

They are used not only to feature the latest innovation in creativity, but also to achieve publicity on an international scale for their fashion accomplishments. This type of show introduces the designer's concept of what the world of fashion enthusiasts will wear for the coming season.

The audiences are made up of several different components. Included, of course, is the press who can make or break a designer's season with favorable or unfavorable reports that appear in both trade and consumer publications. Store buyers are also mainstays of these audiences, eager to make purchases for their couture collections. Finally, individual private customers are in attendance by special invitation from the design houses. This group, comprised of the designer's devotees from the theatrical world and social circles are typical of the purchasers of such apparel and accessories. Many are often seen in the audiences wearing costumes from the designer's past collections to show their fashion allegiance.

Thus, the purpose of the haute couture show is twofold. One purpose is merely for the publicity that may be afforded it by the media and the other from actual purchases that contribute to the company's profits.

## APPAREL MANUFACTURERS

While the haute couture receives the lion's share of publicity from its fashion shows, manufacturers at many other price points regularly subscribe to these events. Their goal is primarily to sell the lines to attending buyers. Labels such as DKNY and Anne Klein, featuring bridge collections, and Liz Claiborne and Evan Picone, catering to a less pricey market, are typical users of fashion shows to introduce each season's offerings.

Typical attendees of such presentations are those that represent the major stores in the country. Typically, buyers and merchandisers from retail operations such as Marshall Field, Bloomingdale's, Lord & Taylor, Macy's, and Carson Pirie Scott are in attendance. The market representatives from the resident buying offices are also regulars at these shows. Since they are the recommenders of merchandise to the retailers they represent, their presence is crucial to the success of any line. In cases of the more well-known apparel collections, the press is also invited in the hopes that they will glowingly report what they have seen in their publications.

## TRADE ASSOCIATIONS

Within the fashion field, there are numerous groups or organizations that represent specific segments of the industry. These groups are known as trade associations. Among the numerous responsibilities they are charged with are those that center upon alerting their membership to current and future trends and gaining as much publicity for the industry as possible. Organizations such as the Men's Fashion Association (MFA), Leather Industries of America, and the National Cotton Council have sponsored fashion shows that feature the best of their respective industries.

The audiences at these performances include those who participate in the industry so that they may be made aware of innovative directions in the marketplace, the professional purchasers who are alerted to the highlights of a season's offerings, and the press, who is invited in hopes that they will fill their fashion columns with interesting copy about the market.

## CONSUMER PUBLICATIONS

Many fashion-oriented magazines regularly sponsor elaborate shows to present an overview of the latest offerings from the markets they cover. *Bride's Magazine, Seventeen,* and *Ebony* are just a few who offer these events.

While the purpose of these shows is to publicize the industry they cover and call attention to their publications, some have additional purposes for their presentations. *Ebony* magazine, for example, has been involved in fashion show extravaganzas since 1958 not only to present the latest in high-fashion design, but to raise money for a host of charities. In 1993, they reported raising $40 million since they began their efforts.

The audiences attending fashion publication sponsored events may be exclusively made of retailers or, in the case of *Ebony,* attendees are consumers who purchase tickets for the event.

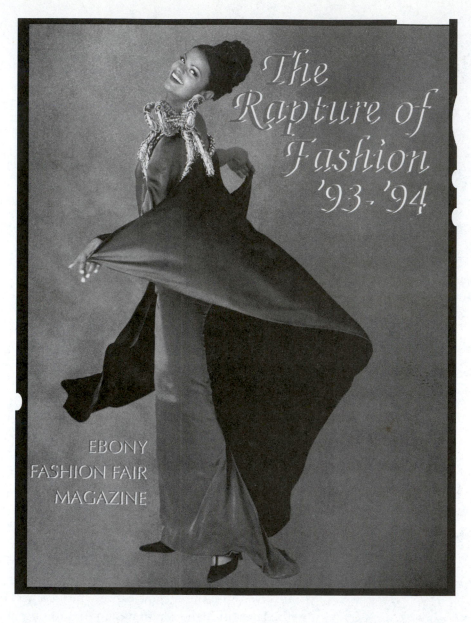

**FIGURE 12-2**

Ebony's *fashion show*

*spectacular (Courtesy*

*of Johnson Publishing)*

## FASHION MARKETING SERVICES

Resident buying offices, reporting services, and fashion forecasting organizations often utilize the fashion show format to present an overview of the latest in fashion creativity. The merchandise featured is representative of the designers and manufacturers of the fashion industry. The marketing services assess the merchandise lines they usually recommend to their clients and choose those pieces for inclusion in fashion shows that make a fashion statement for the upcoming season.

At the resident buying office shows, the viewers are primarily retail accounts they represent. By using this format, the office makes the buyer's relatively short stay more productive. In the short time the buyer has to spend in the market, he or she is able to assess many lines, learn about the directions for the new season, and make arrangements, if necessary, to visit those showrooms whose merchandise generated interest. Without such presentations, the buyer might have to spend extra time scouting lines that might not be relevant to his or her store's merchandising plans.

The fashion forecaster's audience is likely to be the manufacturers who are exploring design direction for the future in terms of such elements as silhouette and color and retailers who might not only wish to learn about trends, but who might want to hear about fashion directions that would benefit private label programs.

## RETAILERS

Store organizations of every size utilize the fashion show format. Through a host of shows that ranges from the formalized runway presentation to informal modeling, it is a means of generating enthusiasm for the viewers.

The shows presented are usually directed at two specific groups. One group is the consumer who is being motivated to buy and the other the store's personnel so that they might familiarize themselves with what they will be selling to their customers. The former is generally offered with more regularity than the show for employees. In a variety of arenas from makeshift runways in the middle of a department, to in-store community rooms, customers are treated to seeing specific collections or general merchandise that the store carries. Many retailers realize an increase in sales whenever these presentations are offered.

## SHOPPING CENTERS

Inspection of the shopping malls across the United States reveals that many have central areas for the presentation of special events, such as Santa at Christmas and the Easter Bunny at Easter time. These areas also serve as arenas where mall managers often present fashion shows that feature the merchandise sold by their tenants.

Generally, these events are free of charge and are merely presented to steer the shoppers to the stores that sell the featured merchandise. At other times, the show might be in conjunction with a specific charity where invited guests buy tickets.

## TELEVISION

From time to time, some television shows present fashion shows. Programs such as *Live with Regis Philbin and Kathy Lee Gifford* have been the sponsors of special fashion events. Formats might be offered that specialize in large-size clothing for women, bridal wear, or active sportswear. With millions of viewers watching television each day, those whose merchandise is selected for viewing achieves immediate publicity that cannot be realized with any other format.

**FIGURE 12-3**

*Retailer and designer*

*collaborate on a show for*

*a charitable organization.*

## CHARITABLE ORGANIZATIONS

As a means of fund raising, many charities sponsor fashion shows. Generally, the format is one in which a dinner or cocktails are served and an accompanying fashion show is presented. It might exclusively feature a particular designer in a store setting, such as the DKNY show that was held at Macy's, New York, where attendees were asked to purchase tickets or a type of merchandise such as bridal or after-five merchandise. The charity shows not only help to collect donations, but also are designed to give business to the participants.

## EDUCATIONAL INSTITUTIONS

At secondary and postsecondary schools, the fashion show has become a mainstay. It might be used merely as a means of giving fashion students the opportunity to learn about fashion show production, to show off the creations of design students, or as an event to raise funds for the institutions that sponsor these events.

The audiences are usually made up of the student body and their friends and relatives. Manufacturers, designers, and retailers are often eager to participate because it is an excellent way in which to make people aware of their companies.

# Fashion Show Formats

There are different types of formats that sponsors use to get their fashion messages across to audiences. They range anywhere from the grand scale presentations to those that are informally structured.

## THE THEATRICAL SHOW

The most expensive of the productions are those that utilize extravagant sets, original music, and scores of actors and models to show off the merchandise. These undertakings are extremely costly, and thus, are infrequently used.

For many years, Milliken, the fiber and fabrics producer, employed the theatrical fashion show, which featured their extensive product line in a variety of ready-to-wear designs. For a two-week period, in the Grand Ballroom of the Waldorf Astoria Hotel in New York City, hundreds of buyers and merchandisers were treated to breakfast and an elaborate fashion show presentation. It was something that was thoroughly scripted and performed by entertainers who regularly toiled in professional theater. Not only did they hope that the buyers would purchase apparel that used Milliken fabrics, but that the invited press would give the company coverage in the fashion pages. With costs extremely high for such productions, Milliken suspended this type of fashion feat. It is only when major companies with significant budgets want to make grand fashion statements that this format is used.

## THE RUNWAY SHOW

The most commonly used format involves a raised runway on which models move from one end to the other, so that the viewers can closely inspect the styles. Typically, the spectators are seated on either side of a runway. The presentation might be formally arranged to include scenery, live or canned music, dramatic lighting, and commentary. For some purposes, the format may be more informally utilized, often relying merely on music and parading models to capture the audience's attention. In the fashion houses of Paris and Milan, runways are used to introduce the latest collections. Most often, it is the music, a large backdrop featuring the designer's name, and the talents of world-famous models that spark interest.

## THE FASHION PARADE

Instead of the formality of the previously discussed formats, some companies prefer the less formal fashion parade. Using a store's restaurant, for example, models parade through the audience wearing the clothing and accessories that are for sale. Most often, commentary is not employed. In its place, models might carry small signs indicating the price of the outfit, the designer or manufacturer name, and the location in the store where it might be more closely inspected.

Sometimes, models may be directed to stop at the various tables to answer questions about the garments they are wearing.

Another approach that involves less production fanfare is one that parades models throughout the store's selling floors. Here, too, the models might carry informative cards or stop to chat with customers offering them information on the apparel and its point of purchase. In order for this type of fashion parade to be effective, the displayed merchandise must be unique or unlike what the customers are wearing. The clothing must stand out from the outfits worn by the shoppers or else they will not attract attention. For this reason, distinctive furs and evening wear are generally best suited for this format.

## THE TRUNK SHOW

Many manufacturers and designers use the trunk show concept to show their lines. The merchandise is brought to the stores in containers or trunks (thus the name) and featured for a day or two. Store customers are invited to these events with the hope that the abundance of one collection might spark interest to attend. A company representative or the designer usually covers the event and mingles with the shoppers to answer any questions about the line. Models are employed to wear the garments and walk through the department or store that is featuring the show. In 1993, Donna Karan participated in such a show at Bergdorf Goodman in New York City. She was on hand not only to greet potential customers, but to answer any fashion questions they might have had.

Not only do these shows give the viewers the opportunity to see an abundance of one designer's work, but it also motivates those that are fascinated with celebrities to go to the store.

# Fashion Show Arenas

There are numerous places in which sponsors may show their merchandise. Some are the standard locales such as theaters, ballrooms, and restaurants, while others include museums, specially erected tents, cruise ships, art galleries, sports arenas, and outdoor parking lots.

No matter which location is selected, it must first and foremost be a place where the merchandise can be easily seen, where a sufficient number of guests may be accommodated, where there is ample space for models to change their outfits, where dressing rooms are convenient to the performance area, where there is sufficient power to generate the necessary lighting, where there is a satisfactory sound system for music and commentary, and finally, where attendees' needs such as rest room usage and coat checking can be addressed.

## THEATERS

A theater or movie house might fit the bill for some fashion shows because they are already fitted with permanent seating that enables guests to have unobstructed views of the stage, sound systems, and lighting facilities. On the other hand, unless it is a formal theatrical production where all of the action takes place on the stage, a runway would have to be constructed. This is sometimes problematical since it must be built across some seats, thus reducing the numbers who may attend and sometimes interferes with access aisles.

## BALLROOMS AND RESTAURANTS

These facilities are used to produce shows that range from the formal variety to others that are more informally oriented. Either place may feature fashion shows that are augmented by sit-down dinners, buffets, or cocktail parties. The premises generally require the arrangement of tables through which a runway might be constructed or the positioning of chairs in rows on either side of the platform on which the models parade to show their costumes.

Unlike theaters that usually are equipped with professional lighting and sound systems, ballrooms and restaurants often have neither. Thus, these elements must be provided so that the show will have a professional appearance.

Another problem with this type of arena is the absence of dressing rooms where participants must make hasty changes to keep the show's rhythm and timing on target. Sometimes makeshift screens are used to house the merchandise to be displayed and as a place for apparel changes to be made.

Since these rooms are not regularly used for fashion presentations, obstacles such as columns might interfere with unrestricted viewing. All attempts must be made to alleviate such problems that could hamper visibility.

If a runway is not constructed for the show and models dance and prance at floor level, segments of the audience will not be able to see the action at all times. This often causes lulls in the presentation and contributes to noise from conversations among the guests waiting to view the models. If extreme care is exercised in preparation of the facility, the ballroom or restaurant is fine for fashion shows.

## TENTS

Sometimes, tents are constructed to house a show. This requires that a facility must be erected and properly housed to guarantee positive results. Without any electrical lines for sound and lighting, permanent seating, stages or runways, and changing rooms, the undertaking requires considerable planning. One of the problems in such places is the elimination of sounds from the outside. Vehicular traffic, if the location is in a central district, such as Bryant Park in New York City where the Council of Fashion Designers sometimes sponsors fashion shows for well-known designers, often causes outside noise.

While this type of arena adds festivity to a fashion show, it is imperative that many potential problems are addressed to ensure the presentation's success.

## SPORTS ARENAS

If the show is targeted to very large audiences, sports arenas are sometimes the only viable place to use. The major problem in these vast halls is often the size. Even with the most carefully constructed stages and runways, many people are too far removed from the action to benefit from the performance.

In such cases, television monitors might be used to bring the action closer to those in the remote seating areas. Sound systems must also be carefully chosen so that the commentary can be heard throughout the stands, without the potential for echoes.

## OUTDOOR FACILITIES

Often, an outdoor fashion show is the chosen scene. The Chicago Apparel Center, for example, sometimes uses the premises adjacent to its structure to house such events. In these cases, weather may be a problem that must be dealt with. Not only will rain or snow demand postponement, but crosswinds could easily hamper the movement of the models on the runway and adversely affect the sound system. Of course, a perfect day or evening turns such events into fashion happenings.

## MUSEUMS

The beautiful surroundings of many art museums often enhance the clothing that is being featured in the fashion show. Many productions have been presented in specific wings of the facility or central halls. Like some of the other makeshift arenas, the transformation of a facility that is arranged to move people from artwork to artwork requires considerable rearrangement. Seating, lighting, sound systems, and the like must be brought in for the one-time function. Of course, the artistic nature of some designer collections make this type of arena the perfect setting.

## SHOPPING MALLS

More and more major malls have set aside common areas in which merchants parade live models for the shoppers to see. Some are equipped with permanent stages and amplification systems that make such offerings simple to present. The only real drawback is the inevitable throng of passersby that might interfere with the performance.

## MISCELLANEOUS LOCATIONS

The facilities that house fashion shows need not be limited to those discussed thus far. The creativity of the producer often leads to locations that might not be typical places for such events. Cruise ships, either in the theaters or restaurants, gymnasiums, zoos, concert halls, art galleries, fairs, and parking fields have all been used. What is most important is that the facilities can be transformed to make them excellent settings for the presentations.

# The Elements of a Fashion Show

For a fashion show to provide excitement and achieve its goals to sell merchandise and promote publicity, it must be comprised of a number of different elements. These elements, or components, of the show will differ from presentation to presentation depending upon its size and budget. The following elements are generally those that are essential for most productions.

## MERCHANDISE

Central to the success of any fashion show is the merchandise to be featured. Whether it is a designer collection at the highest price points or a moderately priced assemblage of items from a retailer, the items selected must be appropriate for the invited guests. That is, if the audience is comprised of a conservatively dressed market, the apparel should emphasize this fashion direction. While fashion-forward, avante-garde costumes generate more excitement, these characteristics will not motivate the viewers to purchase them.

The number of different outfits should be limited to anywhere between sixty and seventy-five, which can be modeled in approximately half an hour. Although longer shows are sometimes presented, thirty minutes is the right amount of time to hold the audience's interest. Merchandise lines should be refined to show that number and should include those items that will expect to generate the most interest.

Even if the show features more traditional, conservative styles and silhouettes, it is appropriate to intersperse outfits that are somewhat more daring than this audience is apt to purchase. Fashion shows that feature clothing for the fuller figure might present, for example, a bright red beaded dress during a formal wear segment although the audience is more likely to purchase one that is black and basic. Although the red entry might never be a good seller, it might lend some excitement to an otherwise lackluster collection.

At the end of most women's fashion shows is the obligatory bridal gown. This not only signals the production's conclusion, but it also provides for a final highlight. To make this feature even more exciting, the gown might be one that is unlikely to be seen at traditional weddings. Perhaps it could be a bridal creation with a miniskirt or one that departs from the standard white. If it is different, it is apt to generate discussions, both for and against, from the departing audience and give the show some last-minute pizazz.

## MODELS

One of the most important components in the fashion show is the model who parades the clothing. A look at any of the major French or Italian runway shows on television immediately reveals a host of individuals who have more than just good looks and perfect forms. Their facial features might be unique, or their manner of walking might be distinctive; something about them makes the clothing exciting. Of course, models of this caliber are extremely expensive to employ and are only within the budgets of a few companies.

Except for some charity shows where the models may be recruited from within the ranks of the organization or school-sponsored events where students participate as models, professionals are preferred. Although the use of amateurs considerably reduces expenses, they do not have the attributes, characteristics, and expertise to carry a show.

The seasoned model who may give the simplest design a specific elegance merely by the way he or she walks will be able to make changes from one outfit to the next within the allocated time, thus avoiding lapses in the timing and will be able to handle emergencies that may arise like appearing out of sequence when something in the changing room goes awry without making the audience aware of the error. The professional need not be trained in walking and turning techniques for each show since such moves become second nature, nor be convinced that the outfits they are to wear need not personally appeal to them.

If amateurs must be used, a great deal of time must be spent in their selections and in the finer points of modeling. While professionals have the right measurements, the average man or woman rarely has the height or weight necessary for many outfits. Because amateur models may not be perfect fits, garments may require considerable alterations

**FIGURE 12-4**

*Models are one of the fashion*

*show's main components.*

that would prevent them from being sold. These volunteers do not look at the presentation as a business promotion for the sponsor, often are disgruntled if the assigned outfits are not to their liking, are careless in the handling of the items, are unaware of the importance of timing, and pose problems that might ruin the show.

The only way "amateur night" can be successful is if a great deal of rehearsal time is built into the plans.

## FACILITIES

Many different types of places are available for the performances, as was discussed in the section on fashion show arenas. When the specific locale is decided upon, it is imperative that it be checked to determine if it has the right amount of space, chairs for the guests, sufficient wattage, and so forth.

One of the more important aspects of facilities evaluation is the amount of space available for the show's central viewing stage, the runway. While some theaters and convention centers are equipped with runways, others are not. In cases in which a runway must be assembled, attention should be focused on the right dimensions. The best height is approximately three feet high. This enables even those in less-than-perfect locations to get a full view of the action. The width should be a minimum of three feet, with more space if possible. The wider platform allows for several models to parade their outfits, side by side. This is especially important if specific merchandise groups within a collection are better featured a few at a time. It helps create an impact for the particular designs, silhouettes, fabrications, or any fashion statement that is being emphasized.

Besides making certain that the runway is of the appropriate dimensions, its construction should be sufficiently solid to guarantee the safety of the models doing their turns. If there is not any direct access from the wings onto the runway for models to enter and exit, a set or two sets of steps should be planned. There should be a public address system for the commentary and any other announcements. A microphone with adjustable positions is a must so that people of different heights may make the necessary adjustments for their use. At the microphone station, a high-intensity spotlight is best so that the script may be read with ease. Without specifically addressing the components of the facility, situations might arise that could hamper the show's effectiveness.

## LIGHTING

A simple arena may immediately be transformed into a perfect setting for a fashion show if the proper lighting is utilized. Before and after the presentation, the room's conventional fixtures, such as recessed high hats or decorative chandeliers, are perfectly suitable for overall illumination. With this lighting, the guests are able to converse with each other and find their places for the show. Once the event begins, however, this type of lighting is of little value. The spotlight should focus on the models who will be prancing and dancing down the aisles. Not only must their outfits be easily seen, but so must the accessories that are used to enhance the costumes.

There might be footlights used at the front of the stage or around the base of the runway for dramatic effects. They might be adjusted throughout the show, sometimes turned off to indicate that the next segment is about to begin. If the setting is a theater, footlights, as well as spotlights that follow the action on the stage, are usually part of the facility. In other places, portable spotlights should be acquired.

Lighting should not be left to the inexperienced. A professional knows how best to illuminate the action. They also are aware of the possibilities of blown fuses or burned out bulbs and are sufficiently seasoned to carry extras if the need arises. How tragic it is if a show is ruined because of lighting failure.

## PROPS

Depending on a show's budget and the magnitude of the event, different types of props are used. In the days of the extravagant Milliken shows, elaborate sets and props were common. Today, the emphasis is more on the costumes, with props playing a secondary role. The elegant couture shows concentrate specifically on the clothing and feature a stage that merely uses a large backdrop with the designer's name.

To augment specific merchandise groupings, props might be carried or used by the models. For active sportswear, it might be tennis rackets; for travel, luggage could be carried, or bicycles used to denote casual wear. Models on roller blades are being used for shows that feature junior merchandise.

When the facility permits, unusual props might lend significant excitement. A unique college fashion show housed in an old airplane hangar on its campus generated a great deal of excitement when all of the models entered the facility perched in open convertibles. It certainly set the tone for a fun evening.

## MUSIC

Whether it is a live band, a pianist, or canned music, it must be planned so its selections will enhance the merchandise and the tempo of the show. Live music, of course, is preferred. Not only can it emphasize the fashions being paraded, but it may also be used to entertain the audience as a warmup just before curtain time. A good conductor and musicians can help set the pace and cover for any shortcomings of amateur models.

If the budget does not allow for live music, recorded music may be used. Care should be exercised to make certain that the right melodies and tempos fit the merchandise and theme of the show. It could require specially recorded tapes for the occasion. However, a model's failure to appear on cue cannot easily be addressed with canned music. As in the case of lighting, attention must be paid to potential problems. An extra music system should be on hand in case a primary system malfunctions.

## BEHIND THE SCENE NECESSITIES

Although the action takes place on the runway, backstage is a place that must be carefully fitted to guarantee a smooth-running show. There must be ample space for the models to make quick changes, tables and proper lighting for the application of makeup, racks on which clothing may be assembled in the order they are to be shown, and tables on which accessories can be arranged. All too often, the emphasis is placed on the arena of the presentation and too little on the back room.

## THE STAFF

For the show to maximize its potential, there must be a staff that is capable of planning the presentation as well as carrying out the plans. The number of people involved depends  on the magnitude of the event and the allocated budget. At the very minimum, there should be a director, stage manager, and commentator. Of course, larger productions require additional staffing.

**FASHION SHOW DIRECTOR.**   The overall responsibility of the performance rests with the director. He or she plans the merchandise sequences, selects the outfits and the accompanying accessories, chooses the models and oversees the fitting of them, and  sometimes  writes the commentary. The coordination of the music, lighting, and prop selection are other responsibilities performed by the director.

**STAGE MANAGER.**   If props are to be used along with accompanying sets, it is the stage manager who is responsibile for making certain that they are in the right places at the designated times. The pace of the show is contingent upon this person's ability to move things along and handle any emergencies that might arise during the performance.

**COMMENTATOR.**   Although many fashion shows eliminate the use of a commentator, some still utilize them. If this is the case, the commentary should be brief and used only to enlighten the audience to such details as fabrications, price, and so forth.

The individual assigned the task should be a qualified fashion specialist who is familiar with the language of the trade. If the commentary is entirely scripted, a good reader is a must. In situations in which the words are ad-libbed, a person with a complete understanding of the language of the trade is essential. They must know about silhouettes, color, trends in such details as skirt lengths for women's shows, fabrication, and so forth.

Some organizers of fashion shows prefer to hire celebrities to perform the commentary. This is one way in which the show might gain better attendance in cases where fund raising, for example, is the goal. In such situations, the celebrity should be given a script, which can be read as the models parade on the runway. It should be understood that while these people are accustomed to appearing before live audiences in theatrical productions or other performances, they are often unfamiliar with the fashion industry's terminology.

The commentator should be appropriately dressed for the performance. Often, the outfits worn by these people are from the collections featured in the show. Finally, the experienced commentator will know how to respond to models that appear out of sequence, lags in time

**FIGURE 12-5**

*The commentator*

*delivers the fashion*

*message.*

when the model does not appear as planned, or in emergency situations that might occur from accidents or mishaps.

**COMMENTARY WRITER.**   If the decision is made to use a written commentary, it should be prepared by a fashion expert who has experience with such presentations. The script should be developed to include the number of each garment and its place in the lineup, the amount of time each will appear on the runway, and the specifics of the music that will be used. In this way, the reader will be able to assure that the proper words will accompany each costume and the show's timing will be on target.

**MUSIC DIRECTOR.**   If live music is the choice and a band is being used, the leader should be provided with the script so that he or she might note musical cues in the appropriate places. This individual also should select the music that best suits the show's theme. In cases in which there is only one musician, such as a pianist or guitarist, this person should serve as both music director and musician.

**DRESSING ROOM ATTENDANTS.**   For a performance to be carried out in the allocated time, it is imperative that a sufficient number of dressers be on hand. They must be assigned to particular models, take charge of the outfits each will wear as well as the accessories that are used as enhancements, and be capable of handling emergency situations. All too often these unsung heroes are called upon to strategically place pins in hems that have come down or calm the models who might be having stage fright. The latter occurrences are generally reserved for the inexperienced performers.

**MISCELLANEOUS PARTICIPANTS.**   Depending on the magnitude of the fashion show, there might be a need for some other staff members. An electrician might be appropriate if the production is a major one that requires special wiring, a seamstress if the garments might require last-minute adjustments and repairs, backstage scenery changers if elaborate sets need to be changed, and a choreographer if the models are called upon to dance on the runway. Of course, as stated earlier in this discussion, the all-important budget must be considered before any of the aforementioned are considered.

## The Budget

No matter how large or small the planned fashion show will be, a budget must be decided upon before any other planning may take place. Even in a situation in which the show is one that is presented by a charity, the models are members of the organization who will not be paid, and much of the production's elements are donated, there might be some costs. Of course, at the other end of the spectrum, where businesses are using the fashion show with the intention to ultimately bring a profit to the company, the costs might be considerable.

The following is by no means a budget outline to fit all of the possible fashion show formats, but one that merely suggests the areas of consideration.

The facility (for the day of performance and rehearsal time)
Invitations
Programs
Show advertisements and promotion
Tickets for admission
Runway (rental or construction costs)
Props
Model fees
Musicians
Production staff
Chair and table rentals
Rental of public address system
Racks and tables (to hold outfits and accessories)
Lighting equipment
Photographer and videographer
Refreshments for participants

Each expense area should be investigated to determine the approximate costs. Since this is a time-consuming task, it should not be undertaken by one individual. The fashion show director should delegate specific budget inquiries to other people on the staff. At a prearranged time, all of the participants should be in attendance to present their findings. At such meetings, others might make suggestions as to how some of the costs might be reduced. The fashion production is a team effort and only when those charged with specific responsibilities in terms of budgeting perform their tasks, will the rest of the requirements of the fashion show production be able to be carried out.

## Specialized Product Shows

The vast majority of the fashion shows are dominated by the women's apparel market. At price points ranging from the haute couture to the most modest and presentations sponsored by designers, manufacturers, retailers, trade associations, charitable organizations, and educational institutions, women's apparel holds center stage. The remainder of the market uses the fashion show format sporadically.

## MENSWEAR

Although it is infrequently used, menswear shows are becoming a little more popular in the fashion industry. The MFA, a menswear trade association, for example, regularly focuses the spotlight on merchandise that they believe represents the market. The shows they give are directed toward the industry's retail buyers and the media who hopefully will spread the news about the products with the most potential for consumer acceptance.

Television shows sometimes use menswear in conjunction with women's apparel and, on occasion, feature collections that are exclusively for the male audience. Retailers also use the fashion show format to alert men who are less likely to browse through the store's offerings as their female counterparts to the merchandise that they might wear for a variety of situations.

## CHILDRENSWEAR

The children's market also offers fashion show events to sell to prospective retail customers and to promote the industry. The most famous of the shows, Pitti Bimbo in Italy attracts market professionals from all over the world to its show, which features children of all ages on the runway. The International Kids Show, a trade exposition held in New York, often features informal modeling on ministages by individual manufacturers. Many retailers often spot children's models alongside their adult counterparts in fashion shows.

There is a little more difficulty with this type of performance than any other due to the unpredictable nature of children. It is therefore best to use professional models than those who might develop last-minute stage fright, which could seriously damage the event's effectiveness.

## BRIDALS

Stores that specialize in bridal wear often use formal fashion shows twice a year to show prospective brides the latest of the industry's offerings. They are presented in the retailer's own environments or places off-premises that are better suited to the large audiences these events often attract. Theaters, restaurants, and ballrooms are typical of the arenas used.

In addition to the bridal gowns, these performances usually feature other apparel for the wedding. Men in tuxedos and full dress formal outfits often display elegant outfits and accompany the models down the aisle. Bridesmaid costumes and dresses for mother of the bride and groom are also featured. A host of accessories, such as headpieces and shoes, are also employed to give each prospective bride a complete picture of what is available for her special day.

At such shows, rotating bands on hand to accompany the parading models as well as to showcase their talents for the upcoming weddings, foods from caterers, and centerpieces supplied by florists help make these events spectacular happenings.

## BACK-TO-SCHOOL APPAREL

One of the biggest selling seasons for retailers who sell merchandise that is aimed at the smallest children to those who attend colleges and universities is the period just before school opens. It is a time when something new is needed for at least the first day of classes and full wardrobes for those who attend prep schools and colleges away from home.

Usually the store's own facility is the place selected for these shows; however, on occasion, other more formal locations are utilized. While the merchandise is certainly the most important consideration for these fashion shows, model selection is also of significance.

Stores generally make certain that the models used, most often non-professionals, are representative of the schools the prospective customers attend. When the emphasis is on college clothing, for example, retailers generally select currently attending students from specific schools to serve as models. This gives the attendees a better feeling for the appropriateness of merchandise for campus wear.

## SWIMSUITS

Many manufacturers promote their new collections with fashion shows that feature a wide range of beachwear. The presentations may be

**VANITY FAIR**

MAY 1987                                                              $2.00

**PARTNERS IN STYLE**
*MR. & MRS. CALVIN KLEIN*

**MADAME CLAUDE**
Her Girls Were the Best

**CLUB CULTURE**
The Archaeology of
New York Nights

**THE KING OF KNOPF**
Publishing's New Raja

**SMART ART**
Doris Saatchi on
Ethel Scull

*esigners promote*

*their product lines*

*by promoting*

*themselves.*

*C*ampaigns utilize a variety of mediums such as print, television, and radio to deliver a unified theme and message.

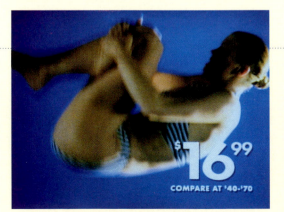

I n-store promotions are an effective way to create excitement and generate instant sales for a line.

**B**illboard advertising

can make an

impressive impact.

Vol. 12, No. 4, August 1990 • $3.00

# Dallas Apparel News

**HOLIDAY CRUISE edition**

Priscilla

*S*pecialty magazines can target large, geographical buying blocks.

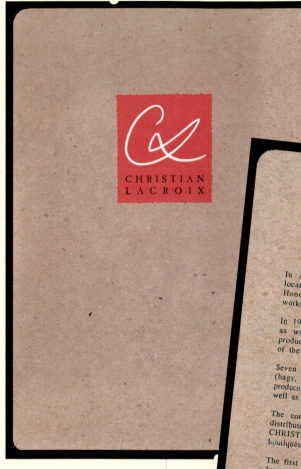

In April 1987, Christian Lacroix inaugurated his Couture House located in an "hôtel particulier" on 73, rue du Faubourg Saint Honoré with the Haute Couture salons, the boutiques, the workshops and the offices.

In 1988, Christian Lacroix presented two Haute Couture collections as well as a Ready-to-Wear line and a Cruise line which are produced and distributed directly by Christian Lacroix Mode, part of the group Indreco, since 1992.

Seven lines of accessories have been elaborated since Spring 1989 (bags, belts, jewelry, shoes, eyewear, scarves and hats) also produced by CHRISTIAN LACROIX, and since 1992, a line for ties as well as a hosiery line.

The company counts a staff of 140 people based in Paris, and distributes its collections in 140 salespoints throughout the world. CHRISTIAN LACROIX counts in 1992 twenty-one exclusive boutiques, one of them in Arles.

The first Christian Lacroix perfume, "C'est la Vie!", was launched in January 1990 and has been followed by its toileteries range in 1991.

For the decor on Faubourg Saint Honoré, Christian Lacroix wanted a place which resembled him, where luxe and creativity are totally conciliated. A universe that only Mattia Bonetti and Elisabeth Garouste could feel and interpret.

From which this mix of primitive and refined materials, baroque and restrained, rich in references to Camargue and to a Provence full of light and gaiety, orange, saffron and fuchsia, in a style which associates rough nails and pure gold.

Christian Lacroix - 73, rue du Faubourg Saint-Honoré Paris 8'. Tel. (1) 42 65 79 08. Télex. 280168. Téléfax. 42 68 0012.

S.N.C. AU CAPITAL DE 1.000.000 F.R.C.S. PARIS N° B 350.555. N° SIREN 347.265 558 APL 05E.

*Creative interior displays and visual merchandising provide a unique look for a store and are a sure way of getting customers into the store.*

as simple as informal modeling in showrooms to major events in hotel ballrooms. For many years, Cole of California staged major runway shows in hotels for prospective store buyers, market consultants, and the media. Other times, television is used to feature the industry's latest swimsuit entries. A major annual event featured on television is the one that features the latest in swimwear selected by *Sports Illustrated*.

More than any of the other product shows, the swimwear production must use carefully selected professional models. While other products may camouflage some of the less perfect figures, the brevity of the swimsuit quickly reveals the slightest imperfections.

## MATERNITY CLOTHING

One of the difficulties of presenting such shows is the availability of expectant mothers to serve as models. Ideally, a pregnant professional is the best choice. Some stores advertise for expectant mothers to appear in these productions, but their inexperience and their present condition often make it difficult to satisfactorily present the merchandise.

Whatever the choice of models, these fashion shows are usually very successful promotions. Many of those in the audience have not been pregnant before and have not a clue about appropriate dress and what is available for them to wear. With so many female executives working right up to their delivery dates, the need for maternity business attire has become important.

## MISCELLANEOUS PRODUCTS

On occasion, millinery, shoes, and sleepwear are presented in shows of their own. Although most often, these are used in conjunction with apparel shows, they sometimes are separate entries. Usually, they are shown in their producer's showrooms for the the buyers to examine.

Extremely important for these presentations is the choice of models. The hat model, for example, must have the right face that will enhance the styles. In the case of shoes, since they are not easily seen by the audience members, producers of these shows often use accompanying slides that show the merchandise close up.

## REVIEW QUESTIONS

1. In addition to designers and manufacturers, which other segments of the fashion industry sponsor fashion shows?

2. What are the three components that make up the audiences at the haute couture shows?

3. Why are resident buyers regular members of the audiences at apparel manufacturer fashion presentations?

4. For what reason would a retailer give a fashion show right in the middle of a department's selling floor?

5. What is the most typically used format for fashion show productions?

6. In what way does the fashion parade differ from the runway show?

7. Describe a trunk show.

8. List some of the different arenas in which fashion shows are presented.

9. With some sports arenas so large, how do fashion show sponsors using that locale bring the merchandise within better viewing range for the audience to see?

10. Are there any drawbacks to using outdoor arenas for fashion shows?

11. What is the most important element of any fashion show?

12. What type of apparel is typically used to conclude a women's fashion show?

13. How does the preparation time differ when amateurs are used in place of professional runway models?

14. What are considered to be the standard height and width measurements for runways?

15. What kind of lighting installation, in addition to spotlights, is used to lend drama to a fashion show?

16. Discuss the pros and cons of using canned music in place of a live band or pianist.

17. Who has the overall responsibility for the show's production?

18. If a commentator is used for a fashion show, what kind of information should the script include?

19. Why is it more difficult to produce a children's fashion show than a women's show?

20. Should more care be exercised in the selection of swimsuit models than those used to model apparel?

## EXERCISES

1. For the purposes of promoting your program at your school and to give students experience, plan a fashion show. To begin the process, it will be necessary to make arrangements to obtain merchandise for the presentation. Some of the sources for merchandise acquisition are from designers and manufacturers, retailers, and if your school has a design program, from the creations of the students.

   Once the merchandise acquisition has been handled, a show should be planned utilizing many members of the student body as participants. Some the areas of consideration in the planning should include:

   - The place for the show to be presented
   - Selection of models
   - Props
   - Methods of promoting the event
   - Lighting
   - Music
   - Selection of a staff
   - Budget preparation

   It would be beneficial to video record the show for use in the organization of future productions and to publicize the school's program.

2. Contact a local department store for the purpose of offering to produce a fashion parade in its restaurant. The clothing selected should be a representation of the men's, women's, and children's wear they carry. The props used should be kept to a minimum and selected from other merchandise sold in the store, such as tennis rackets, bar stools, and so on.

*Santa Claus*

*opens the Christmas*

*selling season.*

*(Courtesy of Macy's)*

# Special Events

fter reading this chapter, the student should be able to:

1. Describe some of the special events that are produced by the various levels of the fashion industry.

2. Discuss the nature of institutional events and how they benefit the companies that use them for promotional purposes.

3. Explain the use of samples as parts of special events for fashion retailers and how they help sell fashion merchandise.

4. Discuss the combined efforts of some producers and retailers in the use of demonstration as a special event.

# Introduction

Each and every season of the year some level of the fashion industry tries to bring attention to its company or product line through the use of events that are not part of their everyday activities. At Christmas time, carolers might be found parading through a store spreading music and cheer and reminding shoppers that it is the season to satisfy that never-ending gift list. During the period that begins at Thanksgiving and ends at Christmas, the cosmetic companies, in conjunction with fashion merchants, do their best to entice passersby with the "gifts with a small purchase" promotion. Newspaper advertisements and store signage that signal the appearance of a prominent fashion designer in an upscale specialty store is yet another special event that stores hope will produce crowds of motivated shoppers.

Whatever the occasion or time of year, publicists, special events directors, and promotional coordinators busily engage in developing yet another special concept that will generate enthusiasm among their customer base. Although the fashion show concept, as discussed in the previous chapter, is the most prominent of the special events to be used by all of the industry's components, it is merely just one of many promotions that companies rely upon to attract attention. A check of the industry's *Fashion Calendar*, trade paper announcements, trade organization newsletters, retailer advertisements, manufacturer and designer press kits, and fashion columns indicate that an endless string of special events is always on the horizon. From costs that might be trivial in terms of a company's overall promotional budget, to expenses that soar in the development and production of a major undertaking, most fashion organizations agree that the investment is generally worth the returns of a successful special event.

# Types of Special Events

Basically, the special events sponsored in the fashion industry fall into two categories: those that are used to bring attention to the company's name and those that are designed to sell specific merchandise. The former, known as the institutional format, might be used to promote goodwill, to emphasize a company's commitment to outstanding service, or to commemorate a specific holiday or event of customer interest. The latter is specifically employed to immediately sell particular merchandise at the time of the event. Often, manufacturers, retailers, and others in the business of fashion use an approach that joins both of these formats into single promotions.

## INSTITUTIONAL EVENTS

More and more fashion organizations utilize the institutional approach in an attempt to bring their names to the forefront of the specific segment of the industry in which they are involved. Many believe that if the event is of a unique and exciting nature, it will not only attract the attention of the markets they are trying to serve, but will also get the attention of the editorial staffs of the broadcast and print media who might supply the company with the desired publicity.

Some of the types of events that fall within the institutional category are one-time promotions. Others are repeated, year after year, regularly capturing the attention of their potential customers.

### LONG-RUNNING SPECTACULARS.

Many companies in the industry have long been associated with institutional events that are repeated year after year. Customers have come to expect these extravaganzas that provide entertainment for the viewers as well as recognition for the sponsors.

Few participants continually subscribe to this type of event as much as Macy's. While others do their share to capture the customer's attention through promotional means, Macy's has found that the annual events bring them a wealth of publicity and business. An examination of some of Macy's endeavors will not only show this retailer's vast promotional program, but will serve to demonstrate the challenge and complexity of institutional events in general.

*The Thanksgiving Day Parade.* Although it is the most well-known of the Thanksgiving parades in the country, Macy's is not the only store or city that subscribes to this type of event. Its popularity stems not only from the fact that it was the first of its kind, but also from its lavishness. Billed as the "longest running show on Broadway," it represents the most challenging undertaking of any retail special event.

To better understand the complexity of this entertainment spectacular that dazzles more than 2 million people who line the parade route

**FIGURE 13-1**  *Macy's Thanksgiving Day Parade is a long-running spectacular. (Courtesy of Macy's)*

and through the wonder of television, more than 35 million people share in the excitement, a look at the planning and behind-the-scenes activities is in order. These numbers indicate that the Macy's event is not one that is solely for New York residents to enjoy, but for the millions of potential tourists who, when visiting New York, will opt for a visit to the store to witness, first-hand, what they have heard about on television.

Thousands of dedicated employees work night and day for months to produce this extravaganza. Specifically, the store's Special Productions Department staff and design artists work the entire year preparing for the event. Among other activities, they audition marching bands and entertainment throughout the country, design and build floats and monumental balloons while restoring past favorites that have been damaged in previous parades, secure celebrity appearances, and enroll and train 3,000 employees who volunteer as clowns, dancers, balloon handlers, and a multitude of other theatrical jobs.

Band selection alone is an enormous task. More than 200 units from all over the country apply for participation, with but a dozen finally making the grade. Those who are selected to participate toil all year long for the event. Thousands of raffle tickets, candy bars, and tee shirts are sold to finance the trip, as well as some less traditional fund-raising items such as Christmas trees and even pepperoni pizzas!

For many, the majestic balloons that ride high in the sky are the parade's centerpiece. With design and construction taking many months, these are a challenge to the Special Productions staff at Macy's. Each year old favorites such as Big Bird, Snoopy, Garfield, Pink Panther, and Ronald McDonald are joined by newcomers. The popularity of the motion picture *Beethoven* led Macy's to create a huge replica of the Saint Bernard that captured the hearts of the American film audience.

The magical parade floats are yet another favorite of viewers. In a former candy factory in Hoboken, New Jersey, Macy's fantasy factory, known as the Parade Studio, the floats are born. From simply big to gigantic entries, the worlds of fantasy, fairy tales, history, myth, literature, and popular culture come to life. Once these magnificent themes on wheels are designed, Macy's employs scores of accomplished actors, singers, and other entertainers who rehearse countless hours to bring the "traveling stages" to life. As with any monumental undertaking, specific details must be carefully adhered to so that the end result will work properly. The floats are no exception. Fiberglass coating is used to answer the potential dangers of inclement weather and collapsible construction is a key to the successful transporting of the floats to the parade site in New York City. With the limited height of the Lincoln Tunnel, the underground connection between New Jersey and New York, these mammoth structures, which soar more than forty feet high, collapse to a size of 12½′

**FIGURE 13-2**

*The July 4th Fireworks,*

*an annual spectacular*

*(Courtesy of Macy's)*

high by 8′ wide. Working through the night before Thanksgiving, the floats are perfectly reassembled at the parade's starting time. While beauty and imaginative design capture the onlookers' attention, it is the behind-the-scenes staff who serve as the unsung heroes of the promotion.

To give one an understanding of the herculean task of mounting such a promotional extravaganza, it might be best told by the amount of time each parade takes to plan and execute. Work on the next year's parade begins practically the day after Thanksgiving!

*The July 4th Fireworks.*  The collaboration between Macy's East and Pyro Spectacular, Inc. brings to the public one of the nation's most spectacular fireworks displays in the nation. Viewed by thousands of people who line the piers in New York City, the many majestic bridges of the area, and the boats that are in the Hudson River, this is yet another spectacular event that brings significant publicity to the department store. As with the Thanksgiving Day Parade, Macy's brings the event to New York's potential visitors through syndicated television showings that reach 150 stations across the country.

The magnitude of this undertaking may be best appreciated by the fact that 11,000 display shells and effects are exploded to create over a million bursts of color and light, playing against a specially written musical score. The fireworks themselves are made in the United States, Australia, Canada, The People's Republic of China, England, France, Germany, Italy, Japan, Mexico, South Korea, and Taiwan, making it an international extravaganza. Each year a new theme is created to make the event one that is truly special.

*The Flower Show.*  The splendor of spring heralds the arrival of yet another annual Macy's adventure in promotion. From the magnificent windows that line the store's entrance to its cavernous main floor, more than 265,000 square feet are filled with nature's finest creations.

For two weeks each year, the store literally comes to life. Pink azaleas, red vein echiantus, evergreen hedges, lilac trees, weeping cherry and birch trees, hydrangea, South African Freesia, weeping evergreens, ficus trees, starry magnolia, and lilac are featured in elegant settings.

Plans for the show begin one year in advance. Floral experts throughout the world are contracted to hold their finest specimens

**FIGURE 13-3**

*The Flower Show*

*signals spring has*

*arrived.*

*(Courtesy of Macy's)*

for the Flower Show. Budding flowers and young plants must be timed for shipping so that they blossom upon arrival at the Herald Square flagship store. One week before the show opens, hundreds of horticultural specialists put over 6,000 rare tropical plants and cut flowers into place while the city sleeps. The finishing touches are made every Palm Sunday just before the doors open.

While the centerpiece of the event is the display of flowers, it is by no means limited to that. To enhance the extravaganza and make it one that huge numbers of people will want to attend, the store plans and executes a number of compatible special events for the two-week period.

Some of these have included:

- a nursery rhyme musical review for children with music and special guest appearances to hold even the tiniest attendee's attention
- musical performances of a classic nature such as the "Classic Duet" of Vivaldi's *Four Seasons*
- singers moving throughout the store serenading shoppers with the songs of springtime
- guided tours of the store that tell everything about the institution's past and present
- table settings designed and created by celebrities such as John Tesh and Connie Selleca, Audrey Hepburn, Liz Smith, Jessye Norman, Bernadette Peters, Ruby Dee, and Ossie Davis
- complimentary photo sessions of the children with Roland Rabbit
- seminars highlighting the professional way to wardrobe the bedroom in a house
- slide presentations by noted garden experts on the arrangement of gardens and growing tips for the spring

Each year, Macy's presents a host of entertainers and performers to make appearances in the flower-enhanced settings. In 1993, for example, the renowned performance group from Canada, Cirque du Soleil, was invited to meet and greet the customers in the stores.

While the aforementioned Thanksgiving Day Parade and Fireworks spectaculars bring a great deal of attention to the Macy's name, it is the Flower Show that actually brings the crowds in to shop since the event takes place on the selling floors.

*Tap-O-Mania.* Always looking for publicity, Macy's constantly dreams up concepts and promotional productions to add to their roster of special events. During the past few summers, they have managed yet another novel entry in their promotional bag of tricks.

For one Sunday each August, a time when shoppers are not really ready to tear the doors down to purchase their fall wardrobes, Macy's puts on the largest tap dancing festival in the world. Participants with or without tapping experience are invited to sign up for the event. All they are required to bring is a willingness to perform and two dancing feet. The event attracts more than 6,000 tappers each year who strut their stuff right in front of the Macy's main entrance to the Herald Square store in New York. Participants are eligible to win a host of prizes ranging from free tickets to theatrical events to complimentary dinners in famous restaurants.

Unlike the other promotions, which cost significant sums of money, this one is relatively inexpensive and brings the crowds right to the stores where they hopefully will enter to shop.

## HOLIDAY FESTIVITIES.

While certain times such as Christmas are a company's major money-making period, other holiday dates are perfectly suited for promotion. These might not warrant extended time commitments, but might be more suitable for a couple of days. Valentine's Day, for example, is one such time. During the winter doldrums among the markdown racks full of leftovers that have not yet caught anyone's fancy and before the freshness of spring has been heralded, the day for lovers has become a favorite to motivate shoppers to spend on their loved ones.

Traditionally, a great deal of attention at Valentine's Day has been focused on candy and greeting cards. While the manufacturers and retailers of those products are often the big winners that time of the year, fashion retailers have come to recognize it is the prefect time to add a little life to their environments. Of course, the intention is to sell merchandise, but the means of getting the customers to the store is often through institutional promotion.

Retailers provide a host of different techniques to draw the crowds, who once inside the store, will make a purchase. Lord & Taylor often uses a variety of promotions that they initially advertise in the newspapers. Each year, for the few days just prior to the holiday, they feature institutionally oriented events such as a pianist playing romantic melodies, silhouette portraits created by an artist, a barbershop quartet that not only sings for the customer's pleasure but is available to personalize a favorite song on tape for a nominal fee, and complimentary calligraphy on gift cards personalized with a purchase.

In addition to the Valentine's period, other institutional endeavors surface during holidays such as Mother's Day. While the goal is to sell something for mother, many stores utilize promotions such as giving a free carnation or floral corsage to every mother who comes to the store. Not only does this kind of event help to boost the store's image, but it tends to sell merchandise to those who attend.

**CHARITABLE ACTIVITIES.** While the fashion show format, as discussed in Chapter 12, is the perfect vehicle for charitable promotions, it is not the only one in which retailers aid those in need. More and more retailers are subscribing to promotions that ask customers to donate used merchandise for the needy. It might be during the winter months when coats are collected or during any other period of the year.

The Benetton stores operated in the United States, participated in such a promotion. Two advertisements featuring the company's founder, Luciano Benetton, depicted his unclad body covered with two messages. One stated, "I Want My Clothes Back," and the other, "Empty Your Closets." The collected merchandise was donated to such organizations as the Red Cross, Red Crescent Society, Gifts in Kind America, Caritas, European Catholic Charity, and numerous local organizations who distributed the goods to people all over the world. The advertisements were seen in more than 150 dailies and 1,000 magazines, promoting the forty-day event.

While this is certainly an institutional event in that it fostered a social drive, it also helped to boost the sales in the individual Benetton stores. Many contributors, while delivering their donations, often were tempted to purchase new merchandise.

**PERSONAL APPEARANCES.** We are all familiar with the appearance of a designer or manufacturer's representative who appears with his or her collection to introduce and sell it to the public. In addition to these promotions, which are product-oriented, many retailers or shopping malls use the personal appearance route just for the purpose of drawing crowds. There is no specific merchandise that is targeted for sale, just the need to bring attention to the store or shopping environment.

In 1993, for example, Regis Philbin, the popular daytime television host was employed by the management of Roosevelt Field—now the country's fifth largest mall—to celebrate its expansion and grand reopening.

Few entertainers can get the crowds to a store or mall as well as the soap opera stars can. Their presence almost guarantees attendance wherever they appear.

Visits to stores by dignitaries may also swell the audience. J.C. Penney once featured a special event that highlighted British-made clothing. During the promotion, Prince Charles and Princess Diana of the British Royal Family were on holiday in New York and decided to visit one of the J. C. Penney stores to review the merchandise from their country. The event attracted scores of people who wanted to get a glimpse of the royal family. Whether it is the opera singer, country-western performer, sports personality, movie star, or the stage or television actor who makes the appearance, the crowds are likely to come.

**THEATRICAL PERFORMANCES.**   Sometimes, a retailer arranges for a theatrical troupe to come to the store to perform some of the songs from a current production. New York stores, for example, with their close proximity to the Broadway stage, often use this promotional format. Sometimes it is merely for the purpose of attracting shoppers, while at other times the intention is to raise funds for charities.

Bergdorf Goodman, the high-fashion Fifth Avenue retailer in New York City, invited the cast of the highly successful *Guys and Dolls* Broadway production to perform excerpts from its prize-winning show. As part of their Valentine's celebration, Macy's arranged for the appearance by cast members of Broadway's *She Loves Me* to entertain; as a special inducement to attend, offered a drawing for a free pair of tickets to the production.

At the Financial Center in New York City, a towering office complex that is enhanced with a high-fashion shopping arcade, there is an atrium center, complete with a stage, used to provide entertainment for the shoppers. Members of ballet and opera companies, jazz groups, song stylists, and others regularly appear. At the times of these special event

**FIGURE 13-4**

*Designer Anna Sui*

*greets the crowds.*

*(Courtesy of Macy's)*

performances, the shopping center's numbers increase, providing the merchants with an opportunity to sell their wares.

**AWARDS SHOWS.**   To reward outstanding individual achieve-ment to companies and designers, most segments of the fashion indus-try sponsor awards presentations. These special events bring a great deal of publicity to the industries at large and help remind customers of their existence. Just as the Academy Awards, Tonys, and Emmys bring attention to the specific fields of entertainment, the awards presenta-tions in fashion similarly focus attention.

The formats differ for the various components of the fashion indus-try. The fragrance industry, for example, offers a number of different award categories. At their annual "FiFi" Awards celebration, members of the international fragrance community are treated to a sumptuous dinner before the presentations are made. Categories such as "Retailer of the Year," "Best Fragrance of the Year," "Best Packaging of the Year," "Best Advertising Campaign of the Year," "Best National Print Campaign," and "Medals of Honor" recognize outstanding participation in the field.

In the field of jewelry, a number of different awards are conveyed. Among them are the De Beers Diamonds International Awards, a semiannual event that recognizes outstanding design and designers from around the world; the Argyle Diamonds Champagne Toasts, that recognize designers for their diamond creations; and the American Gem Trade Association's Spectrum Awards Competition, whose purpose is to promote the creative use of natural colored gemstones by North American jewelry designers.

In the vast field of apparel and accessories, there is a great number of these special award events. Some are organized to garner attention for the entire design industry, such as the annual gala sponsored by The Council of Fashion Designers in America, while others are regionally focused to bring attention to a particular geographical region. The Dallas Fashion Awards, for example, sponsored by the Dallas Apparel Mart and American Airlines, plan the event to underscore Dallas as a fashion market. For eight categories that include accessories, bridal wear, designer dresses, and special sizes, a committee of leaders in the fashion industry nominate the firms or designers for consideration. Buyers who attend the Dallas market each August are then invited to cast their votes for their favorites. In the fall of each year, the recipients are awarded the "Femme" statue for his or her accomplishments.

**TRENDS FORUMS.**   To generate the upcoming season's fashion trends, industry professionals as well as consumers are sometimes invited to attend forums that deal specifically with the latest in the world of fashion. Retailers, with either their in-house fashion directors taking the reins or a well-known fashion consultant providing the information, sometimes use store restaurants or community or special events centers for such purposes. Occasionally, a department in the store is cleared for the presentation. The topics run the gamut from trends in business wear to cosmetics.

At the industry level, these forums have become commonplace at trade fairs and expositions. Buyers and merchandisers, for example, are invited to learn about what is hot in their fields. One very popular international trend forum is regularly held at the Children's International Fashion Show, which takes place in France. The event usually concentrates on different segments of the children's market, such as back to school, outdoors, and celebrations. In addition to the formal presentation at this major children's exposition, round table discussions are held where retailers can meet with the industry's manufacturing professionals to explore a variety of topics.

In some of these forums, audiovisual presentations are used to augment the talks given by the professionals. At the Salon International de l'Habillement Masculin Paris (SIHM), a world fashion menswear exposition, the audiovisual technique is employed.

Some manufacturers even sponsor forums at the start of a new season during market week. One such event that pulls out all of the stops is the grand entry of the Buster Brown Apparel Company, maker of children's clothing. Traditionally, several hundred of the major buyers, merchandisers, fashion analysts, and media that cover the children's market are invited to spend an evening to learn about the direction of the industry. Invited guests first gather at a cocktail reception so they may meet with their counterparts in the field. The next step is a presentation by a leading children's fashion consultant who provides insights into future trends. A slide presentation enhanced with upbeat music and intermittent commentary is the format most often used to generate excitement. An elaborate dinner then follows the informative session, enabling guests to share their thoughts with each other. At the evening's conclusion, the guests are invited to dance the night away.

While the initial purpose of this type of sponsorship is informational, it also serves as a way of having those in the industry who make the wholesale purchases and those who generate publicity fondly recall the name Buster Brown Apparel when serious business decisions are being made.

**CONTESTS.**   A variety of contests are offered by raw materials producers, manufacturers, and retailers to give their industries recognition. Many fashion retailers hold contests in which teenagers are selected to represent the store in a variety of capacities.

The young people are generally chosen to participate as members of "Teen Boards." Those hopeful of being selected are required to complete an application that asks questions relating to the school they are presently attending, any awards or honors they have received, names of their references, and so forth. The store carefully examines each application in order to choose a cross section of applicants from all parts of its trading area.

The purpose is to use the teens to promote the store and its merchandise offerings. They might be called upon to be in a fashion show, participate in seminars for other teenagers concerning appropriate dress for a variety of uses, appear in newspaper advertisements, and anything else that will attract the attention of potential teenage customers.

Retailers offer other contests ranging from selecting the most photogenic babies, with the winners receiving wardrobes from the store, to those that are merely "drawings" that tie in with major promotions. The latter cases, for example, Bloomingdales, known for its store-wide recognitions of specific countries, often run contests that award the winners free trips to the country being saluted.

One of the major contests that is akin to those like Miss America is the Maid of Cotton special promotion. Beginning in 1939, goodwill ambassadors for the United States cotton industry have been selected. Applicants apply to the National Cotton Council's office in Memphis, Tennessee, for consideration. If chosen, the finalist receives a $10,000 educational grant and an all-cotton wardrobe.

Applicants must be United States citizens and residents of a cotton-producing state. The judges look for individuals who have good communication skills, poise, and a pleasant personality. If chosen, the winner receives a thorough orientation on the field of cotton so that she will be able to answer any questions at her many public appearances. Unlike the typical beauty pageants, there are no swimsuit or talent competitions. This requires only an ability to be able to communicate with a wealth of audiences.

After an elimination process, the winner is chosen to represent the industry for a year. The various events in which she participates include an appearance at the Cotton Bowl Parade on New Year's Day in Dallas, interviews on television, and fashion shows throughout the world. Contests of these and other types draw a great deal of attention and ultimately translate into business for their organizers.

**JOINT VENTURES.**   Often, two or more businesses join forces to produce a special event that serves their individual needs. It might be a fashion show, as discussed in Chapter 12, that would benefit the designer's collection and the store that sells the merchandise to the consumer. Fashion shows, however, are not the only game in town where joint sponsorship is utilized for a special event.

One example of such an endeavor is exemplified by Bloomingdale's in their Chicago flagship store. The coparticipant was the Disney organization. To commemorate Mickey Mouse's sixtieth birthday, the event featured Mickey himself along with friends Minnie, Pluto, Goofy, Donald Duck, and Roger Rabbit. Original members of the popular Mickey Mouse Club were also on hand to meet and greet the children and parents who were attending the promotion.

Additional events included an artist drawing Disney characters, animated window displays featuring Disneyland favorites, a charitable component that elicited $2.00 donations that would go to the Children's Memorial Medical Center, and a contest that would give the winner a vacation for four at Disneyland.

This type of promotion, as is the case with the others that are institutionally oriented, give the store and its partner in the production a wealth of positive publicity. Of course, the ultimate goal of any promotion is to generate business. Joint promotions are particularly popular since the costs of development and presentation are shared by those involved.

The list of institutional-type formats goes on and on. It might involve a marathon to underscore physical fitness, invited chefs from restaurants to create and sample their specialties, support of local Little League teams for youngsters, cultural programs, how-to programs, educational seminars on such topics as dealing with the newborn, or anything that will come from the creative minds of those responsible for special events that will bring positive attention to the company name.

## MERCHANDISE PROMOTIONS

While the institutional technique is a subtle way to gain business for those in the fashion industry, practitioners also participate in a number of events that are designed to sell specific merchandise.

### Meet your favorite Disneyland Characters!

Bloomingdale's celebrates Mickey's 60th Birthday with special appearances by the birthday Mouse himself...and his friends Minnie, Pluto, Goofy, Donald Duck, and Roger Rabbit.  From noon to 6 Thursday, Dec. 8 through Sunday, Dec. 11, in Infants on 3.

**Meet the Mouseketeers**
Original members of the Mickey Mouse Club, Sherry Alberoni and Bobby Burgess will be on hand to say hello Thursday, Dec. 8 from noon to 2 in Men's Designer on 2. Got your ears on?

**See Disney Artist in Action**
Stacia Martin draws your favorite Disney characters in a flash! From noon to 6 Dec. 8-11 In Maternity on 3.

### The Disney Shop

Mickey, Minnie and friends make items from the Disney shop a special treat for kids of all ages, from infants to adults. Look for them under the neon in The Next Generation on 3 thru Christmas.

**Disney Animated Windows**
See your Disneyland favorites come to life on 3 near mall entrance.

**Register to win a family trip to Disneyland**
Enter to win an exciting, fun-filled vacation for a family of four at Disneyland in California, visit the newest attraction, Splash Mountain, and continue your celebration of Mickey's 60th year!  Mall entrance on 3.

**Visit the "When You Wish Upon A Star" Tree**
As part of Mickey's Birthday celebration, Bloomingdale's has created a special Christmas tree for Children's Memorial Medical Center.  When you donate $2 to turn on a light...your wish helps a child get well.  Visit our tree on 3 and take home a star to hang on your own tree.

| Dec. 3 - 4 | noon to 6 | Dec. 11 | 10 to 7 |
| Dec. 8 - 10 | 9:30 to 9 | Dec. 17 - 18 | noon to 6 |

**FIGURE 13-5**

*A joint venture between*

*Bloomingdale's and*

*Disney (Courtesy of*

*Bloomingdale's)*

These events range from those that might introduce a new designer label to a store's clientele, to the obligatory clearance sales that are necessary to dispose of unwanted merchandise.

**TRADITIONAL SALES.**   At the conclusion of a regular selling period, it is common practice for retailers to eliminate their unsold inventories at reduced prices. These events might come immediately after Christmas, the Fourth of July, or any time the store feels it must dispose of unwanted inventories.

Sales of this nature are subscribed to by merchants because often the lower prices might bring a new group of shoppers to the store who otherwise might not be able to afford the original prices. Many retailers, therefore, are appealing to two customer bases in their stores.

An extension of the traditional sales event that has become increasingly popular in the industry is to take second and even third markdowns on merchandise. Once the traditional first markdown period has slowed down, many retailers run special sales periods that take even deeper price cuts. These special merchandise promotions usually run for a few days only to make certain that the store will sell off its remaining inventory quickly.

**PRIVATE SALES.**   Using customer mailing lists that have been developed through credit card sales, some retailers use the private sale approach to reach their loyal clientele. Instead of announcing to the general public through advertising means that a sale is about to commence, the retailer informs the customers of a sale "only for them" through direct mail pieces.

For the shopper to qualify for the discount or any other incentives that are offered, a card or invitation must be presented at the time of the purchase. These special sales events for "preferred customers" offer such special considerations as free alterations, free gift wrapping, deferred billing, and gifts with a purchase in addition to special discounts.

Bloomingdale's held an event that proclaimed "this event is not advertised to the public." The sales event offered shoppers gift certificates for future purchases based upon the one-day event's purchases. Customers received gift certificates that ranged from $100 for a $500 purchase to $1,000 for a $5,000 purchase.

**CREDIT CARD SALES.** In an attempt to bolster the use of a store's own credit card or the need for a third-party credit card company to bolster customer usage, retailers sometimes offer special sale prices for those using the appropriate credit card.

Many major merchants wanting to increase their credit card customer numbers offer discounts on any purchases made the day a new account is opened. Sometimes, special discounts are offered by way of

**FIGURE 13-6**

*Special shopping nights*

*promotion (Courtesy of*

*Bloomingdale's)*

THIS EVENT IS NOT
ADVERTISED TO THE PUBLIC

# TWO PRIVATE NIGHTS

JOIN US FROM 5PM TO 11PM
IN BERGEN COUNTY THURSDAY, MARCH 10TH
AND FRIDAY, MARCH 11TH
AND IN GARDEN CITY TUESDAY, MARCH 8TH
AND WEDNESDAY, MARCH 9TH

**bloomingdale's**

promotions from credit organizations such as American Express. In December 1993, American Express in conjunction with Bloomingdale's ran a promotion that delivered discount coupons to American Express cardholders. Each coupon offered a different discount for a purchase at Bloomingdale's. Not only did the credit card company increase its usage, but the store increased its sales volume for the designated period.

**GIMMICK SALES**.    Some retail organizations employ sales gimmicks to attract attention. While the ultimate reward for the shopper is a price reduction, the methods of motivating them to buy are often unique.

Filene's Basement initiated a program that was so successful that it has become a regular part of their special events program. Customers in the company's trading areas receive announcements of a surprise sale that features a covered seal. Under the seal there is a discount indicated that is taken off the customer's purchases. The seal may only be broken at the time the sale is made. Starting with minimum guaranteed discounts of 10 percent and ranging to total free purchases, the customer is invited to participate in this game of chance. Other retailers subscribe to gimmick sales that are labeled "Assistant Buyer Days" or "Manager Days," where special prices are attributed to creative merchandise acquisition by these managerial individuals.

Regular sales have become commonplace and often unnoticed by many shoppers. With the use of sales gimmicks, appetites might be sufficiently whetted to come and shop.

**LIMITED PERIOD SALES**.    When the advertisements announce for "one day only" or for "this weekend" a store is going to reduce a portion of its inventory. After that time, the prices return to their original markups. A & S Department Stores and Macy's are proponents of such abbreviated sales periods as are many other retailers. The purpose is to generate sales during periods that are traditionally slow. In this way, the store motivates customers who probably would not come to the store otherwise.

**SAMPLE SALES**.    Designers and manufacturers of fashion merchandise spend a great deal of money developing product lines each

**FIGURE 13-7**

*Special sales event*

*(Courtesy of Filene's*

*Basement)*

season. Realistically, only a small number of styles created for a collection is ultimately produced for distribution to the stores. At each wholesale season's end, the manufacturers find themselves with many samples that must be discarded before the next season's business may begin.

To dispose of these items and return some of the initial money invested in them for fabrics, construction, trimmings, and so on, more and more designers and manufacturers are conducting "sample sales." Through the use of hand-distributed advertisements and direct mail as well as announcements in periodicals, such as *New York Magazine* in the "Sales and Bargains" column, interested parties are invited to come to the producer's showroom or stockroom to purchase the samples.

So successful are these sales that many manufacturers have expanded them to include overruns of merchandise that they are unable to sell to the stores. Some have become so significant that the producer's own facilities are insufficient for the merchandise offered and the crowds that are attracted. Companies like Hugo Boss have rented space in garment center buildings for such occasions and Escada has taken floor space in the Parsons School of Design for similar use.

**CHARITY SALES.** Some producers in the fashion world dispose of their merchandise in yet another manner, via the charity sale. It has become commonplace for the country's renowned designer names to donate merchandise to be sold at a fraction of its original costs for purposes of raising money for  medical research. The American Cancer Society and AIDS foundations have, among others, been recipients of the monies received through these sales.

While the charities are helped significantly through these events, the companies also derive a good deal of recognition from the consumer at large who might opt to make future purchases wherever the merchandise is offered for sale.

**SAMPLING.** In the cosmetics and fragrance industry, there is often a shared special events effort between the manufacturer and retailer in the promotion of their products. With such a wealth of products vying for the consumer's attention, one of the major ways in which to get an audience is through the use of samples.

Just like the apparel and accessories industries, cosmetics changes take place with each season. As the world of fashion focuses attention on a new color palette for clothing, new cosmetic colors are also added as enhancements.

One of the most popular ways in which to promote cosmetics as well as new fragrances that are being launched, is by way of the sample route. The brainchild of Estée Lauder, cosmetic companies plan special programs that offer samples of their latest products. Typically, at the numerous fragrance and cosmetics counters in the stores, point-of-purchase displays are arranged that spell out the sampling event. Generally, with the purchase of a company's product, the customer either receives, free of charge, a sample of a new product or a "kit" of several products for a nominal charge. Through this undertaking, it is the hope of the manufacturer that the sample will meet with the customer's satisfaction and future business will be the result.

**DEMONSTRATIONS.** Some merchandise lends itself well to demonstration. In fashion, the focus of these events is oriented toward cosmetics and fragrances and certain accessories.

There always seem to be crowds drawn to cosmetic demonstrations where a volunteer is culled from the audience to participate in the promotion. Make-up artists professionally apply a host of products to the chosen individual. While using each formula, the audience is taught the benefits of each one. At the end of the demonstration, the results are generally positive, motivating many observers to purchase the demonstrated products.

One of the accessories that often increases in sales when demonstrated is the scarf. Professionals supplied by the scarves' manufacturers show potential purchasers passing through the stores how a simple square or oblong scarf may be used in a number of different ways.

The demonstration event is usually a combined effort between the producer and retailer. The former is keenly aware that the lifeblood of his or her business lies with the customer's acceptance. While print and broadcast advertising expenditures are significantly utilized to capture consumer attention, it is the hands-on approach that often makes the registers ring and makes the buyers reorder the merchandise. In the same vein, the retailer knows the value of having a professional company representative demonstrate the products. They can best answer the questions and show how the product's use may be maximized. The marriage of the two can help to promote the product and bring profits to the respective companies.

## REVIEW QUESTIONS

1. What are the two major classifications for special events? How do they differ from each other?

2. For what specific purposes are institutional special events promoted?

3. Describe the term *long-running spectacular* as it relates to the special events programs for retailers.

4. What is the longest-running, regularly produced special event that was originated by Macy's and ultimately used by other retailers across the United States?

5. Why have the traditional Thanksgiving Day parades taken such an important place in promotion?

6. If a store such as Macy's does not sell plants or flowers, why does it invest so much money in their display during the Flower Show event?

7. At what time of the year does the fashion retailer spend the greatest amount of money on promotional special events?

8. In addition to Christmas, what other holidays bring fashion retailers increased sales through special events?

9. Discuss some of the different types of individuals used by retailers, as well as designers, to make personal appearances to attract shoppers.

10. List and describe some of the awards presentations used by the fashion industry to recognize outstanding achievement.

11. What is a trend forum? Which segments of the fashion industry use them as promotional events?

12. Explain how a teen board helps the retailer.

13. Discuss the concept of the joint venture and how it is used in the fashion industry for promotional purposes.

14. What is meant by the term *private sale* in retailing?

15. Describe two gimmick sales that merchants use to motivate shopping in their stores.

16. Which segment of the fashion industry uses sample sales as a special event?

17. For which fashion product classification does sampling usually bring great results?

18. How does the demonstration technique differ from sampling?

## EXERCISES

1. Plan a fund-raising special event for your school, fashion club, or any other organization in which you have interest that requires the procurement and sale of fashion merchandise. The event might be used to raise money for a charity, to purchase educational equipment such as computers, or anything else that would serve a charitable or educational purpose. The merchandise may be obtained from a number of sources including fashion designers and manufacturers, retailers, fashion market consultants such as resident buying offices, and so on.

   A carefully planned promotional campaign should be developed using posters, direct mail, telephone solicitation, and so forth to collect merchandise donations and to announce the time and place of the event.

   Committees should be planned for each aspect of the undertaking such as:

   • merchandise procurement;
   • advertising and promoting the event; and
   • facilities planning.

2. Contact a major retailer in your area and present the concept of a teen board to them.

   A contest should be used for the selection of the participants and might include:

   • writing an essay on desire for participation;
   • creating a fashion design; and
   • goals for the future.

   Once the participants have been selected, the students and the store should develop a plan for a special event to appropriately use the teen board.

*Fashion videos*

*lend excitement*

*to a retail*

*environment.*

# *Fashion Videos*

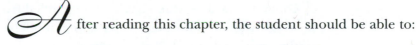

$\mathcal{A}$fter reading this chapter, the student should be able to:

1. Discuss the importance of videos to the various segments of the fashion industry.

2. Describe the different types of fashion videos that are employed by fashion-oriented organizations.

3. Explain how the fashion video has enabled users to get their messages to larger audiences at lower costs.

4. List and discuss the various stages of production of fashion videos.

5. Prepare a script for a fashion video presentation.

# Introduction

When fashion designer Norma Kamali installed television monitors in the window of her retail emporium and used them to feature her entire apparel collection, it was the beginning of a new type of promotion. Passersby, either unfamiliar with the designer's fashion creative genius or unable to spend time to have the merchandise presented by a salesperson, could quickly discover what awaits them if they choose to enter the store. The idea of showing an entire collection in this manner was soon embraced by many others in the industry.

All across the country, major fashion retailers were quick to install television receivers on their selling floors to feature runway shows. These presentations were to all intents and purposes solely produced for attending audiences. By taping them and featuring them on the store's selling floors, endless numbers of potential customers were able to experience the excitement of the original presentations and perhaps, be motivated to seek and purchase the featured items.

The video is no longer relegated to use by retailers to attract consumer attention. Merchants are using them in place of the typical flyers and bulletins that were the major means of spreading their fashion messages to managers and sales associates in the branch stores. Fashion designers are interacting with potential buyers by producing tapes that feature a cross section of their lines, and even the resident buying offices are communicating with their clients via these means.

Today, the fashion video has been expanded from its original simple, straightforward format of parading models, to sophisticated, exciting entries that utilize the originality found in Music Television (MTV) presentations. Replete with original music, unique visual sequences, and dramatic voice-overs, the new generation of videos has become a mainstay of fashion promotion.

# Industrial Users of Fashion Videos

Each day, the production and use of videos in the world of fashion continues to expand. At every level of the industry, companies are embracing the tool as an exciting and generally cost-conserving method of interacting with the field's professionals and consuming public.

**FIGURE 14-1**

*Television monitors*

*show fashion*

*merchandise collections.*

## RETAILERS

Today's merchants have come to utilize the fashion video for two separate purposes. One purpose is as an enhancement to the store's traditional visual presentations and the other is as a means of communicating with buyers, merchandisers, managers, and sales associates about a variety of fashion-related practices.

**SELLING FLOOR VISUAL PRESENTATIONS.**   One can rarely pass through America's major department stores without being greeted by a fashion video. The nature and scope of these presentations range from the runway variety that feature the collections of designers and manufacturers being promoted by the stores, to the upbeat, contemporary entries that offer rock music performances in interesting settings. Each is designed to motivate the passersby to purchase merchandise.

Different departments utilize different video formats. The aforementioned runway shows and specific merchandise presentations are generally found in the departments that concentrate on higher priced lines of merchandise. Each season, for example, the DKNY collection is generally shown within the departments that bear its label. As one moves from one designer area to another, the monitors focus upon the merchandise of a different designer.

With physical fitness preoccupying the minds of many shoppers, retailers have found that "workout" merchandise, when enhanced with the use of action videos, sells in greater quantities. The viewer is shown that the old sweatsuit and gym shorts have been replaced with newer, exciting fashions that are appropriate for the daily exercise routine. The videos that are merchandise-oriented are provided by the vendors in hope that the stores will utilize them in key locations and higher sales volumes will be the result.

In some stores, it is not specific merchandise that is featured, but productions similar to those seen on MTV. In junior departments and specialty stores that cater to the young, the theme generally concentrates on rock music that is augmented with imaginative visual sequences. The purpose is to put shoppers into an upbeat mood that will encourage them to shop. Not only do some stores use individual receivers to feature the videos, but some utilize "video walls" that offer spectacular visuals. Wet Seal, a fashion retail chain that caters to the teenage and young adult female, uses enormous video walls that can be seen by the shoppers who stop to look into the store. In some of their newer locations, a significant part of the rear of the stores have a series of video screens that rival the size of those found in movie theaters. The lively music and the exciting action make the stores come to life.

**COMMUNICATING WITH THE STORE'S PERSONNEL.** The fashion department stores and chain organizations generally manage their businesses from central locations. It is either from a main or flagship store as is the case with operations like Macy's or from company headquarters such as the one operated by J.C. Penney. In either situation, the size of the institutions and the vast geographical territory they often cover make it difficult for management to effectively communicate with their spread-out staffs.

Some of the fashion-oriented tasks that the major retailers regularly deal with concern merchandise selection, familiarization of the upcoming trends for the sales associates, methods for the improvement of visual merchandising, and providing product information.

*Merchandise Selection.*   While most of the large fashion retail operations rely upon their buyers and merchandisers to select products for all of the stores in the group, some believe in the philosophy that different locations require different merchandise assortments. J.C. Penney departs from the traditional centralized merchandising plan where "model stocks" are purely in the domain of the buyer. Using a satellite station that enables top management to interface with the individual units' department managers, J.C. Penney's is able to have the buying and merchandising decisions made at the store level.

Through the use of videos that feature the merchandise recommended by the company's buyers, each department manager is shown the various items on a television screen. After examining everything that is available, they then choose the items best suited for their store in size and color assortments best suited for their needs. Prior to the introduction of the video format, store and department managers had to rely on photographs, drawings, and written documents for their selections. The full-color, lifelike merchandise presentations on video provide for better decision making.

*Trends Familiarization.*   All too often, the store's sales associates have insufficient information about fashion trends. Their distance from the buyers makes dissemination of information a difficult chore. Generally, those in retail sales do not have any advance training about the latest in styling, new color palettes, fabric usage, and so forth. Understanding the nature of the season's latest approach to fashion prepares the salesperson to deal with customer questions and requests.

To improve the lines of communications with the store's sales staff, retailers like Strawbridge & Clothier, the Philadelphia-based department store, have developed videos that feature the season's styles on models that typify their customers. While the runway show is a technique many use to show the collections to sales associates, the

Strawbridge & Clothier video presentation helps the sellers learn about which styles are best suited to their customer's needs.

***Effective Use of Visual Merchandising.*** No matter which department store organization is being evaluated in terms of visual effectiveness, it is the company flagship that garners the most attention. In most situations, the visual merchandising department is located in the main or flagship store and its director and staff is on hand to oversee the installations. The branch stores are often shortchanged when it comes to the intricacies of display. Where and how departments feature their goods and the manner in which they are shown to the customers are usually left to a very small visual staff and to department managers. While the people in the branch visual department are often professionals in their fields, the limited staffing generally restricts them from doing more than the installation and "straightening" of displays that have been poorly handled by shoppers.

To underscore the importance of the department's appearance and to show the appropriate ways in which to feature merchandise that will motivate shoppers to become customers, Neiman-Marcus has developed a video presentation on visual merchandising. Every detail is covered, from how compatible merchandise should be displayed to build sales, to the proper ways to display their products. The video is the work of the flagship's visual team and is sent to the branches to train them in the importance of merchandise presentation.

***Providing Product Knowledge.*** In the aforementioned section on trends familiarization, the emphasis was more on what is new than what makes the product unique and how it might benefit the sales associates if they are more familiar with the construction and merchandising. Many manufacturers are using the video for just those purposes. They are providing their retail customers with tapes that cover such areas as raw material selection, construction techniques, and how to sell the products.

Among those who are using the video as a teaching tool for their retail clientele is Allen Edmonds, a manufacturer of better men's and women's footwear. In their video, *The Making of Fine Shoes*, they teach shoe sellers about leather selection and qualities, shoe construction from the design to the finished product, and the way in which the life of the shoe may be extended. Another user of the video format is the

Amity Leather Company, makers of small leather products that bear the Amity and Rolf signatures. Their presentations also feature the details of product construction and the ways the items should be sold to the consumer. A video that has helped take an accessory that is often lost among the other merchandise and make it into a best seller is *The Wonderful World of Scarves* produced by the Fashion Accessories Association for retailer use. It teaches the ways in which scarves should be displayed in the showcase and the many ways in which the sales associates may manipulate them for different uses.

## MANUFACTURERS AND DESIGNERS

In addition to producing videos that are directed at their retail clients and the consuming public, some manufacturers use them as a means of improving the product knowledge of their sales representatives. In cases in which the organization has regional sales offices and "road" representatives with whom they spend little time, the use of tapes has become a perfect vehicle. The maker of Guess watches uses such a format for educating their representatives about the product's manufacture and the image it wishes to convey to the retail accounts.

Another use of videos by apparel and accessories producers is for showroom viewing by store buyers. During peak selling periods such as market week buyers must sometimes wait to see a collection, even if an appointment has been scheduled. To keep them in a positive frame of mind and to spark interest in what they will shortly see, some showrooms continuously play videos that preview the lines.

Many manufacturers also use the video as a means of enhancing the merchandise that is generally shown without the benefit of models. The use of professionals on the screen who wear the clothing may augment the traditional methods of selling.

## SHOPPING CENTERS

A visit to some of the country's vast retail shopping centers reveals that the video has found still another place where it can help stimulate sales. In the giant shopping outlets such as Sawgrass and Gurnee Mills, with approximately two miles of storefronts under one roof, discovering what is available and exactly where it can be found is a difficult task for shoppers. At these and other centers, management features strategically placed monitors that offer information about the stores, their product mixes, and where they are located. In addition to the individual television receivers, each major section of these shopping centers boasts a video wall that dramatically depicts what is available in the specific section. Enhanced with exciting music, these videos help to move the traffic to the various retailers in the center.

## THE DISPLAY INDUSTRY

Just as the apparel producers use video to promote business, so do many of those companies involved in the manufacture of visual enhancements. Manufacturers of fashion-oriented props, signage, mannequins, and every other display material are using videos to reach their retail markets. Unlike the clothing and accessories designers and manufacturers who are housed in well-defined areas, such as the Garment Center in New York or a specific building like the Chicago Apparel Center, those who produce visual props for the fashion industry are haphazardly located throughout the country.

To present their offerings to the retailing industry, some use videos. One such user is AdMart International, a company that specializes in all types of signage for the fashion retailer. A video featuring how their products are made, the scope of their offerings, and how they can be utilized in the fashion retailer's environment is displayed at trade fairs to attract the attention of the attendees. Those interested in bringing the information back to their companies for further inspection are provided with their own copies of the video.

Another major player in the visual merchandising game is Spaeth Design, creators of animated displays. Examples of their work are always evidenced in the flagships of stores such as Lord & Taylor and Saks Fifth Avenue. They use a video presentation to show potential retailers and fashion shopping malls how their creations are tailored to specific needs and how store windows and selling arenas can be transformed into magical, show-stopping events.

## MARKET CONSULTANTS

More and more market consultants such as resident buying offices and fashion forecasters are communicating with their accounts via video. In addition to the use of traditional direct mail print pieces, many are preparing videos that feature the season's trends, private label collections, methods of promoting merchandise, and other areas of concern for retailers.

# The Elements of Fashion Videos

The different needs of the users of fashion videos results in a variety of types that are produced. Each has its own elements and uniqueness that makes it the perfect tool to promote business and solve problems. Some are rather simple to create and produce, while the sophistication and complexity of others makes their production sometimes as difficult as producing motion pictures. The following includes the various parts that comprise most fashion videos.

## THE CONCEPT

The wealth of those tapes used in the industry include fashion shows that range from the simple runway parade of models to the thematic type that utilizes a story line; instructional entries that teach sales representatives about product construction and the best ways to sell to professional buyers; how-to tapes that teach the viewers the different uses of a single product; motivational pieces such as those that feature aerobic participants moving through their exercise routines in the hope of selling physical fitness merchandise; techniques for the improvement of fashion visual presentations; and industry overviews that prepare buyers for their market visits. The object of each tape must first be determined by a company's promotional director or team. Once the goals have been established, the concept is then presented to a video production company whose names and locations are readily available from directories such as the *Yellow Pages*, advertising agencies, or advertisements in the trade periodicals. The role of trade periodicals is discussed later in the chapter. After the concept has been determined, most projects generally require a script, footage, voice-overs, music, and graphics.

## THE SCRIPT

Most videos that feature a story line begin with the creation of the script. Runway presentations, choreographed exercise routines, and projects of that nature do not generally use spoken words but rely mainly on music to set the mood.

Those that are instructionally oriented, such as the types that teach sales associates about fashion trends or how products are manufactured, a script is a necessary element.

Some of the rules that govern script writing include:

1. The words should be appropriate to the targeted audience. If the market is the consumer, technical terminology should be avoided, with simple sentences used to assure comprehension. For industrial professionals, the language of the trade should be used in the script since they are certain to be versed in such language.

2. Scripts should be as brief as possible, using words only as an enhancement of the live action and music. Too many messages tend to confuse the listener and interfere with the action on the screen.

3. Each phase of the script should be timed to make certain that it specifically coincides with the images on the screen. That is, the words should not last longer than the portion of the tape to which it refers.

## FOOTAGE

It is a matter of preference by some producers as to whether the script comes before or after the action has been taped. Some prefer to get all of the footage "in the can" and then to tailor a script to fit it, while others believe a tightly developed script is a good guideline for what should be recorded. In either case, the taping of the visual portions, or "shoots" as they are referred to in the industry, is of primary importance. It must be remembered that video is a visually oriented medium and the images and sequences captured on tape are the most important aspects of the production's elements. The scope of the project will determine how much time must be spent shooting the raw footage and what should be captured to give the project viewing interest.

The simplest of the video productions is the fashion runway show. The action takes place in an arena, where the camera captures the models prancing and dancing to the music, with some live commentary used to augment the action. If the action merely shows the sixty or seventy costumes being paraded, the end result is likely to be monotonous. The "shoot" should always include action other than just the parade of models. Shots of the audience, the backstage action, the designer helping the models with last-minute adjustments to their garments, dressers hurrying and scurrying to make certain that the right outfit will appear in the right sequence, and the press with their flashbulbs popping all help make the final tape an exciting one. The proper editing of the footage, as discussed later in the chapter, will add to the worthiness of the project.

Often, the new footage may be augmented with "stock" footage; that is, tape that has been acquired from other sources. Photographs, slides, graphs, forms, and other stationary illustrations may also be utilized in certain situations. In the case of a collection being presented that might contrast styles of yesteryear with the designer's current collection, the inclusion of photographs and drawings are necessary since live-action footage might not have been available. These "stills" are then incorporated into the video and "moved" with the director's guidance to give the impression of live action.

## VOICE-OVERS

When interviews are conducted as part of the presentation or instructions are delivered in areas such as product development, the voices heard on the tape are those of the people shown. When action takes place that necessitates commentary from other sources, a voice-over is used. That is, the action is shown, enhanced by spoken words that appear on the tape without the benefit of the individual being seen. People chosen for these tasks should possess trained voices that provide interest to the piece. Professional actors and actresses are usually selected for these tasks.

## MUSIC

The music that is used for fashion videos includes melodies and lyrics that have been published for other uses, compositions that have been specifically written for a particular video, and unpublished pieces that are available from industrial sources for a nominal fee. If published music is chosen, the rights to it must be obtained from the composer and royalties or a fee must be paid for its use.

Music may be the centerpiece to a video, as is the case of those often seen playing in the junior departments of a store. It is the sound that often captures the shopper's attention in these sales arenas.

In other video presentations, the music is generally used as an accompaniment to the action. In the fashion show production, the musical selections play two important roles. One is as an accompaniment to set the pace of the models' movements and the other is to establish the tone of the production.

## GRAPHICS

The graphics used in a fashion video often include company logos and any other headlines and selling terms that the viewer is expected to remember. Major runway videos always have the designer's name prominently displayed as a backdrop so that every time the camera focuses on a model, the viewer will be reminded of whose collection he or she is seeing. The style of lettering that is used to exhibit the designer's name is the same type that is found on the garment's labels and in print advertisements so that they will become synonymous with the creator's work.

Today's graphic designs are usually accomplished by computer utilization. A host of different programs and software are available to accommodate just about every graphic need.

# Producing the Product

Once the various components of the project have been completed, it is the job of the producer to coordinate all of them into a finished product. The complexity of his or her chore is based upon the sophistication required and the dollar amount allocated for its completion.

Costs of video production vary considerably. The novice who merely wants to record a small retailer's fashion show for a charity might merely focus the traditional home video camera on the event and pick up the sounds of the music and commentary. Such an endeavor only involves the cost of the tape, normally the inexpensive half-inch variety and the fee of the cameraperson. The cost may be as little as $250. Those do-it-yourselfers might opt for the purchase of a better quality camera, known as a "high-eight," which produces better quality than the standard equipment.

At the other extreme is the professional endeavor of fashion video production that may cost as much as $150,000. Designers and manufacturers wishing to capture the attention of their markets with carefully designed tapes that utilize professional actors, complete musical scores, and unique special effects often spend a sum in that range. However, much can be accomplished at an exceptional level that costs about $10,000. Typically, the traditional runway taping comes in at that price. These quality productions are either shot on three-quarter-inch tape or Betacam to guarantee clarity. The client receives the master copy on one of those formats and has half-inch reproductions made to send to clients. Although the quality is somewhat diminished on the half-inch tape, it is less costly and usable on the standard video receivers. Showing the video at the three-quarter-inch level requires specialized equipment, which typical viewers and users of the productions rarely have on their premises.

The aforementioned professional production is edited into a finished product through the efforts of the producer and trained technicians. Their job is to follow the details of the script that has been provided. That includes coordinating the visuals, often a combination of live-action footage with photographs and other illustrative materials, inserting the voice-overs at the appropriate times of the action on the tape along with the music, and adding extra visual excitement with the use of special effects.

## EDITING

At the production company's facilities, the components of the project are assembled. The production company houses a host of equipment. Scanners take still slides and transfer them onto tape and, with the technician's aid, institutes "moves" that give the impression of live-action rather than the blandness of the traditional photographs.

The most important task at this stage of development is to faithfully follow the script. It details every aspect of the final presentation. The exact footage that will be used is generally only a fraction of what has been taped on location and in the studio. It is not unusual for a full-day shoot of eight to ten hours to produce about fifteen minutes of usable

## FASHION VIDEO SCRIPT

| VOICE-OVER | VISUALS |
|---|---|
| (Music) Editor:<br>See notes at end of script. | Montage:<br>Each decade is represented by different visuals.<br><br>Graphic: TEENAGE SCHOOL DRESS: THEN AND NOW |
| 1950s<br>1960s<br>1970s<br>1980s<br>1990s | slides 1 & 2<br>stock footage, 16 mm, (12 seconds from opening shot)<br>stock footage, 16 mm, (10 seconds from opening shot)<br>stock footage (Ent. Video Prod., #22   8:52 – 9:02)<br>shoot 1   2:23 – 2:35<br>slides 3, 4, 5, 6, 7, and 8 |
| Teenage dress was certainly not always as we know it today. It has evolved from a more formal approach to one that allows for individual, unique styling! | |
| In the fifties, the dictates of teenager fashion, especially for school, came from educators and parents. | stock footage, 16 mm, 35 seconds |
| As we entered the sixties, the standards changed. The influences came from watching television sit-coms and ultimately from the mod stylings of the Beatles. | stock footage, 16 mm, 35 seconds |
| The seventies were a time for bell-bottoms as the shape of the day and girls were allowed to wear pants to school instead of dresses. | stock footage, 16 mm, 35 seconds |

**FIGURE 14-2**

*Fashion video script noting*

*voice-overs and visuals*

## FASHION VIDEO SCRIPT—continued

| | |
|---|---|
| The advent of MTV provided new entertainers who would set the styles of the eighties. | stock footage (Ent. Video Prod., #22 11:02 – 11:16) |
| Madonna! | stock footage (Ent. Video Prod., #22 12:14 – 12:30) |
| Michael Jackson! | stock footage (Ent. Video Prod., #22 14:30 – 14:45) |
| Movies were also the rage for dictating fashion! | stock footage (Ent. Video Prod., #23 3:23 – 3:35) |
| Saturday Night Fever! | stock footage (Ent. Video Prod., #23 6:28– 6:40) |
| Miami Vice! | stock footage (Ent. Video Prod., #23 15:21 – 15:35 |
| The nineties, at first, carried over the essence of the eighties. | shoot 1    4:24 – 4:40 |
| Kids in sweats and sneakers were solid hits! | shoot 1    5:23 – 5:45 |
| Jeans and baseball caps made major impacts! | shoot 1    7:28 – 7:38 |
| And bell-bottoms resurfaced! | shoot 2    4:24 – 4:40 |
| Today, the fashions are fun and funky, individualistic as well as predictable and more exciting than ever! | shoot 2, mix about 35 seconds from footage to show the styling described in accompanying voice-over |

## FASHION VIDEO SCRIPT—continued

(Music) Editor:
Throughout the video, the music used should be indicative of what was popular during the decades depicted on the screen. When the voice-overs are heard, the sounds should be lowered and raised again when only the action is taking place! Before the music is added, I want to make certain that the selections are appropriate!

**FIGURE 14-2**

*Continued*

tape. Thus, the script must carefully identify the required footage on the script, exactly where it will be used. This procedure, along with identification and placement of photographs, charts, and forms, if used, and any other instructions to the editor, is explored in the following example to show how detailed the editing process is.

The premise of the example, entitled Teenage School Dress: Then and Now, is that it be used as an adjunct to a live fashion show that features contemporary styling for the young. A five-minute production, it is shown to motivate the viewing audience, with the final taped moments coming alive with the in-person show.

**ANALYSIS OF SCRIPTED MARKINGS.** The notations and markings on the script give the editor the directions needed to produce the video. It should be understood, however, that even with the most detailed instructions, postproduction refinement is usually necessary to make corrections.

Some of the more typical markings include:

1. Slide Numbers—Each slide is numbered and used wherever it is indicated. The length of time each slide appears varies from approximately 4–6 seconds, with the amounts determined by the

editor unless specifically indicated. In the example shown, slides are intermingled with 16 mm "stock footage," video stock footage, and special "shoots."

2. Stock Footage—The film or video, as the case may be, is purchased from a company that owns the rights to it. The frames to be used are either specifically indicated or left to the discretion of the editor. The time needed is always indicated in seconds. The name of the company from which the footage is purchased is indicated on the package. In this example, it is from Entertainment Video Productions.

3. Shoots—A term to indicate footage that has been specifically produced as per the instructions of the video producer. The exact footage to be used is indicated first by the number of the tape and followed by exact time frames. To pinpoint exactly what is to be used from the available footage, the times are "burned" into the master tape for easy location. Thus, #23 12:14–12:30 signifies that tape #23 is the one to use, at the "burn-in" markings that read 12:14–12:30 for a total of sixteen seconds!

4. Unmarked Footage—When the selection is left to the discretion of the editor, the script merely indicates the shoot from which it should be taken, where it should be placed, and the amount to use.

5. Music Notations—This is either indicated by the producer or left to the discretion of the editor. If left to the editor, a selection guideline should be indicated on the script.

## POSTPRODUCTION

As has been briefly referred to, a finished product is rarely achieved after the initial editing. Some producers require a review of the project at many steps along the way. For example, there might be an initial evaluation of the tape without the insertion of a voice-over or music. In other cases, the producer might want to see all of the elements coordinated. Whatever the preference, the piece is not considered ready for delivery until all of the "kinks" have been ironed out.

## REVIEW QUESTIONS

1. Which fashion designer is given credit as the first to use video as a major type of promotion?

2. Why is it advantageous for a retailer to feature runway video presentations in selling departments?

3. For what purpose is the MTV type of video used in stores if they do not depict specific merchandise that the store carries?

4. Why does J.C. Penney use the fashion video format to communicate with store managers?

5. How can video be effectively used for visual installations?

6. What value does the fashion video have as a training device for sellers?

7. How do outlet centers such as Sawgrass Mills utilize video in their shopping arenas?

8. In what way can fashion videos help resident buying offices get their messages to the retailers?

9. What is meant by the term *concept* as it applies to fashion videos?

10. Define the term *voice-over*.

11. What are some of the musical sources for videos?

12. Differentiate between half-inch and three-quarter-inch tape.

13. Describe the role of the editor in video production.

14. What is meant by *stock footage?*

15. Describe what is meant by a video *shoot*.

## EXERCISES

1. Using any area of fashion that you wish, prepare a video script, with all of the notations and markings, that would run for approximately

five minutes. Included should be items such as the voice-over, musical selections, sources of visuals, and so forth.

By visiting retailers in your area and watching the videos they feature in their stores, you should get enough information about some of the types you might want to write a script for.

2. Contact a video production company that specializes in fashion videos. Their names may be found in the *Yellow Pages* or at the conclusion of video presentations. Ask for an appointment to interview a company representative to obtain information about the industry. With the knowledge acquired through the meeting, an oral report should be prepared for delivery to the class.

*The press kit is developed*

*to gain publicity for a*

*company, person, or*

*product line. (Courtesy*

*of Ruth Scharf*

*Industries, A Division*

*of Bryan Industries)*

# *Publicity: Obtaining Editorial Coverage*

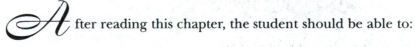

$\mathscr{A}$fter reading this chapter, the student should be able to:

1. Discuss the value of publicity to the fashion organization.

2. Differentiate between publicity and advertising.

3. Explain how publicists successfully place their news stories with the media.

4. Write an announcement or press release that a fashion organization would use to spread its message to the media.

5. Prepare a fashion-oriented press kit.

# Introduction

When Benetton decided to take an unusual advertising approach for its company, it immediately benefitted from editorial coverage that echoed all over the world. Its approach, never before attempted by the fashion industry, was to use social issues as a means of heightening awareness. Rather than focus an advertising campaign on its merchandise collection, which more than likely would not sufficiently intrigue the fashion press to give it editorial coverage, it developed and published a series of advertisements, one of which featured a dying AIDS victim. Whether the intention of the advertisements was to raise consciousness, as they purported, or to merely bring attention to the company name, the concept worked. The promotion not only prompted the trade and fashion publications to give space to the story, but an equal amount of publicity was achieved through commentary by the traditional print and broadcast media.

The use of such a radical advertising approach as the one taken by Benetton, while likely to draw attention, might not always bring positive results to a company. There was risk, indeed, involved in such an approach. Will it present the company name in a light that would increase sales, or would its employment backfire, with rejection of the campaign and ultimately its products. Public relations experts are charged with the responsibility to get favorable publicity for their companies. How they achieve this goal in an environment as competitive as the world of fashion is often a difficult task. Obviously, the public relations specialists at Benetton were happy with the results of their atypical promotion. In 1994, they once again chose the "shock therapy" approach to gain media attention.

The in-store visit of a high-profile fashion designer, a special promotion that is created to increase store traffic, the announcement of a film star joining a company as a "designer," or the development of a new fiber might warrant businesses to develop advertising campaigns to bring the event to the appropriate markets. These occurrences, however, do not guarantee that they will gain additional exposure from the fashion editors.

In-house public relations departments and independent organizations that serve the needs of the fashion industry use a variety of techniques and approaches to achieve the goals of obtaining favorable publicity for their companies and clients. It is the combination of the "newsworthy" story and the know-how of the experts to deliver the message that increases the chances of successful publicity.

## Publicity: An Adjunct to Advertising

To communicate with their current and potential customers, every segment of the fashion industry utilizes some form of advertising. No matter how well-known a company might be, it understands that the regular "feeding" of information to these clients is one of the surest ways to keep their names in the forefront. Whether it is the apparel designer wishing to excite the world with his or her latest collection, the material's producer anxious to tell the manufacturing world of an exciting new fabric, or the retailer hoping to distinguish his or her organization from the competition, some form of advertising is the usual route to take.

In their quest for this attention, companies often strain their budgets. How else might a business control the message that it wants to make and place it where it has the greatest potential for success? If one wants it to achieve maximum exposure, one must have the power to invest in a multimedia campaign and repeat the advertisements as frequently as deemed necessary.

While advertising gives the company control over its own destiny, favorable publicity at the hands of media editorial staffs gives the fashion user a route for unbiased reporting. The message that ultimately finds its place in a fashion journalist's column or on a news broadcast is placed at the discretion of the reporter and may not be in the shape or form that it would be if it were part of a "paid-for" advertisement.

As has already been discussed throughout the text, the advertising message costs a company dearly. This is not the case with publicity. Except for the salaries paid to the members of public relation teams and the expenses attributed to running the office, there are no costs for space or air time, as is the case with advertising. That is why it is often referred to as "free publicity."

## The Tools of Publicity

Reading a newspaper, listening to a radio newscast or watching local and national television newscasts, frequently reveals fashion-oriented items that the press considers to be newsworthy. Headline stories include, "Macy's Files for Chapter XI Protection!", "Gitano Loses the Wal-Mart Account!", "Perry Ellis Dies from AIDS Complications!", and so on. These events certainly bring publicity to the fashion industry, but also negative publicity that might be damaging to the future of a business. It is this type of news that public relations experts would prefer to be minimized by the press. However, with no control over what is being spoken or printed, the world is likely to hear a story without the benefit of input from the company being publicized.

One of the major roles of public relations departments is to get their clients' names mentioned as often as possible in a positive manner. With the enormous competition in every segment of the industry and the seemingly little space that editors provide for such positive publicity, the task is a formidable one. The road to obtaining space begins with any number of tools, including press or news releases, biographical sketches, backgrounders, case histories, fact sheets, interviews, and press kits.

## PRESS RELEASES

Any event that is being touted by a company as being newsworthy generally warrants an investment in some publicity or vehicle that can be quickly disseminated to the press. Often, the choice is the press release, which is generally a one- or two-page document that concentrates on a happening or event. Day after day, public relations professionals prepare the releases in the hope that they will pique the interests of the media to whom they are sent and that either the entire message or a substantial piece of it finds its way into print or on the air.

Every segment of the fashion industry utilizes the press release approach. A fiber company might use it to announce a new fabric that could eventually make a major impact in the field. DuPont, a regular user of the press release, used one in hopes of getting the name of its new material, "Thermax," into the pages of fashion and consumer publications. Cotton Incorporated, the fiber organization that represents American cotton producers, used one that tied in the importance of their fiber to the childrenswear industry.

In both of these examples, the format used was traditional among press release writers.

### FORMAT.

• The messages were typed, double spaced, on white paper. This enables the reader to quickly and effortlessly examine the release, and determine if it warrants inclusion in their publications.

- A company logo or illustration was used to quickly identify the name of the company from whom the message was received. In the case of Cotton Incorporated, its "bursting cotton ball, with the words cotton planted beneath it" immediately identified the sender.
- At the top of both of these releases, the "contact" people for further information, as well as their telephone numbers are prominently displayed for obtaining additional information.

**FIGURE 15-1**

*A press release is used to*

*quickly disseminate*

*information to the media.*

*(Courtesy of Cotton*

*Incorporated)*

COTTON INCORPORATED

1370 AVENUE OF THE AMERICAS • NEW YORK, NEW YORK 10019 • TELEPHONE 212-586-1070

RELEASE **Immediate** CONTACT Bill Daddi
Lisa Anderson

KIDSWEAR GROWS UP IN A NEW COTTON CROP

NEW YORK -- Maybe it's the coming of age of an image-conscious MTV generation. Maybe it's the influence of baby boom parents who are older, better earning, and more fashion aware. Or maybe it's just the continued growing sophistication of the nation's young. But whatever the reason, one fact is evident - childrenswear is growing up.

A quick glance at the childrenswear section of any department store will tell you that kid's clothes have come a long way since the days of frilly dresses with appliques and suits with short pants. Babyish, outmoded and uncomfortable styles have gone the way of penny candy. In their place are mini-skirts, chambray shirts, denim jackets, chinos and a host of other contemporary looks that have much in common with clothing found in adult's closets.

- MORE -

- There was a sufficient amount of space left in the margins for editors to write their comments, such as what to emphasize if the release was to be used.

- The use of journalistic shorthand was appropriately used. For example, the use of the word "more," at the bottom of the Cotton Incorporated release indicated that additional pages follow and in the DuPont example, the use of the symbol ### indicated the end of the release. These are standard markings for all press releases.

- Sometimes, the publicist prefers the release of the news at a specific time. If this is the case, it should be indicated at the top of the front page. In other situations, the word *immediate* is used to suggest quick dissemination of the information. The Cotton Incorporated release indicates immediate release. If there is no direction in terms of a release date, it is then understood to be at once.

- Of course, the message must be cleanly written without any errors and in a style that is appropriate for the ultimate recipient of the message. If it is one that is earmarked for the pages of a fashion-oriented trade periodical that will be read by professionals in the field, the language used may be technically oriented. In cases in which the ultimate consumer is targeted, then simpler, less technical copy is in order.

- The content should be as precise as possible, with a headline used to attract attention, printed in a different type style and size. The headline enables a quick decision to be made as to whether or not further reading is warranted.

It should be understood that editors receive scores of releases everyday that vie for their attention. If they appear to be anything but objective and out of the standard formatting, they are apt to be discarded without having been read.

## BIOGRAPHICAL SKETCHES

In the fashion industry, the name of the designer and information about him or her is often as important as the news about their latest collections. Devotees of certain couturiers and other creative talents often relish the idea of being able to talk about little-known aspects of their past. Fashion magazines and television programming sometimes

October 1990


Bill Blass
550 Seventh Avenue
New York, NY 10018


Bill Blass is one of the most widely acclaimed American fashion designer today, and is the sole owner of Bill Blass, Ltd.  Blass licenses his name and designs to thirty-seven domestic licensees and to seventy world-wide licensees, for products ranging from menswear, women's sportswear and dresses, swimwear, coats, activewear, jeans, homefurnishings, loungewear, hosiery, automobiles and, this year, he introduces three new perfumes.

Within the apparel industry, Bill Blass has won numerous awards.  Three time Coty American Fashion Critics' Award Winner (1961, 1963, and 1970), and life-time member of The Coty Hall of Fame, Blass has also been the recipient of the first Coty Award for Menswear (1968) and has received on three occasions (1971, 1982, and 1983) a special Coty citation for overall excellence. Among many other awards, including those from retailers such as Neiman-Marcus, I. Magnin, and Martha, Blass has received the Gentlemen's Quarterly "Manstyle" Award and the Cutty Sark Hall of Fame Award for menswear design.  In 1987, Blass was given the Lifetime Achievement Award by the Council of Fashion Designers of America.

Bill Blass holds two honorary doctorate degrees.  One is from The Rhode Island School of Design of Fine Arts (1977), the other from Indiana University in Humane Letters (1984).  Also in 1984, Bill Blass received "The New Yorker for New York" Award from the Citizen's Committee for New York City.

Blass served as President of the Council of Fashion Designers of America (1979-1981) and is currently a member of the Executive Board.  Since 1986, he has served on the Board of Trustees of the New York Public Library.  In 1987, the President of the United States appointed Blass to The President's Committee on the Arts and the Humanities.

**FIGURE 15-2**

*Biographical sketch*

*(Courtesy of Bill Blass)*

use a designer focus for their publications and specials. One such television special dealt with Geoffrey Beene and covered his beginnings as a medical student and how he ultimately made the transition to design. An even more dramatic presentation was a Broadway theatrical production that explored the life of the French coutourier, Coco Chanel. Scores of articles and a public television show featured how Ralph Lauren, a former tie salesman, made it to the place he now holds in the industry. These are but a few examples of how important the press and media considers the stories about the world of fashion.

Of course, such in-depth presentations as the aforementioned require a considerable amount of research and cooperation from those being honored in the fashion pages. For less ambitious coverage, the press is more like to satisfy its needs with a biographical sketch.

There are two types of biographies that are used to disseminate information. One is written in a straightforward, matter-of-fact manner that succinctly lists factual information. The other is written in a more interesting manner, or in story form. Either one serves as the basis for further use by the media. Along with the biography, standard procedure involves the inclusion of a photograph that might be used to accompany the published story.

## BACKGROUNDERS

Similar to the biographical format is the backgrounder. Where the former is one that concentrates on a specific individual, the latter focuses on a company or event that it believes to be newsworthy. They are also typically longer than the news release and may run for four or five pages.

When Henri Bendel, one of the fashion industry's palaces of famous apparel and accessories design, decided to move its flagship location to Fifth Avenue in New York City, it produced a backgrounder simply titled "The History of Henri Bendel." It traced the roots of the company and how it began as a millinery store to the time it established itself as one of the most respected fashion emporiums in the world. As the day approached for the new store opening, the press was ready to extract from the backgrouder pages anything that it thought would make for an interesting fashion story.

## CASE HISTORIES

The case history is a favorite tool of a company when it wants to underscore how one of its products helped a user. Textile producers often use this methodology.

DuPont used this device effectively, for example, when they told the world about specific fibers for cold weather use in an expedition by

## THE HISTORY OF HENRI BENDEL

Henri Bendel was founded in 1896 as a millinery store on East Ninth Street. Henri Bendel, who had been raised in the French culture of southern Louisiana, had an innate sense of style and a deep understanding of the importance of personal service. These qualities quickly allowed him to expand his business, first into fur coats and then into made-to-order dresses. In 1912, the Bendel store became one of the first commercial establishments to move uptown to the then exclusively residential area of Fifth Avenue and 57th Street.

The store offered highly personalized service—Mr. Bendel was known for greeting each of his customers by name—and was known in particular for its Parisian merchandise and high style. Mr. Bendel made several trips to Paris each year, returning with creations of the world's leading fashion houses. Lavish in-house fashion shows became social events attended by the city's smart set, including women of the "New York Four Hundred," as well as famous singers and actresses. Throughout this period, Bendel maintained a distinctly French ambience.

The success of Henri Bendel continued as the century progressed, even as pervasive social changes required alterations in the store's marketing strategies. The shift from custom-made clothing to mostly ready-to-wear articles, for example, was achieved without tarnishing the store's reputation for outstanding and smart merchandise. After World War II, as American designers gained popularity, Bendel was always able to offer exclusive designs by the best of these designers.

(More)

**FIGURE 15-3**

*Backgrounder*

Will Steger, an explorer, during his International Polar Expedition. Along with Mr. Steger, a team of arctic explorers and sled dogs pushed off from Canada's northernmost tip towards the northernmost point in the world. The members faced ice surfaces that were as abrasive as broken glass, temperatures that could freeze the breath in their lungs, raging winds, and the constant threat of becoming lost forever in the forbidding landscape. The expedition used no mechanized support,

**FIGURE 15-4**

*Case history*

*publicity piece*

*(Courtesy of*

*DuPont)*

no airlifted supplies, no snowmobiles or arctic vehicles. It was the team and their dogs that got them across the terrain.

While every detail had to be carefully worked out to make the expedition a successful one, as DuPont reported in its case study, nothing was as critical as the clothing that was worn by the participants. With an eighteen pound clothing limit per member, each garment had to provide comfort as well as a guarantee for survival. Staying warm and dry were key to the project's success.

To achieve the proper level of comfort, DuPont engineered fibers and fabrics that were continuously field tested under conditions that were impossible to duplicate in the lab. DuPont fibers Thermolite, Quallofil, and Thermax were employed in the various polar suits, parkas, windbreakers, and parkas worn by the team to meet the challenges of the adventure. Together with the courage of the team and the effectiveness of the fibers and fabrics, the International Polar

Expedition was a success. With their products serving as an important part of the program, DuPont chose to use this "case study" as a means of telling outdoor apparel manufacturers and consumers how these very fibers and fabrics would benefit everyday users.

The formula for this case study and for any others should have the following elements to make it an effective publicity tool:

- A specific problem should be presented that could have applications for others.
- The facts in the case should be carefully spelled out to present a clear picture of the problem to the targeted audience.
- The way in which the problem was solved should be underscored.
- The advantages of the product and how it could serve in similar comparable situations should be highlighted.
- The different uses of the same product by the company for other circumstances should be noted.

All of this is made more effective if it is presented in an interesting writing style and is enhanced with meaningful visuals such as graphs, drawings, and photographs.

## FACT SHEETS

Rather than use the narrative of the typical press release, some companies use the fact sheet as a means of succinctly presenting information to the media. It is a document that is carefully arranged to give the recipient a quick overview of a project, product, or company.

They might be one-page presentations or multipage offerings if the project is a very important one. When using more than one page, however, it is important to list the most important facts on the first page, in case the reader does not have time to examine it in its entirety.

When Bloomingdale's planned its midwest Chicago flagship, it was considered to be a major project. In addition to news releases and other publicity devices, it chose the "fact sheet" route to quickly disseminate information about the company to the press.

In addition to the standard requirements of such a piece as the public relations location and phone number and the person to contact for

**FIGURE 15-5**

*Retailer fact sheet*

*(Courtesy of*

*Bloomingdale's)*

bloomingdale's

Public Relations
900 North Michigan Avenue
Seventh Floor
Chicago, Illinois 60611
312 · 440 · 4515

Contact:   Carol Gies

FOR IMMEDIATE RELEASE

FACT SHEET
BLOOMINGDALE'S CHICAGO

ADDRESS:                900 North Michigan Avenue
                        Chicago, IL  60611

SQUARE FOOTAGE:         250,000 square-feet incorporating six sales and one
                        office floor.

PRE-OPENING EVENT:      September 23, 1988
                        (Benefit for the Chicago Symphony Orchestra)

                        Special Guests:

                        Karen Akers in Cabaret

                        Karl Lagerfeld and a French Haute Couture and Pret a
                        Porter Fashion Show

OPENING DATE:           September 24, 1988

STORE MANAGER:          Brian McMahon
                        Regional Vice President for Midwestern Stores

STORE HOURS:            Monday to Saturday:  10 a.m. to  8 p.m.
                        Sunday:  Noon to 6 p.m.

RESTAURANT HOURS:       Espresso Bar:
                        10 a.m. - 7 p.m., Monday through Saturday
                        1 - 4 p.m., Sunday

                        Petrossian Rendez-vous:
                        11 a.m. - 7 p.m., Monday through Saturday
                        1 - 4 p.m., Sunday

PHONE:                  (312) 440-4460

                                - more -

additional information, it listed the square footage of the store to show its importance to the retail scene, major special events commemorating the opening, hours of operation, and the phone number on the first page. Subsequent pages concentrated on the specifics of the environment, the store's interior theme, a floor-by-floor description, and other information that might appeal to the reader. Fact sheets are either used as independent publicity pieces or are incorporated into a press kit.

## INTERVIEWS

Whether we are turning on the television set to the evening news or to one of the many talk shows, we are invariably invited to watch a well-known person being interviewed. While the format generally explores the individual's background, the emphasis is on something he or she is trying to promote. The world of film and theater regularly parades its stars before the television cameras to publicize the event in which they are appearing. Authors of books are eager to convince the audience to purchase their products.

The world of fashion also makes extensive use of the interview. Designers are sometimes seen discussing their most recent collections and the inspirations for their work in hope of motivating the audience to buy. Sometimes, the interview is sparked with some of the designer's creations, making the impact even greater.

While interviews are perfect vehicles for enormous exposure, given the significant size of the viewing audience, its success is based not necessarily on what is spoken, but the image presented by the individual. He or she must be articulate, well-prepared on his or her subject, and ready to answer any questions that are posed.

Not all interviewees make good subjects. Some are nervous before the cameras, while others might make poor viewing subjects. For the interview to be as successful as possible, many participants require that the questions be given to them in advance so that they will be prepared with appropriate answers. Sometimes the interviews are prerecorded and corrections may be made. In the case of the live performance, there is never too much preparation to guarantee success.

## PRESS KITS

When a company wishes to underscore a major event, it often chooses the press or media kit to do so. This packet of information contains some or all of the publicity tools that we have examined such as news releases, biographical sketches, backgrounders, case histories, and fact sheets as well as reprints from journals and photographs as enhancements.

Some fashion industry segments use the kit on a regular basis, while others reserve the use for special occurrences and events. Fashion designers generally produce a press kit to announce their most recent collection, thus warranting the development of a new one with each change of season. On the other hand, the fibers producer might only use this publicity vehicle when a fiber is being touted for new uses. Retailers might use the press kit at times when special events are featured or when a new branch store is about to open.

Representative of the press kits typically used by fashion industry segments are "Macy's July 4th Fireworks on the Hudson," which publicizes a highly acclaimed special event; the Johnson Publishing Company entry, publishers of *Ebony* and *Jet* magazines, which emphasizes the company's history; Cotton Incorporated, which features news about merchandise made of cotton; and Calvin Klein, a press kit that underscores the importance of the designer. Each is explored to show the different publicity tools used to gain attention from the press that will hopefully find its way into their publications.

**MACY'S JULY 4TH FIREWORKS ON THE HUDSON.**   This is an annual special event from Macy's that is aimed to reach audiences all across the country. While the action takes place in New York City, Macy's recognizes that it has customers who visit the "Big Apple" from just about every state and through a telecast of the event, hopes to reach them as well as the New York residents.

The press kit features a host of different publicity pieces to please the needs of the media who covers such events. Included are:

- Announcements that feature the availability of viewing on television for those unable to be there in person
- Viewing tips for those wishing to attend the performance
- A listing of the agencies involved to underscore the magnitude of the event
- Important moments to look for during the presentation
- A map of the event's location, with suggested viewing areas

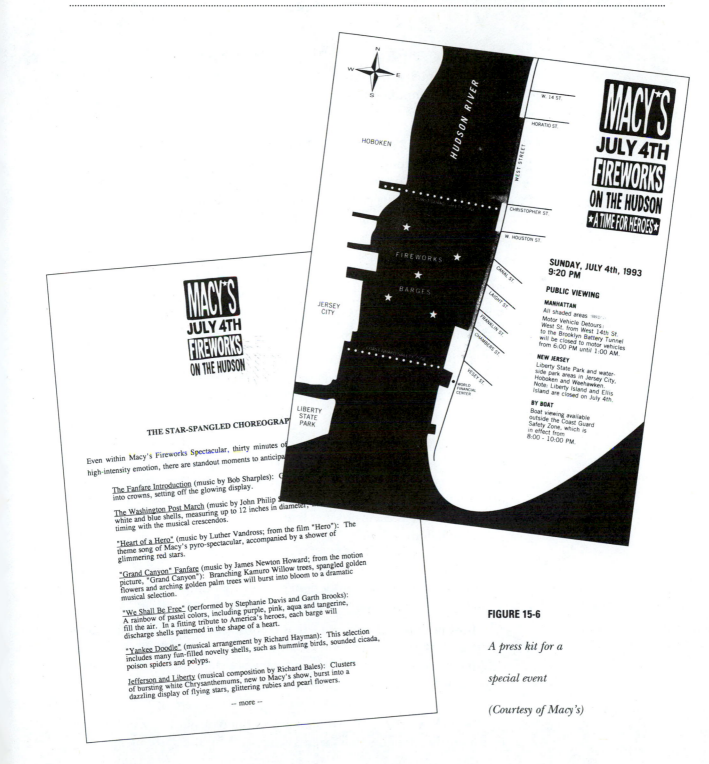

THE STAR-SPANGLED CHOREOGRAP[...]

Even within Macy's Fireworks Spectacular, thirty minutes of[...]
high-intensity emotion, there are standout moments to anticipa[...]

The Fanfare Introduction (music by Bob Sharples): C[...]
into crowns, setting off the glowing display.

The Washington Post March (music by John Philip S[...]
white and blue shells, measuring up to 12 inches in diameter, w[...]
timing with the musical crescendos.

"Heart of a Hero" (music by Luther Vandross; from the film "Hero"): The
theme song of Macy's pyro-spectacular, accompanied by a shower of
glimmering red stars.

"Grand Canyon" Fanfare (music by James Newton Howard; from the motion
picture, "Grand Canyon"): Branching Kamuro Willow trees, spangled golden
flowers and arching golden palm trees will burst into bloom to a dramatic
musical selection.

"We Shall Be Free" (performed by Stephanie Davis and Garth Brooks):
A rainbow of pastel colors, including purple, pink, aqua and tangerine,
fill the air. In a fitting tribute to America's heroes, each barge will
discharge shells patterned in the shape of a heart.

"Yankee Doodle" (musical arrangement by Richard Hayman): This selection
includes many fun-filled novelty shells, such as humming birds, sounded cicada,
poison spiders and polyps.

Jefferson and Liberty (musical composition by Richard Bales): Clusters
of bursting white Chrysanthemums, new to Macy's show, burst into a
dazzling display of flying stars, glittering rubies and pearl flowers.

-- more --

**FIGURE 15-6**

*A press kit for a*

*special event*

*(Courtesy of Macy's)*

- A photograph of one of the fireworks displays
- Photographs of the two celebrities that will participate in the television programming of the event

**JOHNSON PUBLISHING COMPANY.**   To promote its publications, which include *Ebony* and *Jet* magazines, the company uses a standard press kit that immediately satisfies the needs of those who wish to know more about the company, its founder, and publications. To underscore its recognition, the kit emphasizes reprints of articles from prestigious journals and periodicals, as well as factual information.

Included are:

- A fact sheet detailing the company's holdings
- A biographical sketch of its founder, John H. Johnson
- An interview with the company founder
- Reprints of articles about the company that appeared in *The Harvard Business Review, Forbes, United Magazine, Black Enterprise, Madison Avenue Magazine,* and the *New York Times.*

**COTTON INCORPORATED.**   The company that promotes the cotton industry frequently uses the kit approach to keep the fashion media abreast of the latest uses of the fiber. It does not promote its organization with its press kits, but the latest innovations of those in the field who use cotton in their product lines.

Included are:

- A detailed news release that examines the undergarment industry and how famous fashion designers are expanding their offerings to include collections of this type of apparel
- A host of glossy photographs that feature the cotton undergarment designs of such notables as Calvin Klein, Eileen West, Adrienne Vittadini, and Donna Karan to underscore that fashion is no longer relegated exclusively to apparel

**CALVIN KLEIN.**   The designer press kit typically features the ways in which the designer has been recognized by the fashion industry, reprints of articles about him or her, and photographs of some of the items in the current collection.

Included are:

- A biographical sketch of Mr. Klein
- Photographs of him and his wife, who serves with him in the company
- Reprints of articles such as the one from *Vanity Fair Magazine*
- Photographs of some of the styles in the latest collection

No matter what the intention is of the specific press kit, attention must be paid to the following in its preparation.

1. The information should be accurate, up-to-date, and should provide sufficient interest to the media to whom it is aimed.
2. There should be enough elements for the editors to choose from for the particular story they will be writing, such as fact sheets, announcements, news releases, biographical sketches, and so on.
3. If photographs are used, there should be a sufficient number so that there will be a choice for the editor.
4. Reprints of articles from reputable publications should be included so that unbiased observations may be examined.

## Getting the Message Placed

Headlines that read "Gimbels Shut Its Doors After A Century of Business," "The Federated Department Stores File For Chapter 11 Bankruptcy Protection," and "Perry Ellis Dies From Aids-Related Causes" are typical of the negative publicity that plagues the fashion industry. The media is quick to report these calamities without the intervention of publicity personnel.

The placement of a positive message, on the other hand, is not always a simple matter. Fashion editorial staffs are busily engaged in writing columns for their publications or broadcasts and what might seem appropriate for inclusion by some companies does not necessarily coincide with needs of the media. Sometimes, the coverage of a fashion event is so newsworthy that its placement is almost guaranteed.

When Princess Margaret of Great Britain, sister to the Queen, visited Neiman-Marcus for their Fortnight special event, the media was there replete with flashbulbs popping and interviews being conducted. The presentation of such spirited collection openings in the now famous tents of Bryant Park, New York, are certain to bring the most prominent to the pages of fashion. It is the happenings that fall somewhere between the sensational and the less exciting that give publicity people the most problems as items of interest to the media. So enormous is the fashion industry, with all of its segments, that events of relative importance and interest are being offered everyday for the press to write about.

Developing a good relationship with the people who write the stories is essential. These are individuals, like any others, who for one reason or another relate better to some companies and their staffs and have "favorite" designers, stores, and other fashion institutions that seem to capture their attention. If the company or individual represented by a publicity team doesn't have the "ears" of the press, there are some general rules that should be followed to improve their chances of getting favorable media coverage.

## THE PRINT MEDIA

For fashion publicity, newspapers and magazines are the best of the available media. While television, with its visual excitement, is a natural for fashion-oriented happenings such as design collection introductions, it still is the medium that focuses more on news items of general interest. In focusing attention to the print media for coverage of an event, it is necessary to address some fundamental principles before embarking upon the task.

**PUBLICATION SELECTION.**    Each newspaper and magazine is targeted toward a specific market. *The New York Times*, for example, appeals to more affluent readers than any of the other dailies and features columns that would be of interest to them. With its pages filled with fashion advertisements, it seems quite natural that the *Times* will contribute space to covering the newsworthy events of that industry. In the Sunday edition, the Style section is a natural for publicists to try to get their events covered.

Magazines are also directed toward specific interest groups. *Harper's Bazaar* has long been a leader in high-fashion news and would be the appropriate place for the likes of Donna Karan and Ralph Lauren to obtain publicity space.

The seasoned publicity professional must examine every conceivable publication with potential for publicity before going after its editorial staff to gain coverage. This may be accomplished by carefully reading several back issues of the publications to make certain that your stories are typical of what they report about.

In addition to the newspapers and magazines, which are consumer-oriented, trade periodicals are excellent places to gain recognition for the fashion industry. Whether it is the pages of the nationally prominent *Women's Wear Daily*; regional trade papers, such as the *California Apparel News* or *Visual Merchandising and Store Design*, a monthly magazine that focuses on retail industry; there are hosts of these publications for every segment of the fashion industry. Careful study of what is available and what they focus their attention on could benefit those wishing to publicize their stories.

**DEADLINES.** To make certain that the story will be inserted in the desired edition of the publication, it is necessary to know the times by which a story must be delivered in order to be considered. Although the dailies are available up to press time for the latest news story, columns or articles that might feature fashion happenings often require earlier deadlines. The Sunday edition of a newspaper is produced in a number of sections, each carrying a different deadline schedule. Magazines, with their more complicated publishing procedures, have considerably earlier deadlines than those of the newspapers. The easiest way in which to determine the deadline schedule is to call the publication directly.

**DELIVERY OF THE PUBLICITY PIECE.** Unless the item is extremely important to the publication, it is rare that a last-minute delivery of the item will find its way into print. For the fashion industry in particular, rarely is an important event that warrants publicity a last-minute story. Of course, a major retailer's decision to close its doors might be a sudden occurrence, but this is not the type of news that publicists are anxious to get covered.

The introduction of a new fiber, the appearance of a world renowned celebrity at a fashion emporium, the introduction of a new collection to be designed by a movie star, or a fashion show for a worthy charity all take significant time to plan. Because of this, the publicity people should be prepared to deliver the story considering the time needed by the publication for possible placement in their pages.

The event should be carefully presented in written form in any of the publicity tools, such as press releases, fact sheets, backgrounders, and press kits, as discussed earlier in the chapter. Delivery should be via the mail and addressed to the individual specifically responsible for that type of news. The names are easily obtained directly from the publications. The telephone should not be used to present a story, unless it is absolutely a sensational newsworthy event that warrants it.

**AVOIDANCE OF EXCLUSIVITY.**   While it might at first seem that the promise of an exclusive story will help get it published, there is a risk potential in such a practice. The interview of a famous coutourier in a single publication might antagonize the others who wish for the same coverage. For future attempts at placement of stories in those papers, the editors might recall the "insult," and disallow any coverage. Stories should be made available to the media in general by way of news releases or kits, with usage left to the discretion of those in power to print them.

**THE FOLLOW-UP.**   Getting the message printed is certainly a credit to the publicist. To improve the chances of achieving subsequent publicity space, it is imperative that a positive relationship is developed with the press. Once an article is written, a cordial note of appreciation would be appropriate complimenting the flavor of the story and its attention to the facts.

## THE BROADCAST MEDIA

Although television and radio are sometimes interested in covering fashion-oriented events, the time that they have for such endeavors is extremely limited. National and local news of a general nature get preference, with the "soft" news stories often used as filler.

**SELECTION OF THE OUTLET.**    There are two different types of programs that provide publicity for the airwaves. One is the news broadcast and the other "broadcast magazines." The former is the standard type that viewers may see at times throughout the day and night that covers timely news reports. Interspersed between the "hard" news items are stories that might include something related to fashion. The new wave of television "magazines" that cover a few stories, in detail, once a week, such as *Prime Time Live* and *Twenty Twenty* occasionally might give coverage to a fashion story.

Some programs, such as those on public television, from time to time feature fashion-oriented stories that provide significant publicity. *Adam Smith's Moneyworld*, a public television program, featured an entire program that concentrated on Banana Republic, Esprit, and Benetton.

When the item is simple and maximum exposure is the goal, news releases are best sent to every news director in hopes that a spot will be assigned to the story. If the event is one of a special nature and extended time is necessary for maximum publicity, only the most appropriate of the television or radio shows should be contacted.

**DEADLINES.**   As previously discussed in the section on print media, deadlines for broadcast are also important to understand. While a story in a newspaper can be inserted right up to press time, the insertion on a television program takes more time. The piece must be taped and carefully edited to fill a specific time slot. Unless it is of vital importance to the viewing audience, the piece will only be considered if it there is sufficient time to produce the segment.

**INTERVIEWS.**   Radio and television are natural choices for interviews. Stations are always eager to allocate time to individuals who have something to say that is newsworthy. While fashion might not seem to be a universally acclaimed topic, interesting interviewees often provide interest for the audience. If the individual is a "colorful" character in terms of appearance or communication, he or she might be a good choice for the station. Taped clips of the celebrity often help the program directors determine whether or not the interview will be successful.

If the personality is a designer, then a sampling of his or her designs for a television show would make the interview more exciting. Straight talks, without "cutaways" to visuals often become monotonous and avoided by producers.

**THE FOLLOW-UP.**    As was the case with the print media, letters of appreciation are always in order once the segment has been used. The key to continued exposure for a company is to develop a relationship with the individuals in charge of getting the program on the air.

## REVIEW QUESTIONS

1. Discuss the risk taken by Benetton with its departure from traditional advertising and its attempt for favorable publicity.

2. What are some of the newsworthy types of events with which the fashion world might hope to achieve publicity?

3. How does publicity differ from advertising?

4. Is publicity always a favorable vehicle for the fashion-oriented company?

5. What is a press release?

6. List the essential ingredients in the format of any press release.

7. When do publicists often release biographical sketches to the press about designers?

8. Describe the purpose of the case history as a publicity tool.

9. How does a fact sheet differ from the standard press release?

10. Is the interview always a good technique to use to introduce a fashion figure to the public?

11. Describe some of the ingredients of a press kit.

12. How does the publicity agent learn about which publications best serve the needs of the clients represented?

13. What is meant by the term *deadline* as it applies to publicity placement?

14. Should the publicity piece be sent in written form to the press or telephoned to them?

15. Why must the rights to exclusive stories generally be avoided by publicists?

## EXERCISES

1. Visit a fashion retailer in your community for the purpose of preparing a press kit about the company. An appointment with a store owner, manager, or someone in authority should be arranged so that information about the organization may be obtained.

   Once the interview has been completed, prepare a kit using as many of the elements discussed in the chapter. The final project should be reported to class beginning with the manner in which information was obtained and how the "package" was designed.

2. Make arrangements to visit a fashion organization to discuss any upcoming events it would like to publicize. They might include a private label for a store, a designer's latest collection, a special event such as a fashion show, or the opening of a new branch store. After gathering information about the event, write a press release about it, adhering to all of the rules explored in the chapter.

*Simple fixturing and mannequin placement creates a stimulating visual presentation.*

# Promoting Fashion Through Visual Merchandising

fter reading this chapter, the student should be able to:

1. Discuss the importance of visual merchandising and the proper display of merchandise.

2. Describe the different types of environmental settings used in industry that visual merchandisers enhance to highlight merchandise.

3. Explain the different approaches used by the various segments of the fashion industry.

4. List and discuss the various elements that constitute a visual presentation.

5. Explain how display is used to augment advertising and sales promotional endeavors.

6. Discuss the direction of visual merchandising as influenced by store design concepts.

# Introduction

Ralph Lauren is known internationally for his design excellence in different fashion merchandise classifications. His understated approach to apparel and accessories design as well as furnishings for the home are regularly heralded by the industry's critics and connoisseurs. The typical Lauren collections epitomize what a great number of shoppers seek for their personal needs. As one examines piece after piece, it is obvious that he has captivated an endearing audience. Product design alone, though, is not the sole element that accounts for the fascination vast numbers of shoppers have for the merchandise.

When one enters the Lauren flagship store in New York City, a regal building on Madison Avenue that was once home to the Rhinelander family, he or she is immediately treated to a feast for the eyes. Nestled within the five-story mansion that is laden with antique furniture of yesteryear, paintings that immediately capture the essence of a period long gone by, elaborate chandeliers that lend magic to the environment and provide illumination, and bits and pieces of memorabilia that underscore the grandeur of the once-inhabited residence is the very same merchandise that department and specialty stores stock for their customer's pleasure. The difference in this monument to fashion is not the clothing or home furnishings it houses, but the emphasis on the elegant visual presentation.

One need not be a merchant who deals at the level of a Ralph Lauren collection or a merchandiser of couture to warrant painstakingly, carefully executed visual merchandising. Close examination of the product line of the Disney Corporation immediately reveals garments of simple design and construction. The imaginative setting that focuses upon animated Mickeys, Minnies, Donald Ducks, and other signature characters quickly transforms the merchandise into even more appealing products. While the children and their attendants are feasting their eyes on the novel settings that echo Disney productions of the past, they are soon sufficiently motivated to purchase the various items available for sale. The very same merchandise unimaginatively stacked on traditional shelves without benefit of the animated environments would probably sell at a fraction of what the spectacular Disney stores realize.

Visual merchandisers, with their bags of simple and complex tricks, transform even the most ordinary products into those that shoppers eagerly purchase.

# Visual Merchandising Environments

Each segment of the fashion industry makes use of visual merchandising to improve the desirability of its products. While the materials producers, designers and manufacturers, market consultants, and trade expositions utilize some form of visual presentation, it is the retailer who spends the most significant sums on this aspect of promotion.

## RETAILERS

With the enormous amount of competition in retailing today and the similarity of much of the merchandise that is found in stores, one way the retailer differentiates his or her offerings from the rest is through visual merchandising endeavors.

If The Gap, for example, is examined in terms of the merchandise they sell and the manner in which it is presented to the public, the presentation often makes the impact even before the merchandise is handled. One of the keys to the success of their presentations is the neat stacking of merchandise according to specific styles and colors in abundance that immediately impacts upon the shoppers who enter the store. The displays are neither fancy nor intricate, but simply eye-appealing. On diamond-shaped display tables filled with the latest in the store's offering, which are featured right at the entrances, an immediate impact is made. One of the tricks used to ensure attention is the painstaking care given to the display's appearance. Salespeople are responsible for continuous care of these presentations and are always ready to make the necessary adjustments whenever customer handling seems to hamper the otherwise "perfect" piles of goods.

Each retail organization, be it the mass merchandisers such as Wal-Mart and Caldor who sell fashion merchandise at the lower price points, to the upscale designer boutiques such as Escada and Chanel, must establish a concept that best enhances its offerings. Each store must put its best foot forward in the space and specific settings it has to help transform shoppers into customers.

### STORE WINDOWS.

The most memorable settings for fashion merchandise displays are the typically large windows that are found surrounding the entrances to the department store flagships. Most major fashion department stores, with their downtown central district locations, are

**FIGURE 16-1**

*The store's windows generally house the most eye-appealing displays.*

generally fortunate to have scores of shoppers pass their premises every day. Buyers and merchandisers regularly vie for their turn to show their best items in such showcases. With the significant number of departments in each of the stores, however, not every one is allocated an abundance of "window time" necessary to strut their stuff. In addition, specific holidays and events are earmarked for institutional displays, such as the animated extravaganzas at Christmas time, taking even more time away from merchandise displays.

Augmenting these focal points of window display are other types of display cases. There are shadow box configurations, vitrines, and other smaller structures that are used to entice customers to buy. The purpose of these exterior environments, of course, is to show the passersby what merchandise is available for sale. Those presentations that capture attention and motivate people to enter the store are fulfilling the purpose of window displays.

While the flagship's main windows are a company's major way of stimulating in-store traffic, the spiraling costs of retail space have seriously curtailed the use of such showcases. In the same stores that feature these dramatic exterior stages at their headquarter environments, the branches rarely have the same external environments to dress up to attract attention. With mall locations the place of choice for most department store branches, the space that was once given to majestic windows now are used to locate departments. The typical branch now features large panels of glass through which the customers may peer into the store and some limited windows that generally take the form of the aforementioned shadow boxes or "open back" windows that feature a platform for a less formal presentation.

Other retailers, such as the apparel chains like The Limited, Victoria's Secret, Banana Republic, MerryGoRound, and Wallachs; and those that specialize in fashion for the home, such as Crate & Barrel, generally make less use of formal window structures and make more use of the types that permit limited window display and ease in customer observation of the store's interiors.

Some fashion retailers from units of chains to independent retailers who line America's main streets, use different types of window configurations such as "arcades" that allow for more merchandise to be formally shown to those passing by.

**INTERIOR SETTINGS.**   A walk through any retail operation immediately reveals a wealth of potential display settings in which merchandise might be featured. They include platforms strategically placed throughout the store near escalators or other major traffic areas; display counters on which sales associates may sell accessories or other small items; free-standing, glass-enclosed island pedestals known as vitrines; tops of merchandise fixtures that house hanging garments; and platforms that are sometimes found at the entrance to a department. With less attention being focused upon the previously discussed, large window structures, these interior spaces are carefully utilized to feature the store's most eye-appealing items.

The assignment of space in these interior locations is simpler than that of windows. For the most part, the display fixturing is part of a department and therefore is within the department's jurisdiction. Thus,

**FIGURE 16-2**

*A boat suspended in midair enhances an interior setting.*

no space assignment is necessary, as in the case of windows, to assure equal usage by all.

Visual merchandising of the interiors is often the dual responsibility of the visual department and the individual managers of each section of the store. Installations that require new backgrounds and props are usually accomplished by the visual team. In cases in which a mannequin may need a new outfit or an accessory may need replacement after it has been sold, the department manager is usually the one who handles such tasks. Since no major changes are required, the individual department often tackles such display requirements.

Some retailers arouse customer interest through the installation of interior props that signal a new season's arrival or perhaps, a major storewide promotion. Such undertakings are generally as complicated and time-consuming as major window changes. For such promotions, the store's visual team is the one that develops the concept and performs the transition. When one thinks about the Christmas season, for example, with all of the glitter that signals the most important sales time for fashion retailers, the work of the visual merchandising team may be best appreciated.

## MARKET CONSULTANTS

Those in the fashion world who often help cement relationships between manufacturers and retailers are known as market consultants. More specifically, they are the resident buying offices and fashion forecasters. Each of these fashion segments relies somewhat upon visual presentation to augment the promotional and personal techniques they employ to service their clientele.

Resident buying offices primarily serve the needs of manufacturers by presenting their merchandise lines to potential retail customers and retailers by alerting them to the market's wares. While selling and mass communication techniques are the forte of such organizations, they also use visual presentation and display to underscore the various products they are endorsing.

At the resident buying offices such as Henry Doneger Associates, the largest fashion consulting firm in the United States, different visual merchandising techniques are employed. Typically, walls of slatboard or other display props are used to feature the highlights of the season's newest colors, silhouettes, and styles. Sometimes mannequins are spotted throughout the premises, in hope that the visiting store buyers will be able to better visualize fashion's trends.

Fashion forecasters, experts who assist designers with anything from fabric selection to color emphasis for a future collection, and retailers in making their purchase decisions, use a different type of visual format for their work. The industry's leading forecasting companies, such as the internationally renowned Promostyl, regularly cover the walls of their facilities with an assortment of fabric samples and other materials in the color ranges they are predicting for future consumer acceptance. Some forecasters develop wall boards that include specific themes they are touting for future periods of fashion. These boards are replete with photographs, material swatches, and drawings that have been created by the forecasters themselves. One of the industry's most legendary forecasters is David Wolfe, whose predictions are carefully evaluated by his clients. His visual presentations feature the storyboards as well as vast original trend books that speak of fabrication, color, silhouette changes, and styles. The trend books offer a complete visual presentation to buyers so that they will become familiar with the merchandise that will be shown at the various vendor presentations.

## MANUFACTURER AND DESIGNER SHOWROOMS

In garment centers and fashion wholesale markets throughout the world, designers and manufacturers maintain showroom space to which the store buyers come to make their purchases. While one-on-one selling is the major method of doing business, a great number of these companies make use of visual merchandising in these premises. The approaches used are quite varied.

The most significant wholesale center for children's fashions in New York City features a series of glass-enclosed shadow boxes in the grand lobby in which manufacturers show their latest creations. Buyers from all over the country "shop" these windows and often make their way to the showrooms to see the rest of the line.

Other wholesale centers such as the Chicago Apparel Mart, a major regional facility for producers to show their lines, utilize the store window concept for purposes of display. Each showroom features a window much like those found at the retail level for buyers to examine before deciding which should be entered.

Inside of these individual selling arenas, various other visual presentations are utilized. Some use showcases that feature accessories for sale, some use wall boards that display the items the company is wishing to highlight, while others use mannequins and other props for merchandise enhancement. Just as the retailer wishes to attract its clientele's attention, so do those that sell at the wholesale level.

## TRADE EXPOSITIONS

Many of the designers and manufacturers and the materials producers of the fashion industry participate in trade expositions to show their

**FIGURE 16-3**

*The NADI trade exposition features a holiday prop display designed to catch the professional merchandiser's attention.*

goods. A significant number of menswear manufacturers, for example, introduce their new collections as part of the NAMSB trade show; women's companies do the same at the Larkin-sponsored International Boutique Show, also in New York; and the world's renowned childrenswear producers feature their lines at Pitti Bimbo in Italy.

Retailers from all over the world come to these special events to shop the lines and make their selections for the upcoming seasons. The competition for these merchants' dollars is enormous, much like the competition among retailers for the consumers.'

At these convocations, the participants are assigned floor space on which to display their merchandise. Each uses some form of visual merchandising to its best advantage. All, for example, make use of signage that quickly announces the names of the companies at the entrance to the individual booths. Others use a variety of graphics such as oversized photographs that are prominently displayed and feature certain styles. Still others use a variety of props ranging from stands that hold some items to mannequins that feature some of the individual collection's highlights.

Dramatic lighting, on-going video presentations, imaginative backdrops, and other tools of the visual merchandiser's bag of tricks are also used to highlight the different merchandise lines.

## MATERIALS PRODUCERS

Textile mills, fabric converters, and leather tanners are just some of the fashion industry's materials producers who use visual presentation to enhance their merchandise. In their showrooms, a variety of display props are utilized to capture the client's attention. The textiles industry, for example, often uses giant panels that are covered in the latest fabrics and used by sales personnel to show the line. Others use storyboards of apparel designs that feature their materials. Some even use mannequins to display finished garments made of the company's textile line.

Some companies underscore the size of their manufacturing operations with enormous graphics and photographs of their production facilities and the workers who produce the materials. Very often, sufficient confidence is gained by calling a potential client's attention to the magnitude of the company.

Leather tanners often use a series of photographs or actual displays that take the customer through the various stages of the tanning process. This often helps to educate the less informed purchaser of the complexities of materials processing and production.

# The Creators of Visual Presentations

The fashion industry uses a variety of approaches in the creation of the visual presentations on their premises. The choice is dependent upon how much emphasis is placed on display, how often they are totally changed or rearranged, and the budgeted amounts earmarked for such merchandising activities.

By and large, except for the retail industry, where visual merchandising is a major promotional tool, the approach taken is to use free-lancers to perform the visual tasks. In the visual merchandising of fashion at the store level, different approaches are taken to satisfy company needs.

## FREE-LANCE SPECIALISTS

There are a great number of specialists within the visual merchandising community. Some limit their practices to one segment, such as menswear retailers, while others play a more generalized role, dealing with a variety of display installations.

**RETAIL FREE-LANCERS.**   Rarely can an independent merchant employ someone full-time to create and install visual presentations. Even the smaller chains are generally unable to afford the expenses of an in-house display person. In these cases, merchants call upon individuals who operate their own visual merchandising companies.

There are numerous approaches to the use of these display specialists. Some require a formalized contract which spells out the number of times, annually, that services will be rendered, the responsibility for props acquisitions, preparation of the merchandise to be featured, and the financial arrangements for services rendered. Other, especially those with less recognition of their work, are likely to work on a per-display arrangement. The retailer notifies the freelancer of when his or her services will be needed and the extent of the desired services, and pays for them each time an installation is made.

**FREE-LANCERS "TO THE TRADE."**   Aside from the retail arena, other fashion industry components make use of these part-time visual specialists. Rarely does an apparel designer or manufacturer have a sufficient need for full-time assistance with its visual presentations. Whether it is in a permanent sales facility or a booth at a trade show, there is only limited need for visual merchandising endeavors. Retailers, however, have a steady stream of customers coming to their premises and might need, as will be discussed later in the chapter, a full-time specialist to perform display duties.

Showroom presentations are changed with the arrival of a new season. In the menswear industry, with its traditional two-season merchandising, the changes are routinely made twice a year. Similarly, trade fairs and expositions are run just a few times a year, warranting only the limited services of the free-lancer.

## IN-HOUSE STAFFS

At the other end of the approach to visual merchandising is the on-premises staff that works exclusively for a fashion organization. Those whose companies require such arrangements are usually the major department stores and chain organizations. Specifically, there are two major ways in which these businesses utilize in-house staffing. One involves a separate division of the store in which a number of specialists develop, coordinate, and actually complete the installations. The other, generally subscribed to by the fashion specialty chains, involves a centralized approach in which a small group of visual merchandisers plan the presentations and the managers or assistants in the individual store units carry out the plans.

**ON-PREMISES STAFFING.** The attention paid to visual merchandising by full line department store organizations such as Macy's, Bloomingdale's, Marshall Field, and Dayton Hudson, and those of the specialty variety, such as Saks Fifth Avenue, Neiman-Marcus, Henri Bendel, and Bergdorf Goodman, require staffs that number anywhere from two or three for the branches to more than twenty-five for the flagships.

Stores of this nature subscribe to the belief that visual merchandising is an important element to their store's success and originality and creativity are necessary to assure customer attention. When one visualizes the magnitude of the Christmas displays that transform the selling floors into holiday wonderlands, the special events that are enhanced by imaginative visual presentations, and the Easter Bunny's surroundings that are magnets for the children and their parents, only then can the complexity of the tasks fulfilled by the visual merchandisers be appreciated.

Usually headed by a director, or in some stores an executive carrying the title of vice president, the teams utilize people who develop the themes for each display, design or purchase the props that are used, select the vast numbers of mannequins and other forms that feature the

**FIGURE 16-4**

*An in-house visual*

*merchandiser should*

*always be available for*

*display chores.*

merchandise, paint the settings, create the graphics and signage, and finally, complete the merchandise installation task. In addition to the development of these formal settings, the team is also charged with the responsibility of making certain that the displays on the selling floor are kept as fresh as the day they were first erected. At the Lord & Taylor stores, for example, each day members of the visual staff make the rounds of the departments adjusting the mannequins and other forms that might have been carelessly handled by shoppers.

Teams made up of designers, carpenters, signmakers, painters, and merchandise trimmers work diligently each and every day and often long after the store has closed, to assure that the visual presentations will satisfactorily complement the store's merchandise.

**CENTRALIZED VISUAL MERCHANDISING TEAMS.** Many of the major apparel chain organizations, such as The Gap, and home furnishings companies such as Williams-Sonoma, are equally concerned about the visual impressions they make as their department store counterparts. The task, however, for such companies requires a different approach. Unlike the department stores with so many different types of goods to feature requiring different types of themes and attention, the chains are generally comprised of units all with identical or similar product lines and premises that are somewhat uniform in design. Thus, the task of visual presentation is less complex at the chains. No matter if there are twenty stores in the company or one thousand, the requirements of display are often reduced to a "formula" approach.

Typically, the larger organizations prepare their visual presentations at the company's headquarters. With a small team, the theme or design is planned, developed, and executed. Sample windows, for example, are "trimmed" and then photographed for use by the individual stores. The picture is accompanied by a narrative and drawings that completely describe the focus of the display and how it is to be easily recreated. Signage, props, and any other materials are sent along with the plan for use in the installation. So simple are most of these installations to follow, they are the responsibility of the store's manager or assistant. Arrangements like this one enormously reduce the need for a large display budget and guarantee a level of display uniformity.

**REGIONAL VISUAL TEAMS.** Those chains that want a degree of professionalism in the displays in their stores, but find it unaffordable to have a separate visual merchandiser in each unit, often make use of regional teams. The inspiration and design for the entire organization is usually centrally developed, as previously discussed, but the installations themselves are the efforts of display teams. In a company, for example, with several hundred stores geographically dispersed, they might divide the organization into a number of regions in which each is served by a specific team. Responsibility might be for a dozen stores, with the visual merchandisers visiting a different one in a two-week period. Using this approach assures visual presentations that are centrally developed for uniformity and carried out in a professionally prescribed manner.

# Elements That Constitute a Visual Presentation

Whether the visual presentation is one of enormous proportions such as Lord & Taylor's famous animated Christmas windows or a minor installation that merely occupies an interior niche in a department, there are specific elements that become part and parcel to the promotion.

It must be understood, however, that there is one element that might not be included. In institutional endeavors, the presentation might be void of merchandise. When Macy's, for example, prepares its annual Flower Show, the visual presentation focuses upon the greenery and flowers and not merchandise that the store sells. In those installations, props, different types of materials, lighting, color, signage, and graphics are creatively coordinated to produce the visual event.

## MERCHANDISE

Each segment of the fashion industry is in business to promote and sell merchandise. The customers, whether they be professional purchasers or household consumers, are interested in seeing the merchandise available for sale. Except for the institutional mode, which is designed to promote an image or raise consciousness of a particular audience for a specific charity, the merchandise is the first element that must be considered during the visual planning period.

In manufacturers' showroom facilities, fashion forecasters' meeting rooms, buying offices, or the floors of a trade exposition, the merchandise is central to every theme. It is selected by the individual companies and arranged by the visual teams chosen for the installation.

At the retail level, the selection of the merchandise is generally the responsibility of the buyer. With more product knowledge about specific items than most other store employees, the buyer chooses the items with the most potential for success in his or her department.

The general procedure for the initiation of any merchandise display begins with the completion of a form by the buyer. In it, questions concerning materials, construction techniques, key selling points, available colors, potential uses, and price are asked. Once the questionnaire has been completed, it is attached to the merchandise that will appear in the display.

In this way, the visual team may study the items, examine the pertinent information about each that has been provided by the buyer, and then develop a theme or story that can best enhance what the store wishes to sell.

## PROPS

Few visual displays achieve excellence without benefit of props. They may come from a display house that specializes in their creation or from unlikely places such as junk yards and attics. What treasures have been found in those places by people with great imaginations!

Stores and other fashion businesses generally visit display trade shows to examine the inventions and productions of those in the visual field. One of the more well-known events visited regularly by the fashion industry is the one sponsored by the National Association of the Display Industry (NADI). Prop manufacturers from all over the world come to these semiannual events, one held in June for Christmas selections and the other in December for spring and summer. Visual merchandisers and other industry representatives visit the various vendors to learn about new ideas for visual presentations and to purchase what they think best suits their needs.

Rarely does a company have a budget that is large enough to satisfy all of its visual merchandising needs. Through borrowing and using everyday household products that might double as props, the monies allocated for display are stretched. Antique shops are excellent resources for unusual display pieces. An old picture frame, musical instrument, carousel pony, watering can, or anything else that might be available just for giving credit to the lender in the display case. Ordinary household items such as chairs, ladders, tables, and desks may be used in their original states or imaginatively painted to augment merchandise.

To keep abreast of the props available for the fashion users and to learn about what is being used for specific display tasks, examination of the industry's periodicals is a must. Monthlies, such as *Visual Merchandising and Store Design,* feature a wealth of prop vendor offerings, as well as photographs and reports on what the major fashion companies are using in their presentations.

## MATERIALS

Visual merchandisers choose from a host of materials as enhancements of their presentations. From the plainest papers to dimensional

**FIGURE 16-5**

*Basic watering cans*

*used as mannequin*

*enhancements.*

types, from fabrics that run the gamut from felt to the fanciest patterned fabrics, and from vinyls, wood, glass, metallics, and plastics from which to select, visual presentations may take on different images.

The wealth of such materials is available from numerous resources. There are fabrics houses, for example, that cater primarily to the professional theater, which are often places for visual merchandisers to find the right choice. Since visual merchandising in business is often considered similar to theatrical presentation, the sources that both industries use for materials might be the same. Other materials resources include wallpaper manufacturers and distributors, display companies that stock every type of paper imaginable in the widest widths, thus eliminating the need for obtrusive seaming, and fabric outlets.

## MANNEQUINS

A fashion business that wishes to feature a full ensemble for its customers to see often chooses a mannequin for the display. While designers and manufacturers sometimes utilize these forms, it is the retailer who is the primary user of the mannequin. Apparel producers deal with professionals such as buyers and merchandise managers who are capable of visualizing a garment's shape and silhouette "in the hand," without the need to see it "worn." On the other hand, the typical fashion consumer, with less ability to appreciate a style on a hanger, would benefit from seeing the garments on a mannequin.

The wealth and variety of mannequins may be best appreciated by examining the display windows and interiors. Styles ranging from the realistic types, such as those created and produced by the London-based company Adel Rootstein, to the more contemporary representational types that come in different forms and materials, are available. The choice is so broad in terms of cost and appearance, that the visual merchandiser must know which type best suits the needs of the company that will use them. High fashion, specialized department stores with significant display budgets, often select a variety of types to fit their different merchandise offerings. Neiman-Marcus might have in its store rooms a selection of traditional models, as well as different stylized types. Stores that specialize in juniors might opt for a less formal mannequin and use only a wrought iron form that might better complement its offerings.

**FIGURE 16-6**

*The epitome of*

*traditional*

*mannequins created*

*by Adel Rootstein.*

As is the case with the selection of props, materials, signage, and lighting, mannequin procurement rests with the visual merchandiser. He or she generally examines the trade periodicals to learn about the latest in mannequin design and visits the producers' show rooms before the final choice is made. Since the mannequin is often considered the mainstay of visual presentation and the right ones can contribute to increased merchandise sales, significant attention is paid to their selection.

## COLOR

One of the most important elements in any visual presentation is color. If properly used, it will capture the attention of the passersby of store windows and interior displays or provide excitement at such events as fashion shows.

The couturier who wishes to make a visual impact on an assemblage of professionals from the media often chooses to focus on a particular color. He or she might parade six to eight models on the runway at one time, each wearing the same color.

In the apparel manufacturer's showroom, segments of the collection are often shown in "color stories," not only underscoring the importance of a particular hue, but also to impart visual excitement. The colors utilized in any installation or presentation should be decided upon by those with a complete understanding of the power it has to attract. Color "sense" is a natural instinct for some people. They understand the psychological impacts of certain colors and how best to use them to gain an advantage. Others with less inherent color comprehension usually rely upon a system of color theory such as the "color wheel," a circular arrangement that features the primary colors, yellow, red, and blue, and the secondaries, orange, violet, and green, or variations of them. The wheel then is the tool for many different color arrangements or schemes. **Monochromatic** concentrates on one hue. **Analogous** pairs are colors that are adjacent to each other on the wheel. **Complementary** is a choice that uses two colors that are located directly opposite each other on the wheel. When properly used, the color wheel helps the users maintain safety in selection.

The emphasis on one color, or a scheme or harmony that employs two or more hues, may lend the excitement necessary to generate greater sales for the fashion organization.

## LIGHTING

The spotlight that focuses on the model parading down fashion's runways or the beam of an intense halogen light bulb that settles on a particular portion of a window display, at once lends drama to the presentation. The proper use of light to augment a merchandise display or an institutional special event requires a complete knowledge of what is available and how enhancement is achieved.

Visual merchandisers are no longer limited to the traditional spotlights and floodlights that once served the industry. Halogen/quartz and high-intensity bulbs give the user greater dramatic qualities than ever before. Neon, decorative, tubular lighting is also being extensively used to create designs as well as illuminate. Once the initial investment is made for the systems and sources, the lighting expense is minimal, generally requiring only the replacement of bulbs and the cost of electricity. Few visual merchandising elements can provide so much for so little.

## SIGNAGE AND GRAPHICS

Every trade exposition, entrance to a designer showroom, and department in a store makes use of signage that are both informative and decorative. Whether they are oversized fabric banners, plexiglass plaques, wooden and brass nameplates, or illuminated directories, each serves a purpose.

At the department store, in particular, with its vast merchandise offerings, it is not only the merchandise that separates one department from the other, but also the signage that announces the separation.

Designer collections that are merchandised as vendor in-store shops are identified by creative signage. It might use a replica of a designer's signature, a company logo, or any other insignia or symbol that identifies someone such as the red, white, and blue nautical motif that is used on Tommy Hilfiger signs.

More and more graphics are being used by visual merchandisers. They include oversized photographs of fashions on models, well-known personalities such as the designers themselves or celebrities, athletes, panoramic views of countries that influenced the merchandise being featured, and so forth. One of the more exciting types of graphics is the "backlit transparency." Through the use of a colored transparency that is illuminated from within by special lighting, the graphic takes on a dramatic, exciting look. It is being used extensively, in particular, by cosmetic companies that wish to show the vibrancy of their products. When graphics and signage are used as integral parts of visual merchandising, they often help make the presentation's statement more meaningful to the viewer.

The perfect arrangement or blending of these elements requires attention paid to a host of design principles. They include positioning merchandise appropriately with attention paid to balance, emphasizing a segment of the display by concentrating on a central

**FIGURE 16-7**

*Graphics enhance*

*much of today's retail*

*environment.*

*(Courtesy of Nike)*

or focal point, making certain that there is a flow to the merchandise created by rhythmic considerations, selecting goods and props that are proportionally suited to the space they occupy, and assembling all of the elements in a harmonious fashion.

## Enhancing Advertising and Promotion With Visual Merchandising

The purpose of any advertisement or promotion, whether it is one that is merchandise-oriented or institutionally based, is to boost company sales. Each promotional endeavor of a fashion organization begins with some special event or undertaking that will capture the attention of its potential customer. Designers, for example, participate in fashion shows that will hopefully motivate retailers to purchase their collections and the press to provide editorial coverage of the event. Retailers engage in a host of devices that will help stimulate customer awareness and eventual purchasing.

The amounts spent on any one promotion may range from a few hundred dollars for a modest event to tens of thousands for those of significant magnitude such as the Thanksgiving Day parades. The monies earmarked for these extravaganzas are certainly worth the cost if the end results are positive. Those at the helm of a company's promotional activities, whether it is the public relations director, special events coordinator, sales promotion vice president, or any other titled person responsible for directing such tasks, recognize that development of the promotion alone is not enough to guarantee success. The company's potential customers must be drawn to the special event.

Once the event has been planned, a team of experts must concentrate on getting the message out to the appropriate audience. Designers and manufacturers, for example, might run advertisements in the trade papers to generate excitement for a fashion show, while retailers generally use the consumer newspapers to advertise the special event.

### THE VISUAL MERCHANDISING CONTRIBUTION

For most events to be successful, the visual merchandising team must utilize its "bag of tricks" to glamorize and dramatize them. It might be the simple use of topiary trees and trellises to give a fashion

**FIGURE 16-8**

*The residential*

*environment*

*underscores the store's*

*elegance.*

*(Courtesy of J.T.*

*Nakaota)*

show stage a feeling of spring or the hanging of a designer's banner and oversized photographs to indicate whose collection is about to be seen. More elaborate presentations, such as storewide celebrations used by Bloomingdale's in their salute to a specific country, require the transformation of the entire store into one that immediately captures the essence of that land. In such cases, the visual merchandisers toil behind the scenes for many weeks or months designing props and building them, creating signage and graphics, and finally, undertaking the actual installations. Without the benefit of visual merchandising, fashion businesses will be less likely to distinguish themselves from their competition.

## Store Design, Conceptual Direction, and Visual Merchandising

More and more fashion-oriented companies are subscribing to the concept of planning environments that provide permanent settings that do not require periodic changes by visual merchandisers, as in the case of Ralph Lauren's previously discussed flagship store. By contrast, the typical department store or chain unit storefronts and interiors are often functional and basic, requiring that the visual team regularly change the premises for different themes and seasons.

In the specialized retail arena, the trend seems to be focusing a great deal on the environmental concept, with leaders such as the Los Angeles based J.T. Nakaoka Associates Architects creating store designs that utilize this new direction. The concept utilizes the combined talents of the store designer and the visual merchandiser to develop a plan that makes the premises one that is functional, attractive, and, of itself, an environment that does not require constant display and background changes.

Companies such as Bergdorf Goodman Men, Easy Spirit, both designed by the Nakaoka team, and Victoria's Secret use the **residential** direction, while others such as Comme des Garçon, an upscale fashion retailer and Soho Cobbler, a New York shoe emporium subscribes to the **minimalistic** concept, and Reebok, Aeropostale, and Disney, the **thematic** approach.

## RESIDENTIAL

Some retailers believe that for their particular product lines, the feeling of a home or residence is the most appropriate setting. Such an environment gives the shopper the feeling of warmth and familiarity not often found in the typical store designs.

One of the great examples of the residential feeling is evident at Bergdorf Goodman Men. Bergdorf's president and chief executive officer wanted the store to give the impression of "an English club with a comfortable, masculine atmosphere." The anticipated design, however, was not to be laden with the trappings of the typical English clubs, but the magnificence of the grand British chateaus. There would be many grand rooms, each featuring a different merchandise classification with an overall feeling of grandeur and elegance. The woodwork, cabinetry, and furnishings chosen had to enhance the overall residential design. Instead of the typical fixturing, great armoires, similar to those found in grand homes, were built to house clothing and antique-type tables were used to display ties and small items. When the shopper entered the store, he or she had the feeling of entering a stately mansion, rather than a store.

Victoria's Secret, a company owned by the Limited Corporation that specializes in ladies' intimate apparel, uses a residential approach that emphasizes a boudoir setting. Armoires, setees, accent tables, and other pieces of period furniture, enhanced with feminine type wallpapers, fabrics, and gilded mirrors transform the space into an environment that befits any discerning female. Where warmth and comfort are considered the essentials to successfully merchandise a line, there is little other than the residential approach that accomplish them.

## MINIMALISTIC

The clutter that is dominant in many traditional stores is the antithesis of minimalistic design. Rather than have an overwhelming display of the retailer's inventory, minimalism relies upon simple lines and a sparse display of the products.

Typically, metal, concrete, and glass are the materials of choice for the fixturing. Soho Cobblers subscribe to this design philosophy in their shoe stores. Alfi Mawardi, company president, had specific display ideas. "I knew I wanted a clean-looking store—I didn't want that feeling of a thousand shoes on display." The Soho Cobbler, the creation of Demetrius Manouselis, features half-inch-thick clear glass that is embedded in the wall so that the shoes can give the impression of floating in space. Oversized mirrors help to give the impression of greater space and glass, metal, and marble were chosen to compliment the leather of the shoes.

Comme des Garçon also subscribes to the minimalistic look. Clothing hangs sparingly on uncluttered racks, with some pieces merely spread out on glass tables. The store design is faithful to the simplicity of the apparel design. As in other stores of this type, the materials used are primarily glass, steel, and concrete.

In designs of this nature, the merchandise is the focal point, with everything else playing a subordinate role.

## THEMATIC ENVIRONMENTS

One of the first retailers to concentrate on a theme was Banana Republic, a chain that featured merchandise for "Safari." The shops used all of the elements that would bring jungle adventure to its customers. Jeeps, bamboo poles for fixtures, netting, pith helmets, and the like made the visitor feel like he or she was actually in the jungles of Africa. Eventually, the company broadened its merchandising philosophy and abandoned the Safari look. In the world of visual merchandising, however, it proved to be a road to take for other retailers' environments.

Reebok and Aeropostale followed the lead of Banana Republic using themes of their own for their stores. Beginning with its first store in Boston's Back Bay, Reebok converted a former carriage house into a showcase that immediately enthralls the visitor. Calling it a "concept store," it is an environment that relies heavily on a sports theme. Featuring 3,000 products that include footwear, apparel, socks, gym bags, and caps, the customer is treated to a memorable visual experience.

A huge inflatable sneaker at the store's entrance, an enormous abstraction of an athletic shoe sole on the ceiling, mannequins in

**FIGURE 16-9**

*Theme designs are*

*particularly important*

*in children's stores.*

*(Courtesy of SDI)*

physical fitness poses, huge graphic images such as the company's "pump" logo, photographic images depicting lifestyles from advertising campaigns, backlit transparencies, and video monitors are just some of the elements that make this a visual merchandiser's dream to properly show the goods.

Aeropostale, the Macy's spinoff, features unisex sportswear. To enhance its product line, which emphasizes a very casual merchandise concept, the company uses a theme that calls to mind the men in their flying machines. Using replicas of airplanes, parts of the hangars in which they are stored, metal fixturing that resembles lockers, and other airplane memorabilia, a permanent setting is established in which all of its merchandise may be shown without regard to season or a particular theme.

Stores like Disney and Hanna Barbara also use the thematic approach and find that their childrenswear is best shown in this format.

It should be noted that not every retailer subscribes to these forms of visual presentation. Many still prefer the traditional approach where displays and installations are changed to suit the needs of different holidays, store events, and seasons.

## REVIEW QUESTIONS

1. Which segment of the fashion industry spends the most on visual merchandising?

2. How does The Gap try to draw customer attention to the displayed merchandise?

3. Why have the major department stores departed from use of the oversized window configurations found in their downtown flagships when building the branches?

4. Describe the storyboards used for fashion presentations by some fashion forecasters.

5. What is a trend book? Which segment of the fashion industry uses it as a visual enhancement?

6. What specific display element is used by all participants in fashion trade expositions?

7. Describe the role of the free-lancer in visual merchandising.

8. Why does a fashion manufacturer use a free-lancer in the sales showroom instead of employing a full-time specialist?

9. Which type of retailer often requires the services of in-house staffs for their visual presentations?

10. What are some of the activities carried out by display personnel?

11. Discuss the concept of centralized visual merchandising?

12. Why do some major chains subscribe to the centralized approach to display?

13. What is meant by the term *regional visual team*?

14. In retailing, which members of the store's management team selects the merchandise that will be displayed in windows?

15. Aside from the purchase of props from display houses, where else might they be found?

16. Why do manufacturers make less use of mannequins than do retailers?

17. What color system is often used to make certain that specific hues work well with each other?

18. Describe backlit transparencies.

19. How does the visual team enhance the efforts of the special events department in a retail operation?

20. In what way does store design enhance visual merchandising?

## EXERCISES

1. Pretend that you are a fashion forecaster and have been called upon to create a storyboard for the next fashion season. Select a merchandise category such as swimwear, men's sportswear, home furnishings, and so on, and create a storyboard that uses all of the materials necessary for a complete presentation. Use a storyboard constructed out of "foam core" or a similar material.

2. Visit a mall to select a store that uses an interior design concept that incorporates visual merchandising into its premises. Ask permission to take photographs or slides of the entrance, interiors, and any fixtures that underscore this type of store design.

Make arrangements with your instructor to use an "opaque" or slide projector to show your pictures and explain to the class why you think the store you selected makes a visual impact on its customers.

3. Study the store windows of a fashion shopping center and take photographs of five different types of mannequins used to feature apparel. Discuss in an oral report why you think these particular types of mannequins were selected by the retailer.

# Glossary

**account director**—Chief manager of the clients' accounts in an advertising agency.

**affiliate**—A television station that is related to one of the four major networks—CBS, NBC, ABC, and Fox.

**agate line**—The technical term for lines in a newspaper.

**analogous**—A color arrangement that pairs colors that are adjacent to each other on the color wheel.

**answer print**—The final version of the commercial with the sound and film intact.

**asymmetrical balance**—One of the two types of balance used by layout designers where balance is achieved through the use of different elements on either side of the advertisement's center that when properly placed give the impression of equal weight.

**bleed**—This term means that there is no border around the printed matter, with all of the copy and design reaching right up to the edge of the paper.

**book stock**—This type of paper is used most in direct advertising.

**broadsheets**—An extravagant foldout in a brochure that opens up to pages that are sometimes larger than double-spread newspaper advertisements.

**bullpen artist**—An assistant who prepares mechanics or does paste-ups.

**campaigns**—A series of related advertisements that is placed in one medium or a variety of media for a prescribed period of time.

**car cards**—Advertisements that are mounted on panels inside of buses and subway cars.

**classified advertising**—A smaller type of advertising that is primarily used by the fashion industry segments to attract the attention of individuals who are looking for jobs.

**color separation**—A four-color production method that involves the reduction of the original piece of colored artwork into four halftone negatives.

**combination approach**—A term used when two types of messages are blended in a single advertisement.

**compiled lists**—A customer source list that may be rented from a direct mail list broker; this type of list features those people with single, valuable characteristics that would be appropriate for direct mail advertising.

**complementary**—A color arrangement that uses two colors that are located directly opposite each other on the color wheel.

**cooperative advertising**—An arrangement fashion retailers participate in that provides for the cost of the advertisement to be jointly funded by the manufacturer or designer and the store.

**cover stock**—A stronger type of paper that is generally used for the covers of booklets.

**creative director**—The most coveted position in an advertising agency, this person sets creativity standards, understands the needs of the client, and runs the entire show.

**desktop publishing**—A term used to describe computers and software applications that produce copy ready for production.

**dissolves**—One of the different effects that can be added to the footage of a commercial that produces an overlapping effect when one scene slowly fades from view as another fades in.

**evaluative research**—Tests to measure advertising effectiveness.

**focus groups**—Panels of approximately a dozen individuals whom advertisers study to elicit information that will be helpful in the planning of an advertising campaign or a direction the company might take for its advertising and promotional programs.

**font**—The basic set of letters, numerals, and punctuations that make up a typeface.

**four-color process**—A printing system that involves the use of red, yellow, blue, and black to achieve an infinite number of colors.

**frame-by-frame tests**—A research technique wherein each frame of a television commercial is examined separately.

**free-lance**—A term used to describe those who are in business for themselves; for a fee, they produce fashion shows for designers, manufacturers, and retailers.

**full position**—A term used when the location of choice for an advertisement is at the top of a column or directly alongside news matter; an additional cost is charged for this position.

**group head**—A position in an advertising agency that has administrative as well as creative aspects.

**house lists**—A list of a company's customers, used as a source of names for direct advertising.

**institutional format**—A type of advertising that focuses on topics such as the store's awareness of social issues, services that they feature, and the prestigious collections that they exclusively stock for their customers.

**interstate commerce**—Businesses that have operations that cross over state lines.

**junior art director**—A person who specializes in preparatory work such as preparing mechanicals or paste-up.

**junior producer**—The second step in the career ladder to the position of producer; among other things, the junior producer tests advertising concepts.

**leading**—The space between the lines of type.

**letterpress**—The oldest form of printing, which involves the use of a raised surface to which ink is applied.

**line art**—Drawings produced with black ink on white paper.

**management director**—Chief manager of the clients' accounts in an advertising agency.

**milline rate**—A measurement tool used in the fashion advertising industry; it is not an actual rate charged by any publication, just a means of comparing costs.

**minimalistic**—An approach used in visual advertising that relies upon simple lines and a sparse display of the products.

**monochromatic**—A color arrangement on the color wheel that concentrates on one hue.

**offset lithography**—A photochemical process that involves shooting a photograph onto a thin aluminum plate.

**off the card**—Refers to the advertiser's ability to negotiate with a magazine publisher for a reduction of the published rates.

**open-rate**—The price paid for a one-time, full-page insertion in a magazine advertisement.

**outdoor networks**—Developed by the fashion industry, these networks overcome the problems associated with advertising placement.

**permanent bulletin**—A type of painted advertisement that remains in one location.

**physiological testing**—A research technique that measures emotional reactions to advertisements.

**pica**—The unit of measurement for the width of type.

**point**—The unit for measuring the size of type in terms of height.

**precoded**—In questionnaire use, when the forms used to collect the data have specific numbers assigned next to each response in a category.

**preferred position**—A desirable advertising location, which costs more than run-of-paper placement.

**primary research**—Research that provides information that is gathered from original or firsthand sources.

**probability sample**—One type of sample used in surveying in which everyone in the market has a potential for inclusion.

**product advertisements**—Advertising used to tell the consumer about the various styles available in the store's inventory.

**production assistant**—Usually an entry-level position; a person in this position will begin up the career ladder to the position of producer.

**project director**—A research entry-level position in the career ladder toward research director; this person amasses background information for the client.

**promotional advertising**—A type of advertising in which the stress is on price and terms such as "clearance" and "closeout" dominate the copy.

**random sample**—Another type of sample used in surveying that uses mathematical regularity to choose names from a list.

**regular preferred position**—A term used when fashion advertisers are willing to pay more for specific space on a regular basis.

**release print**—The copy of the commercial that is used for airing throughout the country.

**remnant space**—The last-minute available space in a magazine advertisement.

**research director**—A position at the helm of the research division of an advertising agency.

**research supervisor**—The second step in the career ladder toward research director.

**residential**—An approach used by retailers in visual merchandising wherein a setting gives the feeling of the home.

**response lists**—A list used for direct advertising that is developed from customer response.

**rotary bulletin**—A type of painted advertisement that may be dismantled for replacement at different locations.

**rough cut**—The preliminary version of a commercial.

**run-of-paper (ROP) placement**—A term used when the newspaper charges a basic rate for an insertion and positions the advertisement anywhere there is available space.

**runs**—Designations of car cards sold for subway use.

**sample**—A representation or segment of a group that a fashion business may survey to assess a specific market.

**secondary research**—Research that provides information that has already been published.

**short rate**—A higher advertising rate paid by the advertiser when less than the contracted amount of advertising space was used.

**symmetrical balance**—One of two types of balances used by layout designers where both sides of the advertisement are identical to each other.

**television pilot**—A show that is about to go on the air.

**thematic**—A concept used in visual merchandising where a specific theme, or approach, is used.

**typeface**—A term that denotes the style of type.

**type family**—Two or more series of typefaces that have variations on one design.

**voice-overs**—Voices heard but not seen on the commercial.

**wipe**—One of the different effects that can be added to the footage of a commercial where the new scene moves the previous one off the screen from one side to the other or from top to bottom.

**writing stock**—A type of paper that is used to advertise with a letter; it comes in a variety of weights, finishes, and qualities.

**zoom**—One of the different effects that can be added to the footage of a commercial, which brings close-ups of distant shots.

# Index